Comparative Law — Engaging Translation

In an era marked by processes of economic, political and legal integration that are arguably unprecedented in their range and impact, the translation of law has assumed a significance which it would be hard to overstate. The following situations are typical. A French law school is teaching French law in the English language to foreign exchange students. Some US legal scholars are exploring the possibility of developing a generic or transnational constitutional law. German judges are referring to foreign law in a criminal case involving an honour killing committed in Germany with a view to ascertaining the relevance of religious pre-scriptions. European lawyers are actively working on the creation of a common private law to be translated into the 24 official languages of the European Union. Since 2004, the World Bank has been issuing reports ranking the attractiveness of different legal cultures for doing business. All these examples raise in one way or the other the matter of translation from a comparative legal perspective. However, in today's globalised world where the need to communicate beyond borders arises constantly in different guises, many comparatists continue not to address the issue of translation. This edited collection of essays brings together leading scholars from various cultural and disciplinary backgrounds who draw on fields such as translation studies, linguistics, literary theory, history, philosophy or sociology with a view to promoting a heightened understanding of the complex translational implications pertaining to comparative law, understood both in its literal and metaphorical senses.

Dr Simone Glanert is a Senior Lecturer at Kent Law School where she teaches comparative law, French public law and legal interpretation.

Comparative Law –
Engaging Translation

Edited by
Simone Glanert

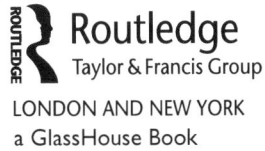 **Routledge**
Taylor & Francis Group

LONDON AND NEW YORK
a GlassHouse Book

First published 2014
by Routledge

Published 2014 by Routledge
2 Park Square, Milton Park, Abingdon, Oxfordshire OX14 4RN

and by Routledge
711 Third Avenue, New York, NY 10017
a GlassHouse Book

Routledge is an imprint of the Taylor and Francis Group, an informa business

First issued in paperback 2015

British Library Cataloguing in Publication Data
A catalogue record for this book is available from the British Library

Library of Congress Cataloging-in-Publication Data
Comparative law – engaging translation / edited by Simone Glanert.
pages cm
ISBN 978-0-415-64270-5 (hardback) -- ISBN 978-0-203-38089-5 (ebk) 1.
Law--Language. 2. Comparative law. 3. Semantics (Law) I. Glanert, Simone,
1973- author editor of compilation.
K213.C65 2014
340'.2--dc23
2013048960

ISBN 978-0-415-64270-5 (hbk)
ISBN 978-1-138-10026-8 (pbk)
ISBN 978-0-203-38089-5 (ebk)

Typeset in Galliard by
Servis Filmsetting Ltd, Stockport, Cheshire

Contents

PART III
Translation beyond translation

Notes on Contributors

C.J.W. (Jaap) Baaij, who holds degrees in law and philosophy, is an Assistant Professor at the Faculty of Law, University of Amsterdam. He teaches contract law and dispute resolution, in both national and transnational contexts. His scholarship concentrates on the intersection of law and language, specifically the role of legal translation in comparative legal research and the multilingual process of legal integration. He teaches seminars on these topics throughout the European Union and in the United States, and frequently provides professional training for translators and lawyer-linguists of the European Commission and the European Council. He is the founder of the 'Amsterdam Circle for Law and Language' (lawandlanguage.eu) and the editor of a multidisciplinary volume on *The Role of Legal Translation in Legal Harmonization*, The Hague: Kluwer, 2012.

Raluca Bercea, a qualified lawyer with an academic background in linguistics and law, is an Associate Professor at the Faculty of Law, University of Timişoara. She has appeared before the European Court of Human Rights and has acted as visiting professor in France, Italy and Hungary. She is the co-founder of the *Romanian Journal of Comparative Law* and the author of 'La leçon de Picasso: quand les tableaux évoquent la fabrication de la comparaison des droits' (2011) 1 *Romanian Journal of Comparative Law* 213 and 'Toute comparaison des droits est une fiction', in P. Legrand (ed.) *Comparer les droits, résolument*, Paris: Presses Universitaires de France, 2009.

Shawn Marie Boyne is a Professor at Indiana University School of Law. Her research interests span the intersection of criminal law, politics and culture. In her recent scholarship, she examines the meaning of prosecutorial 'objectivity' in Germany's civil law system. In her new book, *The German Prosecution Service: Guardians of the Law?*, Berlin: Springer, 2014, she uses ethnographic research to explore how German prosecutors interpret and enact their mandate to view evidence from a neutral standpoint. She argues that, despite the fact that statutes prescribe a form of 'ritualized objectivity', the working meaning of 'objectivity' can be found in collegial decision-making practices rather than in the law. In 2011, the American Society of Comparative Law selected the working draft of her article entitled 'The Many Faces of Objectivity: A Look at German Sexual Assault Cases' (2010) 67 *Washington and Lee Law Review* 1287 as one of six papers to be discussed at its annual work-in-progress workshop held at Yale Law School. She is currently researching the role of defence counsel in civil law systems.

Michael Cronin, a member of the Royal Irish Academy and co-editor of *The Irish Review*, holds a Personal Chair in the Faculty of Humanities and Social Sciences, Dublin City University. His research interests include Irish translation history and translation with specific reference to globalisation. He is the author of *Translation in the Digital Age*, London: Routledge, 2013; *Translation Goes to the Movies*, London: Routledge, 2009; *Translation and Identity*, London: Routledge, 2006; *Translation and Globalization*, London: Routledge, 2003; *Across the Lines: Travel, Language and Translation*, Cork: Cork University Press, 2000 and the co-editor of *Transforming Ireland: Challenges, Critiques, Resources*, Manchester: Manchester University Press, 2010, with D. Ging and P. Kirby; *The Languages of Ireland*, Dublin: Four Courts Press, 2003, with C. Ó Cuilleanáin; and *Unity in Diversity? Current Trends in Translation Studies*, Manchester: St. Jerome Publishing, 1998, with L. Bowker, D. Kenny and J. Pearson.

Luca Follis is a Lecturer at Lancaster University Law School. He works at the interface of socio-legal studies and political and social theory exploring how democratic orders rationalise, legitimate and explicate punitive choices. His current project focuses on the centrality of penal exclusion to the United States' political imaginary and on the historical relationship between criminal dispossession, citizenship and the emergence of the local state. Recent publications include 'Resisting the Camp: Civil Death and the Practice of Sovereignty in New York State' (2013) 9 *Law, Culture and the Humanities* 91 and 'Discipline Unbound: Patuxent, Treatment and the Colonization of Law' (2014) *Law, Culture and the Humanities* (forthcoming).

Pascale Fournier is an Associate Professor at the Faculty of Law, University of Ottawa where she holds the Research Chair in Legal Pluralism and Comparative Law. She previously served as Law Clerk to Justice Claire L'Heureux-Dubé at the Supreme Court of Canada and graduated from Harvard Law School (SJD) as a Fulbright and Trudeau scholar. She has lectured at the State University of Haiti, McGill University, the University for Peace in Costa Rica and the Institute for Women's Studies and Research in Iran. Her major research project investigates the migration of the Jewish *get* and the Islamic *talaq* to Canada, France, Britain, Germany and Israel, and explores through field interviews the effects of such migration on Jewish and Muslim women. Her book, *Muslim Marriage in Western Courts: Lost in Transplantation*, was published by Ashgate in 2010. A French version has now appeared as *Mariages musulmans, tribunaux d'Occident*, Paris: Presses de Sciences Po, 2013.

Jean-Claude Gémar is Emeritus Professor at the Université de Montréal and the Université de Genève. He is the author of *Traduire ou l'art d'interpréter*, 2 vols, Montreal: Presses de l'Université du Québec, 1995 and the co-editor of *Jurilinguistics: Between Law and Language*, Brussels: Bruylant, 2005, with N. Kasirer. A former member of the editorial board of the *Quebec Private Law Dictionary*, he sits on the editorial board of *Meta: Translators' Journal*, a leading Canadian journal in translation studies. Professor Gémar founded the GREJUT (*Groupe de recherche en jurilinguistique et traduction*) at the Université de Genève. Since 1992, he has been responsible for the French Judgment Writing Seminar offered to Superior Court judges by the Canadian Institute for the Administration of Justice. He has also worked as a freelance translator for Canada's Translation Bureau.

Simone Glanert is a Senior Lecturer at Kent Law School. She has repeatedly acted as visiting professor at various European universities and regularly lectures in the United States and Canada. She has also visited at the Université de Montréal. Her research focuses on theoretical issues arising from the practice of comparison in the context of globalisation and Europeanisation. She is the author of 'Foreign Law in Translation: If Truth Be Told ...', in M. Freeman and F. Smith (eds) *Law and Language*, Oxford: Oxford University Press, 2013, with P. Legrand; *De la traductibilité du droit*, Paris: Dalloz, 2011; 'Comparaison et traduction des droits: à l'impossible tous sont tenus', in P. Legrand (ed.) *Comparer les droits, résolument*, Paris: Presses Universitaires de France, 2009; and 'Speaking Language to Law: The Case of Europe' (2008) 28 *Legal Studies* 161. She is undertaking further work on the relevance of Hans-Georg Gadamer's philosophical hermeneutics for comparative legal studies.

Jennifer Hendry is a Lecturer at the University of Leeds School of Law. Previously, she wrote her doctoral thesis on '*Unitas in Diversitate?* On Legal Cultures and the Europeanization of Law' at the European University Institute (EUI) in Florence and spent a year as a post-doctoral research fellow at the Institute for Comparative and Transnational Law (TICOM) at Tilburg University. Her main research interests are in the areas of legal and social theory with specific reference to comparative law and comparative legal studies. In particular, she is interested in the concepts of 'legal culture' and 'legal pluralism'. Her publications include 'Legal Pluralism and Normative Transfer', in G. Frankenberg (ed.) *Order from Transfer: Comparative Constitutional Design and Legal Culture*, Cheltenham: E. Elgar, 2013; '"Unity in Diversity": Questions of (Legal) Culture in the European Union' (2008) 3 *Journal of Comparative Law* 289 and 'Contemporary Comparative Law: Between Theory and Practice' [Review of E. Örücü and D. Nelken (eds) *Comparative Law: A Handbook*, Oxford: Hart, 2007], (2008) 9 *German Law Journal* 1313.

Pierre Legrand directs the postgraduate programme in 'Globalization and Legal Pluralism' at the Sorbonne. He acts as Distinguished Visiting Professor of Law at the University of San Diego School of Law and also visits at Northwestern University School of Law. In addition to Georgetown University Law School, previous visiting professorships include the universities of Copenhagen and Toronto. He has lectured repeatedly in Australia, Brazil, China and Singapore. Some representative publications include *Pour la relevance des droits étrangers*, Paris: IRJS Éditions [Institut de recherche juridique de la Sorbonne], 2014; 'Foreign Law: Understanding Understanding' (2011) 6(2) *Journal of Comparative Law* 67; '"*Il n'y a pas de hors-texte*": Intimations of Jacques Derrida As Comparatist-at-Law', in P. Goodrich and others (eds) *Derrida and Legal Philosophy*, New York: Palgrave Macmillan, 2008; 'On the Singularity of Law' (2006) 47 *Harvard International Law Journal* 517; 'Issues in the Translatability of Law', in S. Bermann and M. Wood (eds) *Nation, Language, and the Ethics of Translation*, Princeton, NJ: Princeton University Press, 2005; and 'The Same and the Different', in P. Legrand and R. Munday (eds) *Comparative Legal Studies: Traditions and Transitions*, Cambridge: Cambridge University Press, 2003.

Kwai Hang Ng is an Associate Professor of Sociology at the University of California, San Diego. He is primarily interested in studying institutionalised language practices in the common law tradition and has undertaken empirical research on the bilingual legal system of Hong Kong and on the use of court interpreters in the United States. His book, *The Common Law in Two Voices: Language, Law, and the Postcolonial Dilemma in Hong Kong*, Stanford, CA: Stanford University Press, 2009, joint recipient of the Distinguished Book Award, American Sociological Association's Section on Sociology of Law, explores how the introduction of Chinese into the common law has reshaped the social and moral character of the law in Hong Kong. He is working on a comparative study of several post-colonial common law jurisdictions in Asia.

Alexis Nouss (Nuselovici) is Professor of General and Comparative Literature at Aix-Marseille Université. He researches in the fields of European culture and translation studies. Representative publications include *Paul Celan: les lieux d'un déplacement*, Lormont: Le Bord de l'Eau, 2010; *Plaidoyer pour un monde métis*, Paris: Textuel, 2005; *Métissages*, Paris: Pauvert, 2001, with F. Laplantine; *Dire l'événement, est-ce possible?*, Paris: L'Harmattan, 1997, with J. Derrida and G. Soussana; *Le Métissage*, Paris: Flammarion, 1997, with F. Laplantine; and, in the 'Que sais-je?' series, *La Modernité*, Paris: Presses Universitaires de France, 1995. He is the director of 'Non-lieux de l'exil' (http://www.nle.hypotheses.org), a research group working on exilic experiences, and gives a seminar on the same topic at the Collège d'études mondiales, Paris. He sits on the editorial board of *Traduction, terminologie et rédaction* (*TTR*) and on various reading committees. He has taught as visiting professor in Brazil, France, Spain and Turkey.

Ferdinand Prinz zur Lippe is a German lawyer. In addition, he holds degrees in political science, psychology and philosophy. He is a Private Lecturer at Trinity College Dublin and a Lecturer at the German Army University in Munich. He also practises law at a leading law firm in Munich where he specialises in the fields of commercial and corporate law, distribution law, cartel law, real estate law and construction law.

Bénédicte Sage-Fuller, who studied law in France and Ireland, is a Lecturer at the Faculty of Law, University College Cork, where she directs the 'Law and French' and 'Law and German' degrees. Before her appointment, she worked as Law of the Sea consultant and principal researcher in pan-European maritime research projects (DG TREN). Since 2009, Dr Sage-Fuller has been involved with UNCTAD and the Dublin Port Company on 'Modern Port Management'. This programme is aimed at providing aid in the form of teaching on sea ports in developing countries. She is the author of *The Precautionary Principle in Marine Environmental Law, with Special Reference to High Risk Vessels*, London: Routledge, 2013.

Régine Tremblay is a Doctor of Juridical Science (SJD) candidate at the University of Toronto. She holds a Bachelor of Civil Law (BCL) and a Bachelor of Laws (LLB) from McGill University in addition to a Master of Laws (LLM) from the University of Toronto. She has also been a member of the Barreau du Québec since 2011. She is a co-editor of *Les Intraduisibles en droit civil*, Montréal: Thémis, 2014, with A. Popovici and L. Smith, and sits on the Editorial Committee of the *Private Law Dictionary of the Family*, F. Allard and others (eds), 2nd edn, Montréal: Éditions Y. Blais, 2015 (forthcoming).

Acknowledgements

Earlier versions of the chapters in this volume were presented at an international conference entitled 'Comparative Law — Engaging Translation' held at the Kent Centre for European and Comparative Law, Kent Law School, Canterbury, UK on 21–22 June 2012. I wish to thank Jenny Harmer, Susanne Krauss and Anita Barylska for helping to organise the event. I am also indebted to Christopher Goddard for assisting with the preparation of the initial drafts and to Nicola Prior for her excellent copy-editing. I am grateful to Sally Sheldon and Paddy Ireland for offering a meaningful financial contribution from the Kent Research Support Fund. At Routledge, I was fortunate to be able to count on the trust, proficiency and forbearance of Dr Colin Perrin, Rebekah Jenkins and Thomas Lodge. Finally, I want to emphasise how much I owe to the many reviewers who generously agreed to provide expert advice on the various submissions. They know who they are.

S.G.

Chapter 1

Translation matters

Simone Glanert

'All forms of comparison are problems of translation and all problems of translation are ultimately problems for comparison'

Aram Yengoyan (2006: 151)

As languages are deterritorialising on an unprecedented scale, as monolingualism is being denaturalised, not least on account of the emergence of global assemblages such as the European Union, translation is materialising as never before. *Everything* is being translated. However, it remains the case that *nothing* is translatable. Indeed, it has become trite to observe that 'secularism' does not carry the same meaning as *laïcité* or that 'contract of sale' does not mean the same as *Kaufvertrag*. Law, immingled as it is with language, could not have escaped this aporetic manifestation of linguistic post-nationalism. Or could it? Can French law, for instance, exist in a significant manner (that is, in the sense that it would make *sense*) beyond the French language? Specifically, can the German translation of an English casebook usefully account for English contract law in the German language?

To move one step further, is it possible to design a law that would mean the same thing across various legal languages and that could therefore legitimately claim the status of 'uniform' law? Can the language of the law really unbelong, that is, detraditionalise itself? Or does it have a border, in French *un bord*, that would suggest an inside and an outside of it, that would entail that it can find itself, at some juncture, *débordé* (or overcome), facing something like intractable alterity? But then, does legal translation need to imply (as it is reflexively assumed to do) sameness, isomorphism, commensurability and *adaequatio*? Could it not depart from the philological tradition and legitimately involve something other than fidelity to an original text? Is legal translation not an original work in and of itself?

In an era marked by an increased interaction between different legal cultures, one would expect that comparative law would offer a privileged space for reflection on the many issues arising from legal translation. Indeed, the process of legal comparison implies the activity of translation since the task of the comparatist is to explain, using her language, a foreign law, which moreover is generally formulated in a different language. Unsurprisingly, then, recently some scholars have repeatedly urged comparatists to recognise the importance of translation in comparative legal research (Weisflog 1996; Großfeld 2003; Pommer 2006; Curran 2006; Legrand 2008; Brand 2009; Glanert 2011; Pozzo 2012).[1]

However, many academics writing in the field do not show any interest in translation. For example, neither Konrad Zweigert and Hein Kötz's textbook *Introduction to Comparative Law* (1996), which has dominated comparative legal studies both in Germany and the United Kingdom for the past 40 years, nor René David's monograph *Les Grands systèmes de droits contemporains* (2002), which after 11 editions is still highly regarded in France, addresses difficulties arising from legal translation. Other comparatists also fail to apprehend legal translation as problematic for comparative legal studies. In particular, H. Patrick Glenn argues, in the most recent edition of his *Legal Traditions of the World*, that 'differences in languages are obstacles to understanding and communication, but not insuperable ones. The translation industry in the world stands as testimony to this' (2010: 49).

Finally, there are comparatists who, while they show themselves to be sensitive to translation issues, do not provide their readership with the requisite theoretical background. For example, Werner Menski, although he emphasises the need for the comparative lawyer to take into account irreducible linguistic pluralism, refrains from exploring the issue of legal translation at any length (2006: 78). In effect, the pressing practical significance and considerable theoretical interest raised by questions of translation has hitherto been neglected by most comparatists. As such, a recent guidebook to comparative constitutional law, an emerging field within comparative legal studies engaging various aspects of national constitutional law and investigating, among others, the possibility of a generic or transnational constitutional law, does not feature any serious analysis of language and translation issues over its many hundreds of pages (Rosenfeld and Sajó 2012).

But why are comparatists so reluctant to discuss the matter of legal translation? At least four reasons seem to explain the absence of a meaningful focus on translation in comparative legal studies. First, comparatists tend to lack interdisciplinary knowledge. Very often, a lawyer will have developed an expertise in her own field but know little about other disciplines. Spanish philosopher José Ortega y Gasset famously referred to such a person as a 'learned-ignoramus', that is, someone who 'will act in all areas in which he is ignorant, not like an ignorant man, but with all the airs of one who is learned in his own special line' (1930: 98). Many comparatists therefore find it difficult to come to terms with writings that are not deemed 'legal' in the traditional sense. Indeed, a French comparatist laments how 'complex cultural and interdisciplinary comparison [...] renders the discipline so complicated' (Fauvarque-Cosson 2006: 61).

Secondly, there are comparative lawyers who do not undertake interdisciplinary research for what they regard as practical reasons. The underlying idea governing these comparatists is that they must provide concrete solutions to specific legal problems involving foreign law. In this respect, one comparatist, showing great scepticism with respect to interdisciplinary approaches, argues that 'this new material is not likely to be of use to applied research of the kind that judges, legislators, and practitioners would ever wish to consult' (Markesinis 2006: 142).

Thirdly, the ascendancy of law may explain some at least of the comparatist's unwillingness to take an interest in translation studies. Traditionally, law has been envisaged as more prestigious than other disciplines such as anthropology, sociology or linguistics. For example, in France, during their first year of studies, law students learn to distinguish between 'the law' and 'the auxiliary sciences of the law' (Aubert and Savaux 2012: 47–51; Cornu 2007: 128–32).

Fourthly, in civil law countries, where statutes are considered to constitute the epistemological substance of the law and where most legal knowledge is articulated around the idea of 'law as science', there is but little epistemological room left for the interaction of law with other fields of knowledge (Kiesow 2010). Against this background, it is perhaps not so startling after all that the majority of comparatists tend to ignore, minimise or disqualify translation issues.

In this introductory chapter, I briefly address what I deem to be some of the most important problems arising from translation in the context of comparative legal studies. In the first part, I foreground the impossibility of translation. Contrary to unexamined assumptions, law simply cannot be faithfully translated from one language to the other. Turning to the second aspect of my argument, I claim that the comparatist must, however, make the impossible possible. Despite the irreducible differences across languages and cultures, the comparative lawyer cannot refrain from translation. Moreover, she must choose, among the various available strategies, an approach to translation that values the otherness of the foreign law. In my third section, I introduce the various contributions to this volume, which all offer comparatists' invaluable insights into the theory and practice of translation in comparative legal studies.

In a paper entitled 'Issues in the Translatability of Law', Pierre Legrand suggests that 'the task of comparatists-at-law is to measure the gap or the *écart* between laws, not unlike the way in which literary translators constantly seek to apprehend the distance between languages' (2005: 41, original emphasis). For example, comparatists should not assume that the French words *plaider coupable* could account for the US legal 'reality' as it is expressed in *plea bargaining*. The comparatist should also be aware of the fact that the German expression *Eigentum* ('property') cannot adequately reflect the French legal landscape where the matter is about *propriété*. The whole history of translation in fact shows that faithful renderings from one language into another are impossible. Indeed, the numerous retranslations of literary or religious texts, such as Shakespeare's plays, Dostoyevsky's novels or the Holy Scriptures, demonstrate that a 'true' and 'ultimate' translation cannot be achieved. In fact, all translators, including legal translators, have to face at least two important challenges.

First, *languages do not signify identically*. In his influential essay 'The Task of the Translator', published in the early 19th century, German philosopher Walter

Benjamin explains that the disparities between languages are essentially due to there being different 'modes of intention [*Arten des Meinens*]' at work (1923: 75). The translation of the German word *Brot* (bread) into the French *pain* strikingly illustrates this phenomenon. In the two languages, what is 'meant' is essentially the same. Both the word *Brot* and the word *pain* thus refer to 'bread', that is, a consumable good made of water, salt, flour etc. Therefore, the German and French expressions are readily presented as equivalent. However, in the two languages, the 'modes of intention' are not the same. Certainly, one would not want to schematise national behaviours. Nevertheless, one can reasonably assume that a German, when using the word *Brot*, will probably be thinking of *Vollkornbrot* (whole-grain bread). By contrast, the French person, when referring to *pain*, will most likely have in mind a *baguette*. Because of the different 'modes of intention' – whole-grain bread and *baguette* – the two words ultimately signify something different for the German and the French. In the event, *Brot* and *pain* are therefore not interchangeable. Indeed, they can be said to *exclude* each other.

It is important to keep in mind that languages evolve in particular economic, geographical, historical, legal, social and political contexts. In his famous essay on the 'The Misery and the Splendor of Translation', Ortega y Gasset highlights the fact that the German word *Wald* (forest) cannot constitute a faithful translation of the Spanish expression *bosque*, although most dictionaries present these two words as equivalent (1937: 96). Indeed, for a German, the signifier *Wald* evokes the idea of an immense terrain with a significant number of trees. By contrast, the Spaniard associates the signifier *bosque* with probably only a small parcel of land featuring only a small number of trees.

These divergences between the German and the Spanish language are a result of the fact that, in Germany, the wooden surface is much more important than in Spain. Here again, the 'modes of intention' are fundamentally different in the two languages, which is why, on reflection, *Wald* cannot be regarded as equivalent to *bosque*. One can even go one step further by asking whether a German citizen of the 21st century from the industrial area of the *Ruhrgebiet* has the same understanding of the word *Wald* as a German painter of the Romantic period of the 18th century during which some trees, such as the oak, were mythified. Appositely, Martin Heidegger observes that translation operates even within a language (1943: 63).

Lawyers should not suppose that legal language is exempt from such challenges, as described by Benjamin and Ortega y Gasset. In this respect, the word 'privacy', which is part of the legal language both in the United States and in the United Kingdom, presents a useful illustration. A close examination of this term reveals that even two legal cultures sharing the same law world (that is, the common law tradition) and using the same language (that is, English) do not have the same understanding of certain legal concepts. The idea of a right to privacy, which commonly refers to the law governing the treatment of personal information (for example, the prohibition on the use of a person's name without consent for trade or advertising purposes), was first addressed within a legal context in the United States. Louis Brandeis (later appointed to the US Supreme Court) and another young lawyer, Samuel Warren, published an article entitled 'The Right to Privacy' in the *Harvard Law Review* in 1890, arguing that the US Constitution and the common law allowed for the formulation of a general 'right to privacy'.

A few decades later, William Prosser, a US tort lawyer, developed specific principles of privacy law (1960). By contrast, in the United Kingdom, there is no independent 'privacy tort doctrine'. The Supreme Court of the United Kingdom, formerly the House of Lords, which refuses to recognise a tort of privacy, requires the claimant to refer either to an existing tort such as a breach of confidence or a specific legal text such as the Data Protection Act 1998. The highest court has repeatedly confirmed its position on this issue, for example, in the landmark cases of *Wainwright v Home Office* [2003] and *Campbell v MGN Ltd* [2004].[2] As a result, the word 'privacy' carries a different meaning for US and English lawyers.[3] The 'modes of intention', as Benjamin would argue, are not the same in the United States and in the United Kingdom.

Secondly, *every act of translation involves a process of interpretation.* Indeed, the translator, before translating from one language to another, must first understand the source text. This act of interpretation is neither neutral nor objective. In his ground-breaking book *Truth and Method*, first published in 1960, Hans-Georg Gadamer, one of the most influential German philosophers of the 20th century, offers useful insights into the matter of understanding (1986). Contrary to the processes prevailing in the sciences, Gadamer argues that understanding never follows a logical method: rules, as precise and rigorous as they may be, simply cannot lead the interpreter straight to the 'right' meaning of the text. The text does not contain 'one' sense that the interpreter would 'discover', for example in the way an archaeologist digs up an amphora that has been lying hidden under stone slabs or a museum director unveils a statue on the occasion of an opening ceremony. On the contrary, an interpreter's understanding of a text or situation is realised through her 'pre-understanding', that is, through an anticipatory apprehension of meaning. Access to the text and to the questions arising from it is already, perhaps unconsciously, fashioned according to the historical tradition to which the interpreter belongs.

The modalities under which understanding takes place can be illustrated through the following example. Suppose a German tourist is visiting New York's Bronx Zoo for the first time, which is often described as the world's largest metropolitan zoo. While walking around, the German comes across an exotic animal, an okapi, native to the Ituri rainforest located in the northeast of the Democratic Republic of Congo, in Central Africa. Now, the German tourist has never encountered this animal before and she is struck by its quite peculiar physical characteristics. The body shape is similar to that of a giraffe, except that okapis have much shorter necks. Further, okapis have dark backs, with striking horizontal white stripes on the front and back legs making them look like zebras. How can the German tourist ascribe sense to this unfamiliar creature? As I have just suggested, she has no choice but to refer to familiar or pre-existing ideas – giraffe and zebra – in order to gain a certain understanding of the animal. Having said that, we can expect that an inhabitant of the Ituri rainforest who has been living alongside okapis all her life will approach the animal from a different point of view and will probably not (need to) think of it as being like a giraffe or a zebra. In other words, her pre-understanding will differ. The point is Gadamer's: the historical tradition to which the interpreter belongs matters to the act of understanding.

The same is the case for the interpretation of foreign law. The comparatist must be aware of the fact that her interpretations of foreign legal texts are never objective, but always conditioned by the tradition that she inhabits and that inhabits her and that forms the substance of her 'prejudgment[s]' (Gadamer 1986: 273). Thus, a translation, which is inevitably shaped by the 'pre-understanding' of the interpreter, cannot allow for an authentic understanding of the foreign language and culture in as much as it can never reproduce or duplicate it. In this sense, Gadamer's hermeneutic postulate according to which 'one understands in a *different* way, *if one understands at all*' can be applied without restrictions to the legal realm (ibid: 296, original emphasis although I have modified the translation). Indeed, Wilhelm von Humboldt, one of the most influential German linguists of the 19th century, rightly stressed that: '[n]obody means by a word precisely and exactly what his neighbour does, and the difference, be it ever so small, vibrates, like a ripple in water, throughout the entire language. Thus all understanding is always at the same time a not-understanding, all concurrence in thought and feeling at the same time a divergence' (1836: 63).

Despite the inherent limits of translation, the comparatist can obviously not refrain from translating; otherwise, legal cultures would be condemned to a monadic existence. In the current context of Europeanisation and globalisation, such a situation is at once impractical and undesirable. The question, however, arises as to how the translator can make the impossible possible. What can be regarded as the most appropriate strategy of translation for comparative legal research?

In my view, the comparatist, whose task is to explain the foreign legal culture, should not adopt a 'fluent' translation strategy. Far too often, translators attempt to produce a transparent discourse by rewriting the original text in the host language. For example, a French translator might offer a French translation of Shakespeare that looks as if Shakespeare had written his text in French. Similarly, a Chinese comparatist could offer a Chinese translation of a German textbook that looks as if the author had written the text in Chinese. In the 18th century, many French translators used this mode of translation, commonly referred to as the *belles infidèles* ('beautiful unfaithful'), with a view to adapting the foreign literary works to French morals and values (Zuber 1995).

The translations of Homer's work into the French language strikingly illustrate this translation practice (Oseki-Dépré 1999: 37). Thus, Madame Dacier's prose translation of Homer's *Iliad* (circa 760–710 BCEa), published in 1699, can be regarded as a rewriting of the original Greek text. In particular, passages featuring elements that French society then considered as too sensual or repugnant were entirely reformulated by the French translator. Only approximately 150 years later, in 1866, did Leconte de Lisle offer a retranslation of Homer's *Iliad* (circa 760–710 BCEb) revealing the richness of the original Greek text to the French readership. A comparison of these two translations shows that the goal of translating in the way in which the author would have written if the language of translation had been her original language is harmful. Such a translation fails to communicate the cultural and linguistic particularities of the foreign text. On the contrary, it produces what one might style an appropriation of the cultural other, which ultimately deprives otherness of its singularity. I claim that a comparatist, who needs to be especially sensitive to the trap of cultural assimilation, cannot accept this approach to translation.

The French translation of the US notion of 'affirmative action' as *discrimination positive* illustrates the salient issues arising from the ethnocentric strategy that I condemn. The words 'affirmative action', an idea originally developed in the United States, imply that positive steps must be taken in order to increase the representation of women and other minorities in the areas of employment, education and business, from which they have historically been excluded (Anderson 2005; Kellough 2006; Leiter and Leiter 2011). In the United States, action is taken in an affirmative way in order to promote a measure of equality between individuals. In 1978, Justice Harry Blackmun, in the case of *Regents of University of California v Bakke*, one of the first US Supreme Court decisions dealing with affirmative action, stressed that 'in order to treat some persons equally, we must treat them differently'.[4]

In France, by contrast, the idea according to which membership of a particular group of people (for instance, an ethnic group) would imply preferential treatment is regarded as contrary to the constitutional doctrine of equality.[5] Rejecting the US practice of 'affirmative action', a French author writes: 'What sense could it have in a country like ours, formed of citizens who, for the past two centuries at least, have not been part of any "race", "ethnic group", "community" or other "minority"?'(Calvès 1998: 339). As a result, French people tend to perceive the idea of 'affirmative action' negatively. It cannot be altogether surprising that the French language has therefore opted for a pejorative translation such as *discrimination positive* (Wuhl 2007; Calvès 2008; Tharaud 2013). Fascinatingly, the French word *discrimination* emphasises the very phenomenon – discrimination – that the United States actively intends to prevent. In the process, the chosen translation appropriates the US initiative to a set of French values and preferences and robs it of its specificity. In the United States, affirmative action is *not* discrimination, contrary to what the French translation would have us believe.

In my view, the comparatist must therefore adopt an 'alienating' strategy of translation, which attests to the particularities of the source text. The result will be a text in translation that purposefully creates a feeling of strangeness. In other words, the translation must give the reader the impression that she is reading a foreign work. Although famous for his 'germanising' translation of the Bible, Martin Luther (1483–1546) offers an early example of someone who occasionally used an alienating strategy of translation with a view to showing greater respect for the specificity of the source language (Bluhm 1965; Bocquet 2000).

In his 'Summaries on the Psalms and the Reasons for Translating Them' (*'Summarien über die Psalmen und Ursachen des Dolmetschens'*), published in 1533, Luther thus stressed that for certain passages where he thought form was especially important, he would not stray from the original text. In such instances, Luther preferred to derogate from the German language than to move away from the Word. For example, as regards the rendering of Psalm 68/19 of the Book of Psalms, Luther explained that he used the literal translation *Du bist in die Höhe gefahren und hast das Gefängnis gefangen* ('Thou hast ascended on high, thou hast led captivity captive') rather than the free translation *Du hast die Gefangenen erlöst* ('Thou hast taken the captives') (Luther 1533: 13). The latter formulation would have conformed better to the fabric of the German language but would have remained too flat to render all the semantic richness of the Hebrew (Bocquet 2000: 88–9). In fact, the German reader had to understand that Christ had not only taken the captives but also the prison itself. In this sense, the prison would no longer be able to imprison any human beings, an idea which implies eternal salvation. Luther's translation is innovative as the German language did not know the expression '*das Gefängnis fangen*' ('capture captivity'). However, Luther wanted to compel the German language to accommodate the specificities of the Hebrew. As a result, a German reader faced with Luther's translation is put on notice that, although she is reading German, she is also reading a text featuring a foreign dimension. In other words, she is made aware that she is reading *German-in-translation*.

In order to highlight the benefits arising from such a strategy for comparative legal research, I want to refer to the translation of the English term 'estoppel' by the French word *préclusion*. In Canada, a country which is at once bilingual and bi-juridical, the French translation of the English word 'estoppel' shows to what extent it is possible to structure language in order to accommodate a linguistic arrangement that is foreign to it. In English, the word 'estoppel', originating from the common law tradition, refers to the idea that an individual is precluded from making a claim incompatible with a legal situation to which she has previously consented. For example, a landlord who informs his tenant that the rent will be lowered on account of major construction works taking place in the building cannot at a later stage, once the tenant has relied on the diminution of rent, change his mind and call for the payment of the usual rent after all. The landlord is legally prevented from acting in this way: he is 'estopped'. In francophone Canada, the word *préclusion*, although unknown to the French language, has been used to convey the English term. *Préclusion* is a literal translation of the English word 'preclusion', which refers precisely to the fact of being prevented from doing something.[6] The introduction of a novel term in the host language,

French, bears witness to the foreign character of a word from the source language which, as I say, is historically connected to the common law tradition.

This approach to translation can be traced most prominently to Friedrich Schleiermacher. On 4 June 1813, Schleiermacher, a German philosopher and translator of Plato, pronounced a path-breaking discourse entitled '*Über die verschiedenen Methoden des Übersetzens*' ('On the Different Methods of Translating'), at the Royal Academy of Sciences in Berlin. In a well known formulation, he outlined two possible translation strategies, which would later be styled as the 'ethical' and 'ethnocentric' approaches to translation (Berman 1999: 78): 'Either the translator leaves the writer in peace as much as possible and moves the reader toward him; or he leaves the reader in peace as much as possible and moves the writer toward him' (Schleiermacher 1813: 49). According to the first scenario, which is said to foster an ethical attitude to translation, 'the translator is endeavoring [...] to compensate the reader's inability to understand the original language' (ibid).

The second scheme, by contrast, which is regarded as promoting an ethnocentric perspective on translation, aims 'to show the work as it would be had the author himself written it originally in the reader's tongue' (ibid: 55). Schleiermacher rejected the latter design because 'the goal of translating just as the author himself would have written originally in the language of the translation is not only unattainable, but is also in itself null and void' (ibid: 56). Strongly arguing in favour of the first arrangement, he reminded translators that the ethical approach to translation 'is founded on two basic conditions: that the understanding of foreign texts be acknowledged as a known and desirable state, and that a certain flexibility be granted to our native tongue' (ibid: 55). Indeed, 'this sort of translation [...] has meaning and value only in a nation whose people are favorably disposed to appropriate the foreign' (ibid).

Schleiermacher's understanding of translation has been defended by leading contemporary translation theorists. In particular, Antoine Berman, a French translator and author of several books on translation theory, strongly advocates what he names an 'ethical' or 'authentic' approach to translation (Godard 2001). For Berman, the activity of translation 'consists in the recognition and reception of the Other as Another' (1999: 74). In the United States, Lawrence Venuti, an influential translation studies scholar and experienced translator, also favours an ethics of translation. In reaction to the ethnocentric practices prevailing on the other side of the Atlantic, Venuti claims, in the name of ethics, 'that translations be written, read, and evaluated with greater respect for linguistic and cultural differences' (1998: 6). According to Venuti, 'the aim is [...] to develop a theory and practice of translation that resists dominant values in the receiving culture so as to signify the linguistic and cultural differences of the foreign text' (2008: 18).

The ethical approach to translation, as advocated by Schleiermacher, Berman and Venuti, did not only have a fundamental impact on translation studies or literary criticism but also on other disciplines such as post-colonial studies. For example, Gayatri Spivak, a prominent feminist, literary critic and translator, emphasises, in an essay entitled 'The Politics of Translation', the need for an ethics of translation that showcases cultural differences (1992). She observes that: '[i]n the act of wholesale translation into English there can be a betrayal of the democratic ideal into the law of the strongest. This happens when all the literature of the Third World gets translated into a sort of with-it translatese, so that the literature by a woman in Palestine begins to resemble, in the feel of its prose, something by a man in Taiwan' (ibid: 204).

Interestingly, some comparatists have also argued in favour of this approach. For instance, Legrand stresses that '[the comparatist] cannot claim, while maintaining the integrity of the comparative process as authenticity of *comparandum*, to represent German law in the English language through a deliberate process of anglicization' (2011: 105, original emphasis). According to this author, 'to translate also entails work on the host language itself in order to allow the uncanny voice of the other to be heard within it' (ibid: 114). Indeed, an alienating approach to translation constitutes the only strategy that is ethically acceptable for comparative legal studies. However, the comparatist should keep in mind that the recourse to this approach does not solve all problems inherent to translation. In the end, translation does remain impossible. Languages do not signify identically. Further, translation always involves an act of interpretation.

Therefore, as Jacques Derrida notes, translation must be seen as necessarily implying a 'transformation' of the original text. Observing that '[w]e will never have, and in fact have never had, to do with some "transport" of pure signifieds from one language to another, or within one and the same language, that the signifying instrument would leave virgin and untouched' (Derrida 1972: 19–20), he adds that 'for the notion of translation, we would have to substitute a notion of *transformation*: a regulated transformation of one language by another, of one text by another' (ibid: 19, original emphasis).[7] Transformation, according to Derrida, captures untranslatability as the negative moment necessary to the recognition and survival of the idiomatic that exceeds one's grasp and to which one's response can therefore be neither sheer reproduction nor meaning transfer. It refers to another *economy*, to an economy of *negotiation*,[8] one where '[w]hat guides [on]e is always untranslatability' (Derrida 2004: 26).

It must be clear that comparatists can no longer ignore or minimise the relevance of translation studies and linguistics for comparative legal studies. Although a closer examination of the possibilities and limits of translation shows that translation is impossible, nevertheless comparatists must make the impossible possible by using an alienating strategy of translation that values the specificity of the source text. It seems apt at this point to enter a quotation from Samuel Beckett, who writes near the end of his novel *The Unnamable* (*L'Innommable*), originally published in French and later adapted by the author in English: 'I can't go on, I'll go on' (Beckett 1953: 418). He adds that 'one must say words as long as there are any' (ibid). In my view, Beckett's injunctions are of the utmost relevance for comparative legal studies. Although the comparatist cannot translate, she must translate and say words as long as there are any.

With a view to responding to Beckett's call and thus making the impossible possible, this edited collection of essays brings together leading scholars representing a wide range of disciplines and national backgrounds. Together, they consider translation issues in comparative legal studies and demonstrate beyond any doubt why these need to be taken seriously by comparatists. The book features three different sections, each of which addresses a specific concern as regards the relationship between comparative law and translation. The first part, entitled 'Addressing translatability', assumes that no serious reflection on comparative law and translation can escape the initial consideration of threshold questions having to do with translatability. To what extent is (the impossibility of) translation possible? Can translation overcome the epistemological encumbrance of the translator? Can a translation ever be said to be true? How much knowledge of a language and culture is required for a valid translation to happen?

The first contribution sets the tone for this collection of essays engaging comparative law and legal translation. In his chapter, 'Translation as ethics', Alexis Nouss shows that translation is much more than a means to an end. Rather than being confined to a strictly mechanical or technical process, translation constitutes in fact a model for ethical thought and ethical practice. Nouss argues that translation is ethical in the way in which it is inherently critical, infinite and subversive. First, translation is critical as it implies a number of 'turning points' or 'points of decision'. Secondly, translation is never final since the translator's decisions are influenced by history. Thirdly, translation is subversive because it questions the ideas of authority and auctoriality. Through a discussion of the works of eminent philosophers such as Benjamin, Gadamer and Emmanuel Levinas, Nouss argues that every translation must be regarded as a unique encounter between the self and the other. As such, the activity of translation gives rise to a full range of questions which are of the utmost significance for comparatists who, as individuals situated in time and space, constantly find themselves having to move across different cultures and languages.

The following chapter, entitled 'Who's in control? Translation, cost and the origins of speciation', is also of signal importance for comparative legal studies as it finds itself exposed to current trends in favour of a dominant global language. It will have been obvious that, in recent times, English has progressively become the common language of exchange and communication across the world. Nowadays, not only EU institutions but also information technology and scientific research as a whole are to a large extent dominated by the English language. According to a common assumption, the development of a simplified global English language devoid of cultural elements would allow for more effective and cheaper international communication. However, the emergence of a common language cannot avoid problematic implications regarding the generation of transferred or devolved costs and changes in the understanding of translation or language – not to mention the role of the translator – which are often ignored or underestimated. Michael Cronin, who comes to the matter from a critical vantage point, urges comparatists to rethink language and translation in a globalising world.

The contribution entitled 'Legal translation and the problem of heteroglossia' offers comparatists fruitful insights into the practice of legal translation. Approaching the matter from the perspective of a sociologist, Kwai Hang Ng challenges traditional approaches to the translation of law. The widely accepted idea of legal translation as a bridge between legal systems, the continuing confinement of legal translation to the translation of texts and the prevalent view that the achievement of equivalence is the main purpose of legal translation do not account for the institutional goals of existing legal translation practices. Contrary to common assumptions, legal translation must be regarded as an institution shaped by the ideologies of law and power relations. Having undertaken extensive field research on bilingual courtrooms in Hong Kong, which belongs to a unique group of post-colonial jurisdictions, Ng develops an institutional theory of translation practice based on two fundamental criteria – interpretive autonomy and permanency – which allows for enhanced understanding of the multiple ways in which law interacts with society.

Jean-Claude Gémar, in his chapter 'Catching the spirit of the law: from translation to co-drafting', reflects upon the very nature of legal translation and ponders the different translation strategies that are available to the legal translator. For centuries, the question of equivalence has been a constant source of preoccupation for translators. It is well known that all translators are confronted with problems of conceptual incongruity across languages. However, legal translators have to face an additional difficulty owing to the specialised character of legal language and the normative function of legal texts. Canada, as a bilingual and bi-juridical country, offers rewarding insights into the theory and practice of legal translation. In recent years, Canadian legal translators have experimented with many translation strategies that are of the utmost relevance for comparatists, ranging from strict literal translation to the co-drafting of bilingual legislation. By way of concrete examples, drawn in particular from the Canadian context, Gémar pertinently illustrates the complexity of legal translation in a multilingual normative setting.

In the light of the investigations conducted in the first part of the book, the next section focuses on the specificity of a comparative enterprise, with foreign law as its object of study. The second part therefore addresses the following kinds of questions: Can the very notion of comparative law be said to be interchangeable with that of translation? Does the fact of normativity that attaches to legal texts affect the translation process in comparative legal studies? Must strategies of legal translation vary according to the type of comparative legal research being pursued? Can the foundations of the dominant theoretical model within the field of comparative legal studies (*praesumptio similitudinis*, functionalism, etc) be reconciled with the lessons derived from a reflection on the limits of legal translation?

In her chapter entitled 'Comparative law and the (im)possibility of legal translation', Jennifer Hendry offers an innovative understanding of legal translation in relation to comparative law. For the lay person, legal translation consists in the rendering of legal writings formulated in one language into another language. However, legal translation involves much more than a linguistic or technical procedure. For example, with a view to engaging a critique of legal comparison legal translation can be conceptualised both as a lens and as a frame. This configuration helps comparatists to appreciate the different strands of thought that have developed within the field of comparative law. Indeed, the specificity of comparative law could be said to lie in the fact that the basic dichotomy within the field – the distinction between functionalist and culturalist approaches – is, in the end, a debate about the (im)possibility of translation. Within comparative law, there are scholars who say all is translatable (the functionalists), while there are others who claim nothing is translatable (the culturalists). Ultimately, therefore, it is all about translation! In sum, Hendry aptly shows how comparative law and legal translation are intrinsically and intricately linked to each other.

In the following chapter, 'Translation and the "contamination" of comparative legal research', C.J.W. (Jaap) Baaij explores two influential translation strategies – the target-oriented and source-oriented approaches – that have been used for the translation of authoritative legal texts in the context of comparative legal research. Baaij argues that, contrary to common assumptions, the target-oriented scenario, which requires the legal translator to adapt the target text to the needs and expectations of the reader with a view to creating equivalent legal effects, cannot be regarded as useful for comparative legal studies. In fact, it is often overlooked that this scheme is inevitably grounded on a comparative legal analysis, which is likely to 'contaminate' subsequent comparative legal research. Since the legal translator aims to create a sense of 'sameness' across languages, the comparatist may find herself entertaining the mistaken impression that she is 'discovering' similarities between the domestic and the foreign law. Emphasising the benefits of a source-oriented strategy of legal translation, Baaij highlights the potential value of literal translation for comparative legal research from a hermeneutic standpoint.

In her chapter, 'Translating civil law "objectivity" with an adversarial brain: an ethnographic perspective', Shawn Marie Boyne invites comparatists to reflect upon issues arising from the interpretation of foreign law. Her study, which is based on extensive field research on the role of prosecutors in Germany, stresses the many interpretive challenges faced by legal scholars comparing the German and US criminal systems. Boyne claims that anglophone comparatists trained in jurisdictions where the adversarial model is used have overlooked the strengths of German criminal justice owing to problems of translation and normative bias. Indeed, having undertaken interviews with German prosecutors, she realised that her own perspective was in fact coloured by her experience as a prosecutor in the United States. This argument reminds comparatists carefully to consider the law in practice, continually to interrogate sources of knowledge and assiduously to take into account the larger cultural context in order to determine the meaning of particular legal concepts. Crucially, comparatists also need to be aware of the fact that their backgrounds can be expected meaningfully to influence their understanding of foreign legal culture.

In her contribution, 'The powerless translator: an argument based on legal culturemes', Raluca Bercea sheds light on the person of the legal translator and on the inherent limits of legal translation. Translators are commonly viewed as authoritative figures who can decide to translate the original in many different ways. Legal translators, however, enjoy less latitude owing to the fact that the source and target texts are generally meant to operate in identical fashion, something which holds particularly true as regards normative texts. However, the legal translator faces serious problems because of the presence of linguistic units, or 'culturemes', that are profoundly marked by a given culture. Genuine culturemes are never equivalent, and the search for alleged correspondence requires specific and refined cultural knowledge. At the same time, legal translators have to find meaningful linguistic units operating similarly in corresponding legal situations, which necessitates excellent legal expertise. In her text, Bercea critically assesses different translating strategies so as to determine their usefulness in a context in which translators may find themselves being deprived of their habitual power.

Against the background of an intensified interaction between different cultures driven by economic, legal, political and social interests, the third part of the book emphasises translation's more figurative senses. Specifically, it refers to the negotiation and emergence of meaning – a fact always already laden with power relations but pregnant with new discursive and material possibilities – through the disorientation or repositioning of traditional identities. Can processes of Europeanisation or globalisation usefully generate a new legal language? Can a practice of constitutionalism be meaningfully referred to in a foreign constitutional context? Can law be translated into economic language so as to allow for the rankings being defended by the promoters of 'legal origins' theory?

In their co-authored chapter on 'Translating religious principles into German law: boundaries and contradictions', Pascale Fournier and Régine Tremblay investigate the extent to which a state can translate religious principles within its boundaries and in line with its laws. This issue is of the utmost contemporary relevance, particularly for countries that are home to different religious groups but who only pay lip service to these communities' religious laws. With a view to clarifying the relationship between religious laws and state law, the authors conducted extensive fieldwork among Jewish and Muslim communities in Germany. Having interviewed a number of Jewish and Muslim women living mainly in Berlin, Fournier and Tremblay claim that religious family law is far from being harmonious. In fact, the parties and their families, not to mention religious leaders, are constantly redrawing the boundaries delineating the competing normative orders. In the absence of marked boundaries between religious laws and state law, the recognition, translation and valorisation of religious principles by the state becomes an endeavour as challenging as it is complex.

The next chapter similarly addresses the peregrine nature of law, although from a very different perspective. In his chapter 'Of friendless and stained men:

grafting medieval sanctions onto modern democratic law', Luca Follis offers a detailed examination of civil death, a concept introduced in the United States through the English common law, which has given rise to translation and transferability problems. In Britain, civil death, which was a consequence of attainder or entry into the religious order, became most significant between the 14th and 16th centuries. When it crossed the Atlantic and was grafted onto the statutes of the new democratic states, it developed into a different legal mechanism closely connected to the penal imaginary and the legitimation of state punishment. As late as 1954, civil death still existed in 17 US jurisdictions. In his chapter, Follis traces the history and nature of civil death in England and the United States as he explores the cultural and institutional factors having prompted the mutation of a common law concept into a strong instrument of legal violence.

Bénédicte Sage-Fuller and Ferdinand Prinz zur Lippe, in their contribution 'Abuse of tax law as a language of morality in modern times: a comparative analysis of France, Canada and Ireland', suggest a foray into the politics of legal language. In states where the rule of law prevails, taxes are regarded as a legitimate means for the organisation of public life. Problematically, however, tax regulations have become increasingly complex. Taxpayers often try to turn this fact to their advantage by seeking abusive interpretations of relevant statutes, thereby causing loss of revenue to the state. Many countries have tried to address this issue through the development of General Anti-Avoidance Regulations (GAAR). Sage-Fuller and Prinz zur Lippe invoke the theory of the language of morality developed by philosopher Alasdair MacIntyre in order to illuminate legislative formulations used in French, Canadian and Irish GAAR. Focusing specifically on the meaning of the word 'abuse' in three jurisdictions and two languages, this critical and comparative analysis shows how the language of morality has significantly changed in modern times.

In 'Withholding translation', the final contribution to this collection of essays, Pierre Legrand argues that there are cases in which translation should not govern. In particular, there are situations of 'overtranslation' to be avoided. 'Legal origins' theory, which was developed in the United States in the 1990s, constitutes a noteworthy example of such 'overtranslation'. According to 'legal origins' theory, a country's economic performance is closely linked to whether its legal system is rooted in the common law or civil law tradition. Since 2004, the World Bank has been issuing reports effectively grounded on 'legal origins' theory, measuring and comparing the ease of doing business in more than 130 countries. The so-called *Doing Business* reports purport to show that, from an economic point of view, common law countries are generally performing better than those that historically pertain to the civil law tradition. Problematically, recourse to 'legal origins' theory implies the articulation of the legal into a strictly computational language with a view to identifying the 'better law'. Now, such mathematisation of law simply cannot account for its complexity nor can it convey any sense of its cultural fabric. Legrand concludes that the effort to reduce laws to diagrams and statistics is ill-informed.

By drawing on fields such as translation studies, linguistics, literary theory, history, sociology, philosophy or post-colonial studies, each of the critical and interdisciplinary chapters contained in this volume analyses, in a specific way, the central role of translation in comparative law. This collective enterprise thereby wishes to set a new agenda for comparative law as a discipline. After all, in the pithy words of a leading contemporary translation studies scholar, 'translation changes everything' (Venuti 2013).

Notes

1 I do not mean to suggest that there is no specialised literature on legal translation (Gémar 1995; Šarčević 1997; Cao 2007) or legal linguistics (Gémar and Kasirer 2005; Mattila 2013).
2 *Wainwright v Home Office* [2004] 2 AC 406 (HL); *Campbell v MGN Ltd* [2004] 2 AC 457 (HL).
3 For a comparison of the US and English laws of privacy, see Neil M. Richards and Daniel J. Solove (2007).
4 *Regents of University of California v Bakke*, 438 US 265 (1978) at 407 (Justice Blackmun, concurring).
5 However, this interpretation allows for exceptions. For a study of legislative interventions regarding gender equality, see Joan W. Scott (2005).
6 See National Program for the Integration of Both Official Languages in the Administration of Justice: Jurilinguistic Component, *Canadian Common Law Dictionary*, *vbo 'estoppel'* http://www.pajlo.org/en/dictionary.php (accessed 1 October 2013).
7 Elsewhere, Derrida refers to a 'mutation' (1985: 206). See also Benjamin: 'For in its afterlife – which could not be called that if it were not a transformation and a renewal of something living – the original undergoes a change' (1923: 74). Benjamin anticipates Derrida.
8 An apposite understanding of the word 'economy' as used by Derrida throughout his work would be 'dynamic interplay' (Johnson 1993: 20). For the idea of 'negotiation', see Jacques Derrida (1986: 85).

Bibliography

Anderson, T.H. (2005) *The Pursuit of Fairness: A History of Affirmative Action* Oxford: Oxford University Press.

Aubert, J.-L. and Savaux, E. (2012) *Introduction au droit et thèmes fondamentaux du droit civil*, 14th edn, Paris: Dalloz.

Beckett, S. (1953) *The Unnamable*, in *Trilogy: Molloy, Malone Dies, The Unnamable*, London: J. Calder, 1956.

Benjamin, W. (1923) 'The Task of the Translator', in R. Schulte and J. Biguenet (eds) *Theories of Translation*, trans. H. Zohn, Chicago: University of Chicago Press, 1992.

Berman, A. (1999) *La Traduction et la lettre ou l'auberge du lointain*, Paris: Le Seuil.

Bluhm, H. (1965) *Martin Luther: Creative Translator*, St Louis, MO: Concordia Publishing House.

Bocquet, C. (2000) *L'Art de la traduction selon Martin Luther ou lorsque le traduc-teur se fait missionnaire*, Arras: Artois Presses Université.

Brand, O. (2009) 'Language as a Barrier to Comparative Law', in F. Olsen, A. Lorz and D. Stein (eds) *Translation Issues in Language and Law*, New York: Palgrave Macmillan.

Brandeis, L.D. and Warren, S.D. (1890) 'The Right to Privacy', *Harvard Law Review*, 4: 193–220.

Calvès, G. (1998) *L'*Affirmative action *dans la jurisprudence de la Cour suprême des Etats-Unis*, Paris: LGDJ.

—— (2008) *Discrimination positive*, 2nd edn, Paris: Presses Universitaires de France.

Cao, D. (2007) *Translating Law*, Clevedon: Multilingual Matters.

Cornu, G. (2007) *Droit civil: Introduction au droit*, 13th edn, Paris: Montchrestien.

Curran, V.G. (2006) 'Comparative Law and Language', in M. Reimann and R. Zimmermann (eds) *The Oxford Handbook of Comparative Law*, Oxford: Oxford University Press.

David, R. (2002) *Les grands systèmes de droits contemporains*, 11th edn, C. Jauffret-Spinosi (ed.), Paris: Dalloz.

Derrida, J. (1972) *Positions*, 2nd edn, trans. A. Bass, New York: Continuum, 2004.

—— (1985) 'Des tours de Babel', in *Psyche*, vol I, trans. J.F. Graham, Stanford, CA: Stanford University Press, 2007.

—— (1986) *Altérités*, Paris: Osiris.

—— (2004) [Interview], *Magazine littéraire*, April, n 430: 21–29.

Fauvarque-Cosson, B. (2006) 'Comparative Law in France', in M. Reimann and R. Zimmermann (eds) *The Oxford Handbook of Comparative Law*, Oxford: Oxford University Press.

Gadamer, H.-G. (1986) *Truth and Method*, trans. J. Weinsheimer and G.W. Marshall, 3rd edn, New York: Continuum, 2004.

Gémar, J.-C. (1995) *Traduire ou l'art d'interpréter*, 2 vols, Sainte-Foy: Presses de l'Université du Québec.

—— and Kasirer, N. (eds) (2005), *Jurilinguistics: Between Law and Language*, Brussels: Bruylant.

Glanert, S. (2011) *De la traductibilité du droit*, Paris: Dalloz.

Glenn, H.P. (2010) *Legal Traditions of the World*, 4th edn, Oxford: Oxford University Press.

Godard, B. (2001) 'L'éthique du traduire: Antoine Berman et le "virage éthique" en traduction', *Traduction, terminologie, rédaction*, 14: 49–82.

Großfeld, B. (2003) 'Comparatists and Languages', in P. Legrand and R. Munday (eds) *Comparative Legal Studies: Traditions and Transitions*, Cambridge: Cambridge University Press.

Heidegger, M. (1943) *Heraklit*, in *Gesamtausgabe*, vol LV, M.S. Frings (ed.), 3rd edn, Frankfurt: V. Klostermann, 1994.

Humboldt, W. von (1836) *On Language: On the Diversity of Human Language Construction and its Influence on the Mental Development of the Human Species*, trans. P. Heath, Cambridge: Cambridge University Press, 1988.

[Homer] (circa 760–710 BCEa) *L'Iliade d'Homère*, trans. [A.] Dacier, vol I, Paris: Rigaud, 1719 [1699].

—— (circa 760–710 BCEb) *Iliade*, Odile Mortier-Waldschmidt (ed.), trans. [C.-M.] Leconte de Lisle, Paris: Presses Pocket, 1998 [1866].

Johnson, C. (1993) *System and Writing in the Philosophy of Jacques Derrida*, Cambridge: Cambridge University Press.

Kellough, E. (2006) *Understanding Affirmative Action*, Washington, DC: Georgetown University Press.

Kiesow, R.M. (2010) 'Rechtswissenschaft – was ist das?', *JuristenZeitung*, 12: 585–636.

Legrand, P. (2005) 'Issues in the Translatability of Law', in S. Bermann and M. Wood (eds) *Nation, Language, and the Ethics of Translation*, Princeton, NJ: Princeton University Press.

—— (2008) 'Word/World (Of Primordial Issues for Comparative Legal Studies)', in H. Petersen and others (eds) *Paradoxes of European Legal Integration*, Aldershot: Ashgate.

—— (2011) *Le droit comparé*, 4th edn, Paris: Presses Universitaires de France.

Leiter, W.M. and Leiter, S. (2011) *Affirmative Action in Antidiscrimination Law and Policy*, 2nd edn, Albany: State University of New York Press.

Luther, M. (1533) 'Summarien über die Psalmen und Ursachen des Dolmetschens', in *D. Martin Luthers Werke*, vol XXXVIII, Weimar: H. Böhlau, 1912.

Markesinis, B. (2006) 'Understanding American Law by Looking at It Through Foreign Eyes: Towards a Wider Theory for the Study and Use of Foreign Law', *Tulane Law Review*, 81: 123–85.

Mattila, H.E.S. (2013) *Comparative Legal Linguistics*, 2nd edn, trans. C. Goddard, Farnham: Ashgate.

Menski, W. (2006) *Comparative Law in a Global Context*, 2nd edn, Cambridge: Cambridge University Press.

Oseki-Dépré, I. (1999) *Théories et pratiques de la traduction littéraire*, Paris: A. Colin.

Ortega y Gasset, J. (1930) *The Revolt of the Masses*, K. Moore (ed.), trans. A. Kerrigan, Notre Dame, IN: University of Notre Dame Press, 1985.

—— (1937) 'The Misery and the Splendor of Translation', in R. Schulte and J. Biguenet (eds) *Theories of Translation*, trans. E.G. Miller, Chicago: University of Chicago Press, 1992.

Pommer, S. (2006) *Rechtsübersetzung und Rechtsvergleichung*, Frankfurt: P. Lang, 2006.

Pozzo, B. (2012) 'Comparative Law and Language', in M. Bussani and U. Mattei (eds) *The Cambridge Companion to Comparative Law*, Cambridge: Cambridge University Press.

Prosser, W.L. (1960) 'Privacy', *California Law Review*, 48: 383–423.

Richards, N.M. and Solove, D.J (2007) 'Privacy's Other Path: Recovering the Law of Confidentiality', *Georgetown Law Journal*, 96: 123–82.

Rosenfeld, M. and Sajó, A. (eds) (2012) *The Oxford Handbook of Comparative Constitutional Law*, Oxford: Oxford University Press.

Šarčević, S. (1997) *New Approach to Legal Translation*, The Hague: Kluwer.

Schleiermacher, F. (1813) 'On the Different Methods of Translating', trans. S. Bernofsky, in L. Venuti (ed.) *The Translation Studies Reader*, 3rd edn, London: Routledge, 2012.

Scott, J. W. (2005) *Parité! Sexual Equality and the Crisis of French Universalism*, Chicago: University of Chicago Press.

Spivak, G.C. (1992) 'The Politics of Translation', in *Outside in the Teaching Machine*, London: Routledge, 2009.

Tharaud, D. (2013) *Contribution à une théorie générale des discriminations positives*, Aix-en-Provence: Presses Universitaires d'Aix-Marseille.

Venuti, L. (1998) *The Scandals of Translation: Towards an Ethics of Difference*, London: Routledge.

—— (2008) *The Translator's Invisibility: A History of Translation*, 2nd edn, London: Routledge.

—— (2013) *Translation Changes Everything: Theory and Practice*, London: Routledge.

Weisflog, W.E. (1996) *Rechtsvergleichung und juristische Übersetzung*, Zurich: Schulthess.

Wuhl, S. (2007) *Discrimination positive et justice sociale*, Paris: Presses Universitaires de France.

Yengoyan, A.A. (2006) 'Comparison and Its Discontents', in A.A. Yengoyan (ed.) *Modes of Comparison*, Ann Arbor, MI: University of Michigan Press.

Zuber, R. (1995) *Les 'Belles infidèles' et la formation du goût classique*, Paris: A. Michel.

Zweigert, K. and Kötz, H. (1996) *Introduction to Comparative Law*, trans. T. Weir, 3rd edn, Oxford: Oxford University Press, 1998.

Part I

Addressing translatability

Chapter 2

Translation as ethics

Alexis Nouss

Introduction

There is an old joke concerning a rabbi who was attempting to quell an argument between two villagers, and therefore asked to meet with each of them independently. The rabbi listens to the first one and concludes: 'You're right'. The man leaves happy. The rabbi listens to the second one and concludes: 'You're right'. And the second man leaves, also happy. The rabbi's wife comes into the room and tells her husband: 'I heard everything. How could you tell the first man and then the second that they're both right? They cannot both be right!' The rabbi stays silent for a moment, and then says: 'You're right'.

This joke represents a perfect vehicle in order to understand what ethics is about: judgment, singularity and pluralism. More specifically, we have to ask: how does one pass a judgment or make a decision in a specific situation, knowing that there is a range of possible choices? This leads to the more general question of how to interpret a situation in order to make a decision. This last question acutely describes the translative process which can thus be utilised here as a heuristic model.

Commenting on James Boyd White's book *Justice as Translation*, Richard Freeman writes: 'Neither the client's story [for the lawyer] nor the law can be perfectly rendered; justice consists in some new and appropriate fusion of the two' (2009: 440). Such an attempt calls for an ethical intervention for which translation could be another name. This issue will be investigated through three theses that I will propose. In their wording, the sentence 'Translating is ethical' is to be understood as: 'Translation provides a model for ethical thinking and practice', one model among others since, by definition, ethics implies plurality, the reason why it should not be taken as a synonym for moral philosophy or for deontology, as is often the case in translation studies.

Each of these theses is defined by a concept and by a spatial metaphor. If time is the prime medium for translation, space should not be neglected as an interpretative grid. *Translatio* is displacement and *translation* retains the idea, being a transfer from one linguistic/cultural space to another. Law, especially comparative law, is in the same way bound to spatial influences and considerations.

First thesis: translating is ethical because a translation is always critical since it expresses a series of 'turning points' or 'points of decision' (recalling the meaning of *krisis* in Greek) without deleting the previous stage of indecision, as on a threshold.

Second thesis: translating is ethical because a translation is never definitive since the decisions it is based on are dependent on historical settings which the translator should be aware of and interpret, like a mariner on a ship's deck looking at a sea of contingencies.

Third thesis: translating is ethical because a translation is naturally subversive since it challenges the very notions of authority and auctoriality, as do Marivaux's or Mozart's characters on stage.

Those three theses could be summarised by the following analogical statement: translation is to the original what ethical decision is to the law (moral or juridical).

First thesis: critique, or at the threshold

'A translation is always critical since it expresses a series of "turning points" or "points of decision" (recalling the meaning of *krisis* in Greek) without deleting the previous stage of indecision'. A translation is a text which the reader knows could have been different – unlike the original. I am not expecting Flaubert to have been able to produce a better version of *Madame Bovary*. I read *Madame Bovary* for what it is. However, with regard to its translations, there are 20 of them in English, the latest by Adam Thorpe, published in 2012 (Flaubert 1856), and nobody will complain. Retranslation is a natural literary phenomenon.

The threshold would be the best spatial metaphor to illustrate this ethical and translative phenomenon. A threshold is the quintessential ethical place, the site of ethics since ethics implies both a status of indecision and a singular situation. In front of a door, for example, I may either enter or not into the room beyond. The reason for my choice will only apply to this particular door. Holding another motivation in front of another door will induce another decision. In each case, my whole subjectivity is involved.

Now, the significance of the notion of threshold is most important to understanding the meaning of translation and vice versa since, contrary to current conceptions, translating means experimenting with the threshold condition as much as enacting the passing-through, the crossing-over. More than the comfort of reaching the other side, translation reflects a measure of fear, the expression of an anxiety born out of being on a threshold and of facing the unknown. One is never sure of perfectly understanding the original text – no more than the original reader, and one never knows what his or her translation will look like. That is the reason why retranslating is a common practice while rewriting is not widely accepted in the general textual economy.

In his *Passagen-Werk* (*The Arcades Project*), Walter Benjamin discusses what he calls the 'threshold magic' or 'threshold spell', '*der Schwellenzauber*' (1927–40:

214). His examination of thresholds is astonishing, given that he stresses the potential threat they are carrying out, the bad omen they could herald, rather than the ideas of generosity, of welcoming, or of hospitality they are commonly associated with. That is precisely the point: welcoming should be commensurate with a sense of ill-coming (Derrida and Dufourmantelle 1997). Order has to be disturbed by the coming of the stranger, a foreigner or a foreign tongue. Otherwise, there is no threshold to pass, no translation but a mere transition between two spaces or, in linguistic terms, a transcoding.

One has to go beyond a pragmatic approach to language in so far as any linguistic act is first and foremost an ethical act; I am always talking or writing *to* someone. Moreover, it is because there is someone to be addressed that I am talking or writing. There is no need to hide Emmanuel Levinas's influence here as his philosophy is invaluable for making sense of a European identity whose DNA features otherness within its elements. Levinas has shown how recognition of the other, as the basis for intersubjective relationships, involves recognition of the other's exteriority (1961). Without such acknowledgement, the relationship soon finds itself perverted and threatened by domination. The vibrant function of language – the *saying* as opposed to the *said*, in Levinas's terms (1974) – is to maintain a distance, to protect and to perpetuate the threshold, and consequently to demonstrate that in any human relation the goal is not to erect a bridge between individuals; it is not, then, to achieve an act of communication. Rather, the purpose of the relationship is the relation itself.

Likewise, for Benjamin, 'a translation that seeks to transmit something can transmit nothing other than a message – that is, something inessential' (1923: 151). The main goal of the translative process is not to transfer a meaning but to put languages together through the agency of a human subject whose subjectivity lay in the matrix of their encounter. This concerns primarily the gathering of the two languages involved, but raises the potential congregation of all the world's languages, which any translative act presupposes.

The associated correlated notions of threshold and of translation have the power to subvert the oppositional logics of inside/outside as does the Parisian passage – which provided the theme for Benjamin's *Arcades Project* as well as its blueprint – whose connecting design leads from one public and external space (a street) to another via a fake 'interior'. Undermining such logics will bring a possible answer to a question vital for a definition of European identity: how does one prevent, let us say, a Frenchman from perceiving a Spaniard as a foreigner while simultaneously recognising, accepting and respecting his alterity? Such a dialectical tension between closeness and remoteness, between proximity and distance, characterises European identity and induces translative belonging patterns. By virtue of being Europeans, both the Frenchman and the Spaniard can see in each other a portrait which is not their own but could have been. As Europeans, each can see a possible resemblance in the other's dissimilarity. To be European means to stand on the threshold of all other possible European identities and to be able to translate (into) them.

Second thesis: interpretation, or on deck

In his seminal essay 'On Linguistic Aspects of Translation', Roman Jakobson asserted the possibility of translation from a semiotic perspective in a famous statement: 'Equivalence in difference is the cardinal problem of language and the pivotal concern of linguistics' (1959: 127). If translation is concerned with difference and not with similarity or equivalence – as claimed by traditional theories of translation – this must means that the performance of any translative act assumes distance.

The text to be translated is indeed always situated at a distance from the translator, be it a historical or a cultural distance, or both. The goal of translation is precisely to go through this distance, to *trans-late* it, but not to cross it. This means, however, exposing the receptor to a reality with which he is not familiar. Now, could the efficiency aimed at by so-called target-oriented translation theories be obtained while maintaining and transmitting to the reader/receiver a sense of distance covered? Hans-Georg Gadamer's philosophical hermeneutics (1964: 101) throws a precious light on the process:

> It may be difficult to understand what is said in a foreign or ancient language, but it is still more difficult to let something be said to us even if we understand what is said right away. Both of these things are the task of hermeneutics. We cannot understand without wanting to understand, that is, without wanting to let something be said.

Comprehension would thus be, from a hermeneutical point of view, less difficult in the case of a foreign language than for a familiar one and translation between two languages would be less difficult than understanding within the same language. The key to this paradox resides in the dimension of strangeness attached to the condition of foreignness. Strangeness is actually more perceptible, its origin more easily located, when it is given as such, when it is part of the code of the message to be received from a foreign language. Freud made this apparent through his notion of *das Unheimliche* (the Uncanny) (1919: 121), uncanny precisely because it is familiar.[1] Translation is in reality different from the mere comprehension of a foreign language; it paradoxically resembles interlingual comprehension because if two texts and two languages are concerned, translation casts only one actor: the translating subject, his experience and history since texts are always grasped within a history, wrapped in a bundle of connotations that the translator must locate, a task which he can do only in relation to his own situation. Translation is a process which calls for perception of the *Unheimliche* factor within the translator's personal process of comprehension while he is facing the world:

> The relationship to self, to thought, to others, comes and goes ceaselessly through language. So there is no ethics without ethics of language, if ethics is

not an ethics of language, through the ceaseless shift for I to you, including the absent, the he.

(Meschonnic 2011: 46)

I, you and he together are setting the triangular stage where, for Levinas, justice could be performed: one self, another one and a third one or rather the third, namely the law (1974). Such a distance and its recognition provide a ground for an ethical concern, unlike a transcendental framing, moral or metaphysical, which would encompass, anticipate and therefore delete any distance. Production of meaning is therefore no longer confined in a kind of heavenly realm of signifiers but accepted as a human responsibility. No longer is history a heavy burden, at times so overwhelming that interpretation is rendered impossible nor as a 'yawning abyss' (Gadamer 1986: 297), which likewise defies understanding, but as an historical distance which, by producing relationships, produces meaning. Hence, hermeneutics presents itself as a third approach away from the sterile opposition between source- and target-oriented theories or between concern for the author and looking out for the readership. The translator should not focus on understanding how the author does or did understand or how the reader does or did understand – at any rate the attempt will be unproductive. He should forget about all the current bland and linear binary oppositions and rather become familiar with a triangle in which the three angles (author/translator/reader) are blissfully spinning on the rhythm of history around a prismatic centre occupied by the text.

This awareness of the working of history ends for Gadamer in what he describes as a 'fusion of horizons' (1986: 305). However, a true hermeneutics of translation would rather see the world of the original text and the world of the translator be connected than blended. The translator or the reader of a translation are like mariners standing on the deck of a ship crossing the water: what is behind and what is in front are simultaneously separated and united by the progress of the moving vessel. In a sea of contingencies, agitated by waves and waves of possible choices, where to head to is a matter of interpretation.

The being of translation is not incidentally subservient to history, the stuff translation is made of *is* history and that is why it carries out ethical duties, language being the very link to all historical horizons. When Antoine Berman talks about the 'truth of a translation' (*la vérité d'une traduction*) (1995: 14), he makes it dependent on the translator's historical position, on his translation project and on his translational horizon; in other words, on the specific conditions under which a meaning set out as transcendent could not be respected. Translation is thus inscribed within the counter-discourse that, in Western metaphysics, emphasises the specific as opposed to the general, the transient to the permanent, the present to eternity, and the ethical to the normative.[2]

Third thesis: subversion, or on stage

Some years ago, I felt it appropriate to sketch a 'Praise of Betrayal' along the lines of Erasmus's *In Praise of Folly* or Marx's *In Praise of Crime*.[3] On the one hand, I was annoyed by the repeated quotation of the adage *Traduttore, traditore* (Translator, traitor); on the other, I was intrigued by Franz Rosenzweig's rendition of Matthew 6:24: 'Translating means serving two masters' (1926: 47).[4] How could it be? In the most important modern translation of the Bible into German, which he co-authored with Martin Buber in the first decades of the 20th century, the German philosopher granted mastership both to Jewish tradition and to German language. As such, this work stands as one of the most ethical enterprises of translation imaginable. Owing to what would eventually happen to German Jewry, this translation can in fact be regarded as an attempt to salvage the very idea of ethics.

Nonetheless, given that betrayal could be considered as a most unethical act, defending it requires justification. First, from an epistemological viewpoint, if we reflect on the kind of scientificity with which we call hard sciences the norm, translating appears to foster a science or a knowledge of inaccuracy to the extent that it establishes precisely how not to look for coincidence or exact equivalence, how not to comply with the rigour of the law, how to proceed accurately by approximation, an idea notion that is the counterpart of Levinas's ethical 'proximity': I am close to the other when I recognise that I will never be up to my responsibility towards him, or in other terms when I understand that I will never cross the distance, that I will never fully obey the moral law, never totally fulfil my moral duty (Manderson 2006).

Secondly, when ethics is the welcoming of alterity, if it is to be itself, it has to be infinite and cannot be expressed in terms of accuracy. That inaccuracy is the truth of translation, making it ethical, is supported by two linguistic facts. The first reveals that *translation* does not translate well: translation is not *Übersetzung*, is not *targum*, is not *çeveri* and so on as the semantic radicals of those respectively English, German, Hebrew and Turkish words are totally different. The second raises again an etymological issue, although a wrong one: 'Romance languages derive their terms for "translation" from *traducere* because Leonardo Bruni misinterpreted a sentence in [...] Latin', George Steiner reminds us (1998: 311, original emphasis). Admittedly, a translation error or a semantic betrayal. But sin calls for possible redemption according to Steiner's belief (ibid: 224) in the duality of truth and falsehood in our understanding of language:

> Falsity is not, except in the most formal or internally systematic sense, a mere miscorrespondence with a fact. It is itself an active, creative agent. The human capacity to utter falsehood, to lie, to negate what it is the case, stands at the heart of speech and of the reciprocities between words and world.

As a matter of fact, *traducere* comes from *tra* (beyond) and *ducere* (to lead), while *tradere* (which produced *trahir* in French and betray in English) is formed from *tra*, indicating transmission, and *dare* (to give). The distance betwee *ducere* and *tradere* is really not vast. Translation is a giving; betrayal as we give somebody up' in English, *donner quelqu'un* in French. No surprise her . it is acceptable to betray when it is for a noble cause – which is what distinguishes betrayal from treachery – as in Mozart's operas or Marivaux's plays, to mention only light-hearted examples. Equally, one has to accept that for a translation to be accurate, it will be at the price of betrayal.

Conclusion

One finds many traitors in Shakespeare's plays. They are there for their obvious dramatic value but also because the Bard knew that any power game has to do with betrayal. For instance, the second act of *Henry V* starts with the elimination of three traitors, although close to the king (the Earl of Cambridge, Lord Scroop and Sir Thomas Grey), as a kind of purificatory action before sailing off to battle in France. And yet, besides or even before being a play about war and peace as it is traditionally presented, *Henry V* is a play about translation. This is not only because of its historical background; the conflict between the kingdoms of England and of France calls for a bilingual text – as indeed the play provides – English with some passages in French. The reason is because such a bilingual situation raises issues of translation, which are indeed connected to political power and expansionist drives.

Translation as an activity appears three times in the play. The first reference is politically neutral and quite humorous. Catharine, Catherine de Valois, daughter of the King of France, is trying to learn English with her lady-in-waiting, Alice (Act III, scene 4). The second instance concerns a violent scene of war (Act IV, scene 4). And the third allusion depicts a meticulous enterprise of seduction, with Henry proposing to Catharine in order to secure their kingdoms' union (Act V, scene 2). These last two occurrences express the dual function of translation: to get to the other in order to exercise mastery over him or to get to the other so as to understand him. In other words, it is about looking for sameness or for difference. Here, the full ethical dimension of translation appears in all its concreteness.

Domination entails ignoring the difference; understanding means respecting it. This is what the third example enacts: 'O fair Catherine, if you will love me soundly with your French heart, I will be glad to hear you confess it brokenly with your English tongue. Do you like me, Kate?' (Shakespeare 1599a: Act V, scene 2). Across linguistic boundaries, Henry wants to be loved, while Catherine does not know if she can love him. She confesses her doubt in her broken English just as a character in Corneille's theatre would have put it: 'Is it possible dat I sould love de *ennemi* of France?' (ibid, original emphasis). Henry replies to this with a wonderful piece of Baroque love rhetoric, which could also conceal a purely manipulative discourse:

No, it is not possible you should love the enemy of France, Kate. But in loving me, you should love the friend of France; for I love France so well that I will not part with a village of it; I will have it all mine; and Kate, when France is mine, and I am yours, then yours is France, and you are mine.

Henry then tries to repeat this declaration in French before concluding with this great definition of translation: 'But thy speaking of my tongue, and I thine, most truly-falsely, must needs be granted to be much at one' (ibid). 'Truly-falsely', this oxymoronic adverb, which François-Victor Hugo translates by performing the betraying act of false truth or of true lie – '*mais il faut avouer que nous parlons, toi ma langue, et moi la tienne, avec une imperfection également parfaite, et que nos deux cas se valent*' (Shakespeare 1599b: Act V, scene 2), brings to bear another Baroque touch. Now, this brief Shakespearian exegesis shows that linking translation and love stresses efficiently the ethical dimension of translation, given that love provides the most ethical situation: an individual chooses to attach himself to another on the basis of the other's otherness. No supplementary motivation is required, no contract needs to be signed. If love was to be driven by any objective motivation, if love could be explained, then it would not be love on any account. There takes place a pure ethical drive: the other one's value lies in his being other.

We began with a *Witz*, a Jewish joke whose hermeneutical value has been well known since Freud. Let us conclude with another interpretive comment from the Jewish tradition, a Talmudic commentary[5] on a passage from the fourth book of the Bible, *Numbers*, whose title in Hebrew is *Bamidbar*, which means 'In the desert' (Numbers 21, 18–19). The commentary (Babylonian Talmud, treatise *Nedarim*) relates precisely to the concept of desert, a core notion within Jewish theology. It explains such centrality by way of an analogy serving an ethical purpose: the human subject should be *camidbar*, as a desert, in the ontological condition of wilderness: *Hefker lakol*, totally ownerless. By forsaking his individuality, the human subject will open up to a superior way of being, linked to the divine will. Along the same lines, another Talmudic commentary states that the more a man renounces mastery of the world, the more the world will belong to him.

Those comments are not mentioned for their theological or inspirational value – how effective would it be? – but for what they suggest when applied to the translative process. For the translator should adopt a similar attitude towards the original text. The more he is open to it, the more he will, in the first phase, forsake his stylistic and textual personality and, in a second phase, be the author of his translation, becoming the author of a second original. Translation sets forth this paradoxical genealogy: the possibility of a second original, a 'second finding', to quote Barbara Folkart's title for her book dedicated, unsurprisingly to Berman: *Second Finding: A Poetics of Translation* (2007). The expression comes from a poem by Richard Wilbur, who writes: 'Wishing ever to sunder/Things and things' selves for a second finding, to lose/For a moment all that it [the beautiful] touches back to wonder' (ibid: 44). For her part, Folkart comments: 'Poetry is a reinventing, a second finding that sunders the real from what we think we know of it. [...] The translation of poetry should be a second finding, one which sunders the source poem from what we think we know about language, poetry, and the real' (ibid: 445–46).

The ethical drive calls for such a constant reinvention since each encounter between the self and the other is unique. Therefore, instead of welcoming the original without leaving one's textual and cultural territory in a kind of fake hospitality, one should delete any territorial presence and welcome in one's being the other text, the text of the other. As the novelist Jonathan Franzen says about his writing environment: 'When I'm working, I don't want anybody else in the room, including myself' (2012). In Talmudic literature, the legal notion of *hefker*, of being without ownership, is used to qualify the desert as a land which is not a property. *Abandoned*, one could say in using a term that is quite relevant because of its other meanings of surrendering one's right and of desisting from a given task. The French *abandon* has the same polysemy, which prompted me to employ it when I rendered Benjamin's essay title *Die Aufgabe des Übersetzers*, usually translated as 'The task of the translator', as *L'abandon du traducteur* (1923).

The semantic connection comes out easily. When one gives up on a task, the consequence applies to the outcome of the task, involving any material element connected to the process. If I had renounced writing this chapter, I could not claim any ownership of it, which does not mean that I would have relinquished my three theses and the ideas they support. This could be an ethical position not unlike Bartelby's 'I would prefer not to' in Herman Melville's story, *Bartleby, the Scrivener*, a story about indecidability for Gilles Deleuze (1997: 68–90) or potentiality for Giorgio Agamben (1999: 243–71). In any case, the scrivener's compulsive answer, 'I would prefer not to', is an opening to all possibilities and, as such, can relevantly configure translation as ethics.

The condition of being abandoned, of being deprived of any ownership, can be understood in a translative context and with regard to the original as implying that there is no primary text potentially claiming authoritative and authorised ownership of its translations. All things considered, the assertion loses its edge if one thinks of the ruling in the European Commission stating that any version of any text in any of the 24 official languages of the European Union bears the same legal value as all others. Put differently, there is no original or, which amounts to the same point, there are 24 originals. Along converging lines, one could engage in a discussion on the issue of translation copyright and ask which understanding should guide its implementation. Ought one to refer to the notion of 'copy' (derivative rights) or to that of 'authorship' (property rights)? Ethical thinking carries another perspective allowing one to break with this binary system. Who, then, is the author of a translated literary work? The text belongs to the author, but the words are the translator's. So, who is the owner? As in the rabbi's joke, it is the responsibility of a third player to decide, specifically the reader. And the reader may well answer as the rabbi did.

Notes

1 Quoting Freud indicates that Gadamer's philosophical hermeneutics should not be referred to in an uncritical manner. Two major aspects of his thought call for thorough discussion: the weight of tradition and the role of the community in the transmission of meaning (Cercel 2009).
2 Berman states clearly that 'the truth of translation [is] ethical and historical' (1999: 46).
3 A fascinating short essay included in the 'Theory of Surplus-Value' section of *Das Kapital.*
4 Matthew says: 'No man can serve two masters: for either he will hate the one, and love the other; or else he will hold to the one, and despise the other. Ye cannot serve God and mammon' (*King James Version*). Beside the irony of quoting from the New Testament in an essay dealing with the translation of the Old Testament, Rosenzweig links the parable to the famous polarity suggested by Friedrich Schleiermacher as regards possible translation strategies: 'Either the translator leaves the writer in peace as much as possible and moves the reader toward him; or he leaves the reader in peace as much as possible and moves the writer toward him' (1813: 49).
5 I owe this reference to Rabbi Philippe Haddad. See his lectures at http://www.akadem.org (accessed 1 October 2013).

Bibliography

Agamben G. (1999) 'Bartleby, or On Contingency', in *Potentialities: Collected Essays in Philosophy*, trans. D. Heller-Roazen, Stanford, CA: Stanford University Press.

Benjamin, W. (1923) 'The Translator's Task', trans. S. Randall, *Traduction, terminologie, rédaction*, 1997, 10(2): 151–65.

—— (1927–40) *The Arcades Project*, trans. H. Eiland and K. McLaughlin, Cambridge, MA: Harvard University Press, 1999.

Berman, A. (1995) *Pour une critique des traductions: John Donne*, Paris: Gallimard.

—— (1999) *La Traduction et la lettre ou l'auberge du lointain*, Paris: Éditions du Seuil.

Cercel, L. (ed.) (2009) *Übersetzung und Hermeneutik/Traduction et herméneutique*, Bucharest: Zeta Books.

Deleuze, G. (1997) 'Bartleby or The Formula', in *Essays Critical and Clinical*, trans. D.W. Smith and M.A. Greco, London: Verso.

Derrida, J. and Dufourmantelle A. (1997) *Of Hospitality*, trans. R. Bowlby, Stanford, CA: Stanford University Press, 2000.

Flaubert, G. (1856) *Madame Bovary*, trans. A. Thorpe, London: Vintage, 2012.

Folkart, B. (2007) *Second Finding: A Poetics of Translation*, Ottawa: University of Ottawa Press.

Franzen, J. (2012) 'The Path to Freedom', *The Guardian US*, 26 May, 'Books' http://thelonggoodread.com/2012/05/27/jonathan-franzen-the-path-to-freedom/> (accessed 1 October 2013).

Freeman, R. (2009) 'What is "Translation"?', *Evidence and Policy*, 5: 429–47.

Freud, S. (1919) 'The Uncanny', in *The Uncanny*, trans. D. McLintock, London: Penguin Classics, 2003.

Gadamer, H.-G. (1964) 'Aesthetics and Hermeneutics', in *Philosophical Hermeneutics*, D.E. Linge (ed. and trans.), Berkeley, CA: University of California Press, 1976.

—— (1986) *Truth and Method*, trans. J. Weinsheimer and G.W. Marshall, 3rd edn, New York: Continuum, 2004.

Jakobson, R. (1959) 'On Linguistic Aspects of Translation', in L. Venuti (ed.) *The Translation Studies Reader*, 3rd edn, London: Routledge, 2012.

Levinas, E. (1961) *Totality and Infinity*, trans. A. Lingis, The Hague: Kluwer, 1991.

—— (1974) *Otherwise than Being or Beyond Essence*, trans. A. Lingis, The Hague: Kluwer, 1991.

Manderson, D. (2006) *Proximity, Levinas and the Soul of Law*, Montreal: McGill-Queen's University Press.

Meschonnic, H. (2011) *Ethics and Politics of Translating*, trans. P.-P. Boulanger, Amsterdam: J. Benjamins.

Rosenzweig, F. (1926) 'Scripture and Luther', in M. Buber and F. Rosenzweig (eds) *Scripture and Translation*, trans. L. Rosenwald, Bloomington, IN: Indiana University Press, 1994.

Schleiermacher, F. (1813) 'On the Different Methods of Translating', trans. S. Bernofsky, in L. Venuti (ed.) *The Translation Studies Reader*, 3rd edn, London: Routledge, 2012.

Shakespeare, W. (1599a) 'The Life of Henry the Fifth', in *The Complete Works*, S. Wells and G. Taylor (eds), Oxford: Oxford University Press, 1986.

—— (1599b) 'Henry V', in *Théâtre complet*, vol I, trans. F.-V. Hugo, Paris: Gallimard, 1941.

Steiner, G. (1998) *After Babel*, 3rd edn, Oxford: Oxford University Press.

Chapter 3

Who's in control? Translation, cost and the origins of speciation

Michael Cronin

In October 1910 at the Enniskillen Quarter Sessions in the north of Ireland, the proceedings were momentarily troubled by the stumbling block of translation. Solicitor John F. Wray was cross-examining a witness and asked: 'Was it the custom for a *mehel* of men to come to the bog to cut turf?'. The word *meitheal*, or *mehel*, as it was spelt in the newspaper report greatly bothered County Court Judge Craig. Judge Craig asked the solicitor what he meant. The solicitor replied that it was an Irish word and that the witness would soon explain what it meant. The judge rebuked the solicitor saying: 'Couldn't you get an English word that would suit equally as well? We talk English in this court, and we have no interpreter here except yourself. Call it something else'. Wray proceeded to explain that *meitheal* was an Irish farming custom whereby farmers would contribute a day's work to help a neighbour cut the turf quickly. At a later stage in the proceedings, Wray asked the witness what was the usual number of men in a *meitheal* but the judge had had enough: 'I do not want your *mehel*. Talk some English. I do not know Irish. It is a very interesting language, but I have not learned it' (Anon 1910: 9).

At the heart of this particular legal exchange is the status of language, or rather, languages and the appropriate role of translation. Is the intolerable residue of the untranslated an affront in a specific historical instance to the hegemonic language of the courts or is it a reminder of how any instance of translation, in legal settings or elsewhere, makes the connection between language and power inescapable?

In this chapter, I will explore a number of developments that impinge on how we might think of or about translation in the contemporary moment, from the emergence of controlled languages to the notion of *lingua franca* and from the role of disintermediation to the nature of scientific communication. In the context of debates around translation and comparative law, it is important at all times to remind ourselves that this object called 'translation' is constantly changing.

Control

One of the core questions faced by translation in the digital age is how one of the tools that humans use to communicate, language, is influenced by the other tools that they use. If time, critical mass and cost are factors informing the organisation of translation as an activity, what happens to language itself in the new regimes of translation?

Beginning with cost, it is currently estimated that it requires US$200 to write, review and republish a new page of documentation. The cost rises to US$1200 if the page is translated into the 23 (now 24) official and working languages of the European Union (EU) (Wignall 2009). The notion of cost is bound with the polysemous nature of language. The more that is said in one language, the more it costs to say it in other languages. As the Business Development Director of SDL phrases it: 'the multiplicity of ways in which we can say the same thing means that we have to review and approve everything that is written. With no way to see in advance what is the "correct" way to say something, writers are continually and unwittingly creating new material' (ibid). So one new sentence in the original language generates 23 new ones, for example, in an EU context. This new material is referred to as 'accidental content' and a reduction in the generation of this accidental content, it is argued, can produce significant savings. However, the rationale for combating the proliferation of 'accidental content' is not just financial. Too much content of this type 'reduces clarity, quality and ultimately ease of use. In extreme cases, it may even impact safety if content is sufficiently inconsistent and confusing' (ibid). The duty of clarity and care come to the rescue of cost in this scenario.

Use of versions of a Controlled Natural Language (CNL) is held to be one way of avoiding the expensive and dangerous chaos of novelty. CNLs in English generally use specific sets of grammatical and style rules, a restricted vocabulary, limited sentence lengths, determiners and the active rather than the passive voice to generate content. This makes texts easier to translate but it also means that more translations can be reused as the likelihood of 'accidental content' being generated in the source language is diminished. The less that is being said, the more often it can be said (in other languages), at no extra cost. Procedural information (eg removing and replacing the casing on a PC), warnings and cautions, component level reuse (eg documentation relating to similar engines and gearboxes reused across different model ranges), all of these lend themselves to the type of content reuse which is viewed as an important element of the economies of scale of larger translation projects.

However, it is useful to reflect more broadly on how natural language and not simply specific corporate CNLs become an object of control in an era of global communication and how actual practices resist specific ideologies of control. Martin Schell, the managing director of GlobalEnglish (http://www.global english.com), sees global rights carrying global responsibilities (2008):

> Our company focuses on promoting and refining the use of English as a tool for global communication. We feel that native speakers of English need to become more responsible about the global role of our language. This means speaking and writing English more clearly so that it can be understood throughout the world.

Speaking and writing English as a *lingua franca* (ELF) involves simplifying syntax by reducing subordinate clauses and modifier phrases, minimising the total number of compound nouns, verbs, adjectives and adverbs and expressing an action as a verb rather than as a gerund. The Global English of Schell, like the Controlled Natural Languages of SDL, is deemed to be simpler, safer and more economic. In addition, it is presented as more culturally sensitive. Whereas it might be assumed that the particular complexity or 'thickness' of a language constitutes its richness and that cultural sensitivity in translation involves capturing and respecting that thickness, Schell's Global English paradigm is strikingly different. The more English is shorn of its difference, the more it is sensitive to difference. Responsible intercultural communication for the English native speaker is to be always already translated, to imagine what it is like to experience English as a translated subject. Removing, not preserving, 'accidental content' is the only way to avoid accidents of misunderstanding, be they real or imagined.

Ironically, the rhetoric of transparency finds support in the 'Fight the FOG' campaign started by translators of the European Commission Translation Service in 1998. FOG is an acronym for a number of expressions such as 'farrago of Gallicisms', 'frequency of gobbledygook' and 'full of garbage' (Taviano 2010: 44). The campaign was prompted by a concern that the English increasingly being used as a *lingua franca* in EU institutions was characterised by wordiness, imprecision and clumsiness. In effect, what the campaign acknowledged was that many of the source documents produced by the EU in English were themselves always already translated in that they had been compiled by multilingual groups who did not have English as their first language. The collaborative and interactive capacities of information technology in addition to the reduced time necessary for the physical production and virtual delivery of documents both facilitates and accelerates the creation of these multi-authored documents.

It would appear then in the increasing prevalence of ELF in the EU (Phillipson 2003) that just as there is technical convergence in terms of norms of exchange and interoperability (eg internet protocols), there is a similar convergence at the linguistic level in terms of a common language of exchange and communication. One operating system. One Language. Is English, then, the Perfect Language that Umberto Eco's scholars have striven for over centuries (Eco 1995), the Language of Eden that communicates its meanings with perfect clarity, its communicativeness a perfect parallel to the instantaneous connectivity of global IT?

Stefania Taviano, in her study of the translation of ELF notes that, in the case of many EU documents in English, what tended to characterise these documents was convoluted syntax (overuse of relative clauses, embedded and subordinate clauses), use of uncommon collocations, Eurojargon, adjectives/past participles in a post-modifier position and extensive use of nominalisation (2010: 27). She further noted the following (ibid: 29):

> Noun phrases tend to be post-modified by a prepositional phrase with an embedded non-finite verb phrase, as in the case of 'the establishment of a

mechanism of structured cooperation with the Member States using methods that have been tried and tested under the Open Method of Coordination was welcomed by many respondents'.

ELF in the corpus she examined was not a language of incisive immediacy but was complex, prolix and, in places, impenetrable. It is the existence of these hybrid, tacitly multilingual texts that led Anthony Pym (2001: 11) to characterise translators not as agents of hybridisation but as practitioners of dehybridisation:

> Contemporary professional non-literary translation in Europe is an agent of dehybridization for the simple reason that source-text generation processes are increasingly multilingual, whereas translation outputs are normally monolingual. Translations in general are agents of dehybridization in the sense that they create and project the illusion of the non-hybrid text.

In an experiment that Taviano carried out with her students (mainly native speakers of Spanish and Italian), she found that they considered the translation of long and complex sentences from English into Italian and Spanish to be relatively straightforward. It was the translation of simple English sentences that proved to be much more challenging. The hybridised texts, owing to the presence of syntactic structures common to Romance languages, had already done the work of dehybridisation for the translators. It was the rendition of terse, more succinct prose that proved more problematic (Taviano 2010: 76–77). The tacit translation present in the production of the documents, in a sense, facilitated the task of explicit translation in their translation into other languages. What is striking is that, as Taviano points out, the widespread use of English, 'seems to contradict the view [...] according to which we should be witnessing the use of a reduced and simplified international language for the sake of global intelligibility and limited translated costs' (ibid: 40). English may be coming to dominate the institutions of the EU but there is no simple or obvious correlation between greater usage and greater simplicity. More means more.

In his study of the translation of EU Green and White Papers into Italian, Arturo Tosi concluded that the translations led to the production of a hybrid, Euro-Italian. The translators, in other words, were engaged not so much in a process of dehybridisation as one of parallel hybridisation of the target language (Tosi 2007). The Italian translations were characterised by relatively high levels of lexical ambiguity, a marked lack of coherence and cohesion owing to a tendency to follow the patterning of the source text and a repeated preference for maintaining more or less the same word count as the English original. What further amplified these trends was the recourse to translation memory and databases, which encouraged the use of previous translations. The multiplier effect of translation technology as noted in Tosi's study gives the lie to more utopian visions of language instrumentalism that characterise particular presentations of translation tools. If English-language dominance of information technology (Microsoft,

Apple, Google, Facebook) has, in part, favoured the widespread dissemination of English, it does not necessarily follow that the fate of ELF for translation is as a language devoid of 'accidental content' or dramatically simplified for the purposes of instantaneous, global communication. On the contrary, the greater incidence of non-native speaker production of text in English can lead to a collaborative hybridisation of the text to facilitate collective production and understanding of the text. The epidemiological effects of digital technology are expressed through the use of translation memories and terminology databases that further the dissemination of new translated varieties of this hybridised English.

Gospel truth

The idea that 'speaking and writing English more clearly so that it can be understood throughout the world' carries with it the assumption that the rhetorical and cultural preferences of one language community can be mapped onto a code of universal communication. In other words, the idea that the use of plain, unadorned speech is the ideal and most effective way to communicate is rooted in the theocratic ideology of Reformation English. An important impulse for the translation of the Bible into vernacular languages was, of course, the notion that in this way the Word of God could be communicated directly to the community of the faithful. No more hiding behind the borrowed prestige of a dead language or dependence on the unreliable mediation of a corrupt clergy, the Word of God would be made directly accessible to everyman and everywoman (McGrath 2002). In a further puritan elaboration of the ideology of directness and immediacy, great emphasis is placed on plain speaking, the simple, unfussy statement of unadorned truth and there is a widespread suspicion of all forms of figurative speech, which made Elizabethan and Jacobean theatre a particular object of opprobrium (Cronin 2005: 13–24). The idea of plain speaking is a rhetorical preference that is linked to a particular set of religious and cultural dispositions, and there is no reason to assume that it can be the expression of, or must found, an idea of universal intelligibility. Indeed, the assumptions that it might are what irritate the German linguist Philip Perlmann in his reactions to the language usage of his American colleague Brian Millar in Pascal Mercier's novel *Perlmann's Silence*:

> The voice formed the words in a completely undetached way. Its tone didn't just show that this was the speaker's mother tongue; the tone wasn't only an expression of the self-evidence with which the language was at the speaker's disposal. There was more at stake: the tone contained […] the message that this was the only language that truly deserved to be taken seriously. *Self-righteous, you understand, his penetratingly sonorous voice is self-righteous. He speaks as if the others were to blame and very much to be pitied for the fact that they, too, don't speak East Coast American, this Yankee language.*
>
> (Mercier 2011: 42, original emphasis)

Perlmann is expressing these opinions to his partner Agnes, who is somewhat sceptical of his sweeping generalisations about speakers of American English. However, what Perlmann fails to observe as a linguist is that circulation deterritorialises a language and that the technology of circulation is not an indifferent factor in the mutation of the language. That is to say, the greater the incidence of English-language usage by non-native speakers of the language, the more probable the translation effects in English of second language usage as is borne out by the development of a particular English language variety in the EU. What gives more permanent presence to these translation effects is that they are in turn captured in translation into different European languages leading to the kind of hybridisation described by Tosi in the case of Italian. An important link in this process of replication is the technology of translation and terminological memory. The technology acts as a powerful multiplier of mutation. In this respect, it is no different from the print technology of Reformation Europe, where the conjoined effects of vernacular translation and print dissemination led to the emergence of markedly different varieties of language, German being a case in point (Sanders 2010). As James Gleick (2011: 400) argues:

> The revolution of Protestantism hinged more on Bible reading than on any point of doctrine – print overcoming script; the codex supplanting the scroll; and the vernacular replacing the ancient languages. Before print, scripture was not truly fixed. All forms of knowledge achieved stability and permanence, not because paper was more durable than papyrus but because there were many more copies.

Stability, permanence, reliability are dependent on the power of duplication. Readers can discuss texts and know that they are referring to the same version wherever they find themselves once they have the same printed edition. What this capacity to reproduce the same endlessly implies is, of course, the powerful consolidating effects of mechanical or technical reproduction. However, what is also apparent is that there are no predictable outcomes in terms of the translation fortunes of Global English or the effects of ELF in translation in a digital age.

One potential translation scenario is the chaste utopia of Schell's Global English or the minimalist functionalism of SDL's Controlled Natural Language. Such developments would appear to dovetail with a digital logic of frictionless, instantaneous convertibility, simplified, monosemic speech circulating even more rapidly along information superhighways. English as a language then would not only reflect the predominantly anglophone corporate dominance of the internet but would also become the preferred language of digital communication through the promotion of highly controlled and specific varieties of the language. Of course, the fundamental impulse for this development is translational. The optimal version of the language is optimal translatability. The easier it is to translate the original document, the more successfully 'global' the language of composition. In other words, ease of translation becomes the implicit parameter for global intelligibility and acceptance. In this scenario, English as Cybertongue is always already translated.

There is, however, another potential path of translation development involving English. In assessing future directions for the evolution of translation, Nigel Reeves (2002: 28) outlines two broad categories of translation activity:

> The first might be called spontaneous translation, done on the spot, often from International English, or direct composition in English by business people, civil servants, scientists, and secretaries, a kind of internalized translation that removes the need for the translator as middleman. The second will be specialist translation in technical, professional, legal, political and cultural domains, included the related studies of summarizing and information transfer.

Implicit in Reeves's distinction is an opposition between English as the source language of global communication that disavows the fact of translation (removing the need for the 'middleman' or, more often, middlewoman) and English as a source and target language for translation that explicitly recognises translation as a constituent part of the cultural identity of particular groups of speakers of the language. This distinction mirrors a familiar one between English as a language of global communication and English as the 'basis for constructing cultural identities' (Graddol 2001: 27). The division in turn maps onto a ready differentiation between the automatic or semi-automatic translation of text for 'global information management (GIM) solutions' (Wignall 2009) and highly particularised forms of translation, involving substantial human input, such as, for example, new renditions of Dostoevsky's novels into English.

However, such translation polarities with their attendant machine/human opposition tend to mask the reality of a global *lingua franca* evolving into distinctive hybrid varieties, which are not necessarily simpler or less complex but are nonetheless distinct. EU English is not the mother tongue of any citizen of the EU but is the recognisable *lingua franca* of the discourse community of its speakers. What gives the language its force is the cyborg interface of humans (translators) and technology (translation memories), which reproduces for the digital age the disseminatory effects of the printed copy in the time of Gutenberg and Caxton. The 'internalized translation' that Reeves speaks of complicates the notion of a reduced pidgin that would serve as the perfect parallel for the binary reductionism of the digital. As a language such as English is more widely disseminated through information technology, it does not follow that Schell's Global English is the inevitable medium of realisation as opposed to a horizon of rhetorical expectation (see also Crystal 2006). On the contrary, the replicative effects of the technology do not so much eliminate the translator as middleman or middlewoman as to turn potentially every middleman and middlewoman into a translator with access to his or her own virtual printing press. This is not to assume that power is evenly distributed throughout discourse communities but it is to acknowledge that the effects of circulation in translation are neither predictable nor homogenous.

Value

The historian and cultural commentator Tony Judt (2010: 1), in a work published shortly before his death, claimed that there was something profoundly wrong about the way people lived their lives in the contemporary world:

> For thirty years we have made a virtue out of the pursuit of material self-interest: indeed, this very pursuit now constitutes whatever remains of our sense of collective purpose. We know what things cost but we have no idea what they are worth.

Even if the 'we' in Judt's claim needs to be qualified and refers to particular parts of the planet where material self-interest can be distinguished from physical survival, he diagnoses a recurrent and habitual concern with cost as the ultimate arbiter of what is of value in many contemporary societies subject to the dictates and constraints of the market economy. Indeed, it is frequently the costs associated with translation that become a core argument in attempts to remove translation altogether from societies and impose a *lingua franca*. One commentator, for example, on the translation situation in the United Kingdom had the following to say:

> It's a shocking figure: more than £100m was spent in the past year on translating and interpreting for British residents who don't speak English. In the name of multiculturalism, one Home Office-funded centre alone provides these services in 76 languages [...]. The financial cost is bad enough, but there is a wider problem about the confused signals we are sending to immigrant communities. We are telling them they don't have to learn English, let alone integrate.
>
> (Rahman 2006: 27)

What is noteworthy is the way the idea of cost itself is constructed. Costs are always a cost to someone, and it is that someone who goes on to define what a cost is but strictly, of course, in one's terms. Implicit in Zia Rahman's argument is the contention that if everyone learned English the unnecessary costs associated with translation would disappear. It is a variation on an argument that is articulated in critiques of the foundational multilingualism of supranational bodies such as the EU. Large sums of money, it is argued, currently being spent on translation and interpreting services would be saved if the sole working language of the EU was a vehicular language like English (Van Parijs 2004). What these arguments centred around cost fail to make apparent is the equally onerous costs of having to resort to a *lingua franca*.

If one takes the example of English, vast sums of money are spent by governments around the globe to teach the language to its citizens (Grin 2004:

189–202). This is a cost that is not borne by English speakers themselves but is incurred by those who do not speak the language and feel the necessity to learn it. In addition, the circulation of cultural goods such as music, cinema and literature in English does not automatically have to bear the translation costs that are almost axiomatic for non-anglophone cultures that seek global circulation of their own cultural goods. In a sense, what is at play here is a practice of what might be termed *transferred* or *devolved cost*, which is characteristic of the redefinition of consumption in digital contexts.

In a practice that originated with low-cost airline operators, intending passengers are invited or, in the case of some airlines, obliged to print out their boarding passes in advance. This entails the passenger having access to the equipment (computer and printer) and internet connection which allows him to enter the necessary details and print out the pass. Both the equipment and the connection are a cost to the passenger or to the entity that has made these available to the passenger. There is the further opportunity cost of the time spent accessing the site, filling in the details and printing out the pass. This is the time that the passenger could have been doing something else. In short, what were formerly production costs for the airline, paying someone to prepare and print out your boarding pass, now become consumption costs for the passenger.

Digital technology allows the transfer of the cost from the producer to the consumer. The labour is done by the passenger not the airline operator so that the surplus value accrues not to the passenger but to the airline. When the argument is advanced that the use of a *lingua franca* eliminates translation costs what one has, in effect, is another form of transferred cost. Whether as consumers of the *lingua franca* or potential producers of the language, those who do not speak it must bear the often considerable costs of acquisition. These costs include not only the monies actually spent on formal education but also the opportunity costs of learning the language, that is, the time that could have been spent pursuing another potentially lucrative activity.

Thus, while much has been said in the context of translation about how digital technology can reduce translation costs, little thought has been given to the notion of cost itself and how it is construed and by whom. Translation is always a 'cost' to the dominant language but the dominant language is supposedly cost free. The costs disappear from view, discreetly transferred to the speakers of the non-dominant idioms. What translation or the demand for translation makes apparent is the nature or existence of this embedded cost for the non-native speakers of a global *lingua franca*. If there is no need to translate this is because one of the parties has spent considerable time and/or money dispensing with that need.

Invisible labour

The making invisible of the language labour encoded in the use of a global language is partly facilitated by the phenomenon of *disintermediation*, which is a

striking feature of economic and social practice in the digital age. As th
writer and economic commentator John Lanchester remarks: 'Every
deal with a phone menu or interactive voicemail service, you're donating your
surplus value to the people you're dealing with' (2012: 8). When you withdraw
money from an ATM or book a flight on the internet, you are doing the job of
an absent human agent. The agent who formerly booked the flight or the bank
teller who handed you your money, the intermediary, is no longer there. Digital
technology allows for the disintermediation and now you do the work. In effect,
what disintermediation tends to favour is an ideology of convenience that masks
the nature of the real costs involved.

There is another dimension to disintermediation, which is not so much to do
with the cost as with the nature of what is being mediated. In a classic Google
search of sites in another language, alongside the results of the search there
is in square brackets the lapidary phrase: 'Translate this page'. By clicking on
the translation option, the results can, of course, be highly uneven and much
occasional humour at gatherings of translators is devoted to providing ever more
egregious examples of what comes out at the other end of online machine translation systems. The jokes may be entertaining but they are not always particularly
instructive. What is revealing about Google Translate is not the limits to what it
can do but the unlimited nature of what it says about what it means to translate.
What we have, in effect, is another form of disintermediation; in this instance,
the translator as intermediary is nowhere to be seen. The labour of translation
is made invisible and the only ostensible labour is the greater or lesser degree
of post-editing on the part of the user as he or she tries to make sense of the
translated passages. However, there is another dimension to this phenomenon of
translation disintermediation, which relates to how the activity of translation itself
comes to be perceived.

Knowledge is fundamentally a matter of distinctions. We understand something by reference to something else: the ways in which a lemon, for example,
is similar to an orange and the ways in which it is different. Of course, what we
choose to compare something with will determine what aspects of it will be to
the fore and what will be marginalised. Thus, Iain McGilchrist argues (2009: 97,
original emphasis) that comparing a football match with a trip to a betting shop
will bring out some aspects of the experience, while comparing it with going to a
place of religious worship will evoke others:

> The model we choose to understand something determines what we find. If
> it is the case that our understanding is an *effect* of the metaphors we choose,
> it is also true that it is a *cause*: our understanding itself guides the choice of
> metaphor by which we understand it. The chosen metaphor is both cause
> and effect of the relationship. Thus how we think about ourselves and our
> relationship to the world is already revealed in the metaphors we uncon-
> sciously choose to talk about it. That choice further entrenches our partial
> view of the subject.

If we assume that the universe is mechanical and take the machine as our model we will find, not surprisingly, that the body and the brain are particular kinds of machines. As McGilchrist (ibid: 98) observes: 'To a man with a hammer everything begins to look like a nail'. If we assume that the mind is a kind of computer, our notion of memory changes, as Nicholas Carr remarks. We begin to think of memory as a static repository of pieces of information, potentially infinitely extendable, its effectiveness determined only by our memory capacity. The fact that human memory transforms and alters the information that it contains and is fundamentally a dynamic and metamorphic process is masked by the dominant, computational metaphor (Carr 2010: 110–11). Whereas a file in a folder will, if uncorrupted, remain the exact same if we retrieve it a year, two years or ten years later, memories of events in our lives often change substantially over time. As we experience more and more, memories are added to our existing store and earlier memories are altered or reconfigured by these new additions. Such is the prestige and power of the digital that a certain, almost inevitable metaphorical leakage occurs so that humans increasingly tend to think of their own memories as similar to the memories in the hard drives of their computers.

An analogous development potentially affects the activity of translation as a result of the emergence of online machine translation. The disembodied, instantaneous execution of the translation task implies that translation is an agentless, automatic function that can be realised in no time at all and that translation is fundamentally a matching or substitutive operation, the text changing as the language is translated but the layout remaining the same. Hitting the 'translate' button or the 'Translate this page' link is more than a keystroke; it is a paradigm shift. Irrespective of the results, what is implied in the form of disintermediation at work is the representation of translation as a form of instantaneous language transfer akin to the automated sub-routines of digital processing. Jerome in his study gives way to the ghost in the machine. Implicit in this representation, of course, is a particular notion of what language is in globalised forms of exchange. Here, the purpose of language is primarily instrumental. Its function is as an instrument of communication, and the quicker the better. As Eric Schmidt, the chief executive officer of Google argues, presenting Conversation Mode, an oral translation application for Google Translate: 'Never underestimate the importance of fast' (2010).

Service language

In order to understand what happens to languages in periods of global change, Pierre Judet de la Combe and Heinz Wismann set up a distinction between what they call a 'service language' (*langue de service*) and a 'culture language' (*langue de culture*) (2004: 33–35). The service language is a language that is seen in the restricted sense of conveying information of an instrumental nature from one speaker to the next, typically, a language like English used at international meetings of experts on climate change or air traffic regulation. Language, of course, does many things, not all of which involve communication in the narrow sense of information transfer. As Claude Hagège (2012: 180) notes:

> Whatever be the case, whether or not the dominant language is the one in which he or she dreams, this capacity of languages to function as a support for thoughts, imagination and dreams, completely overshadows, without of course suppressing it, the instrumental function of communication in language.

Each language features a triple form of distinctness. First, each language has a separate and distinct set of linguistic structures and by extension, to a greater or lesser extent, different linguistic representations of reality. Secondly, each language community has a specific set of social practices that are articulated through language. Thirdly, each language community is a discourse community or set of discourse communities that expresses history, culture, belief systems through the discourses that have evolved within the community (Hagège 1985: 352).

The idiomatic, symbolic and collective fields of reference account for the particular semantic density and historical specificity of each group of speakers. It is this density and specificity that Judet de la Combe and Wismann try to capture in their notion of a culture language. The difficulty, however, with this term 'culture language' is that it suggests that language as a factor of differentiation is largely concerned with areas of high culture and that science and technology, for example, lie mainly in the realms of a service language. From this perspective, putting a Rilke poem into an online translation system would be inviting trouble but feeding in the handling instructions for a combine harvester would not seem particularly anomalous. The culture language and the service language would have different translational outcomes. This is a false dichotomy, in that what is at stake in scientific and technical translation is arguably as important as what is at play in literary translation, although their fortunes are rarely associated.

Laurent Lafforgue, the winner of the Fields medal for mathematics in 2002, claimed that contrary to popular opinion it was not because French mathematics was so strong that French mathematicians continued to publish in French but that it was writing and publishing in French that added to the originality and creativity of French mathematics:

> At a psychological level, choosing French is a sign of a combative spirit, the opposite of the notion of abandonment or renunciation. Of course, a combative spirit is no guarantee of success, but it is necessary. As the Chinese proverb says, the only battles we are sure to lose are those we fail to wage. On the moral plane, that is to say, at the level of values, which are even more important, the choice of French, or rather a distant attitude with respect to the currently dominant language in the world, means that we consider research itself more important than communicating the results. In other words, love of truth takes precedence over vanity. This does not mean not

trying to communicate with others. Science is a collective enterprise that has been pursued down through the centuries, and even the most solitary researcher is wholly dependent on what he or she has learnt and continues to receive every day. Nevertheless, refusing to attach excessive importance to immediate communication is to be reminded of the meaning of scientific research.

(2005: 32)

There is no evidence, of course, to show that writing about science in one's mother tongue as opposed to English is an obstacle to scientific discovery. Mendel, Planck and Einstein wrote in German, Marconi wrote in Italian and Carnot wrote in French. The period from the end of the 19th century to the beginning of the Second World War was characterised by a notable degree of multilingualism in scientific research and the period was rich in innovation in a multiplicity of disciplines (for German examples, see Watson 2010). If scientific research is about, among other things, curiosity, complexity, innovation, risk and creativity, it is difficult to see how it can be left outside the purview of culture language, as these are attributes of our ability to function effectively in the symbolic richness and historical depth of a particular language. Scientific activity is part of the culture of a community and the cultural richness of science is enhanced rather than diminished by the cultural plurality of languages if only because, for example, everybody does not end up reading exactly the same articles in exactly the same language.

The incorporation of science into a notion of culture language is implicit in the very existence of scientific or technical translation, as much as in the practice of literary translation. What translation as a practice is articulating is a notion that the value of any field of enquiry or cultural practice is greatly enhanced by the expressive and hermeneutic resources of a speech community. Allowing scientists to write in their mother tongue is as important a part of the cultural ecology of humanity as allowing sonnets to be composed or novels to be written in the many idioms of the globe. Translation allows this to happen while simultaneously ensuring that the developments in a particular ecological niche inform the other idioms of the globe. In this context, it is possible to argue that translation is crucial to the emergence of *speciation* as opposed that of *specialisation*. Speciation is a term that refers to the development of particular species, usually as the result of certain isolating factors. Specialisation is the tendency of research in modern science to fragment into smaller and smaller sub-disciplines.

The linguist Hagège points to the intense creativity of Ancient Greece, Renaissance Italy and the Germany of the Holy Roman Empire (from the mid-16th century to the late 18th century) as based on the marked fragmentation of the political entities to be found in these periods. The city-states or principalities were both separate and in regular contact, so new ideas could be explored in relative isolation before the stimulating and beneficial contact with other cultures (Hagège 2012: 132–33). In other words, what particular historical *exempla* point to is the possibility of speciation as the precondition and expression of polycultural and polylingual plurality, which is opposed to the prevalence and danger of monocultural and monolingual specialisation, that is, the endless elaboration of dominant models in a dominant language in a state of repressive equilibrium. It is in this context that any future thinking on translation and comparative law must situate itself, as translation scholars try to deal with the reductive fury of the Judge Craigs of our polities who want to discipline the dissenting energies of languages and cultures and make translation more of a reflex than a reflection.

Bibliography

Anon. (1910) 'Judge Craig and Irish: What is a "Mehel"?', *Freeman's Journal*, 3 November, 9.

Carr, N. (2010) *The Shallows: What the Internet Is Doing to Our Brains*, London: Atlantic.

Cronin, M. (2005) 'Double Take: Figuring the Other and the Politics of Translation', *Palimpsestes*, 17: 13–24.

Crystal, D. (2006) *Language and the Internet*, 2nd edn, Cambridge: Cambridge University Press.

Eco, U. (1995) *The Search for the Perfect Language*, trans. J. Fentress, Oxford: Blackwell.

Gleick, J. (2011) *The Information: A History, a Theory, a Flood*, London: Fourth Estate.

Graddol, D. (2001) 'English in the Future', in A. Burns and C. Coffin (eds) *Analyzing English in a Global Context: A Reader*, London: Routledge.

Grin, F. (2004) 'On the Costs of Cultural Diversity', in P. Van Parijs (ed.) *Cultural Diversity versus Economic Solidarity*, Brussels: De Boeck.

Hagège, C. (1985) *L'Homme de paroles*, Paris: Fayard.

—— (2012) *Contre la pensée unique*, Paris: Odile Jacob.

Judet de la Combe, P. and Wismann, H. (2004) *L'Avenir des langues: repenser les humanités*, Paris: Éditions du Cerf.

Judt, T. (2010) *Ill Fares the Land*, London: Penguin.

Lafforgue, L. (2005) 'Le français, au service des sciences', *Pour la science*, March, 32: 8.

Lanchester, J. (2012) 'Marx at 193', *The London Review of Books*, 5 April, 34: 7–10.

McGilchrist, I. (2009) *The Master and His Emissary: The Divided Brain and the Making of the Western World*, New Haven, CT: Yale University Press.

McGrath, A. (2002) *In the Beginning: The Story of the King James Bible*, London: Hodder & Stoughton.

Mercier, P. (2011) *Perlmann's Silence*, London: Atlantic.

Parijs, P. Van (2004) 'L'anglais *lingua franca* de l'Union européenne: impératif de solidarité, source d'injustice, facteur de déclin?', *Économie publique*, 15(2): 3–22.

Phillipson, R. (2003) *English-Only Europe? Challenging Language Policy*, London: Routledge.

Pym, A. (2001) 'Against Praise of Hybridity', *Across Languages and Cultures*, 2: 195–207.

Rahman, Z.H. (2006) 'Hope of Escape Lost in Translation', *The Sunday Times*, 17 December, 27.

Reeves, N. (2002) 'Translation, International English and the Planet of Babel', *English Today*, 18(4): 21–28.

Sanders, R.H. (2010) *German: Biography of a Language*, Oxford: Oxford University Press.

Schell, M. (2008) 'Global English' http//www.globalenglish.info/global.html (accessed 1 October 2013).

Schmidt, E. (2010) 'IFA International Keynote' http://www.youtube.com/watch?v=d4YJO6Xh9gE (accessed 1 October 2013).

Taviano, S. (2010) *Translating English as a Lingua Franca*, Milan: Mondadori Education.

Tosi, A. (2007) *Un italiano per l'Europa: La traduzione come prova di vitalità*, Rome: Carocci.

Watson, P. (2010) *The German Genius: Europe's Third Renaissance, the Second Scientific Revolution, and the Twentieth Century*, New York: Harper Collins.

Wignall, G. (2009) 'Authoring for Consistency and Reuse' http://www.sdl.com/search/results.html?query=Authoring+for+Consistency+and+Reuse (accessed 1 October 2013).

Chapter 4

Legal translation and the problem of heteroglossia

Kwai Hang Ng

Introduction

This chapter straddles the boundaries between translation studies and sociology. It outlines an institutional theory of translation practices. Theories of translation are often prescriptive – they prescribe what good translation does. My goal is otherwise. Here I attempt analytically to describe the diversity of *doing* translation in reality. My claim is that there are multiple uncoordinated, at times even conflicting, yet coexisting notions of translatability in practice. Contrasting notions of translatability impose different demands and norms. They favour different styles; they assert competing claims of authority; above all, they envisage different relations governing law, language and the translation process. I see legal translation as an institution structured by ideologies of law as well as the power dynamics between legal professionals and other social groups. A fully worked out sociological account of legal translation must therefore consider the institutional context in which a particular notion of translatability is singularly valorised.

The account that follows is inevitably influenced by the peculiarities of my own research experience. Two of these should be mentioned. The first is that my primary case study focuses on Hong Kong. Hong Kong's legal system belongs to a unique group of post-colonial jurisdictions that are very much cosmopolitan and outward looking in their orientation. My interest in post-colonial law in general and several post-colonial common law countries in Asia in particular probably explains why I am fascinated with the question of heteroglossia. The term, originally coined by Russian literary theorist Mikhail Bakhtin (1895–1975), refers to the coexistence of distinct varieties within a single 'linguistic code'. It highlights the mixed and dialogic nature of language-in-use and holds that in every speech one can find traces of 'another's speech in another's language' (Bakhtin 1981: 324).

For my purpose, I appropriate the term to refer to the fundamental 'otherlanguagedness' of post-colonial legal systems. A common feature among post-colonial legal systems, particularly those of the common law variant, is incongruence between legal language and the vernacular. These systems almost invariably evolved from the old common law courts that were imposed over the

courts in colonial Africa, Asia and the Caribbean. As such, they
anguages that the general people neither use nor understand. The
_, or 'otherlanguagedness' is thus a salient and yet unique feature of these
systems. As will be seen, to talk about legal translation in the post-colonial context means much more than a mere filling in of terminological lacunae or lexical
gaps but a wholesale reinterpretation of the law for court users.

The second peculiarity of my research experience is that I am primarily an eth-
nographer who likes to get into a courtroom to see how people interact in open
trials. Studying law ethnographically alerts me to the fact that much of the so-
called translation work in courts is done orally, that is, in the form of court interpretation. As both a professional skill and an academic topic, court interpreting
is often treated and taught differently from legal translation. Court interpreters
have to 'translate' simultaneously, that is, in real time without much forethought.
Legal translators take their time to look for the perfect phrase or expression. In
my opinion there are, however, no good theoretical reasons for excluding court
interpreting from a discussion that aims to identify the manifold distinct forms of
translation practices. In fact, a conception of translation confined to textual practices leaves out too many important institutional phenomena deserving scholarly
scrutiny, including court interpreting and other forms of legal incorporation that
are translational in nature and in function.

Traditional understanding of translatability

I would like to begin by offering a tentative definition of the term *translatability*.
What is translatability? The meaning of the concept is quite undefined (Bassnett
and Lefevere 1990). One meaning (a dictionary meaning), simply and quite
intuitively, is the quality or status that makes a word or a phrase capable of being
translated into another language. However, to say a word is translatable may be
to have already invoked a particular definition of translation – the definition then
seeming tautological. In another meaning, more broadly construed, translatability refers to the preconditions for understanding. Translatability is a concept
often called upon for understanding encounters between cultures. For present
purposes, I would like to treat translatability as a *meta*-theoretical concept. I
understand it as a conceptual discourse that defines what is translatable and what
is not. The concept also defines for us what makes for an ideal translation. Let
me elaborate by specifying three major conceptual premises that underlie the
conventional notion of translatability in the context of legal translation.

Legal translation as a bridge between legal systems

It is generally presumed that the bulk of legal translation is done at the international and supranational levels (Šarčević 1997: 15). Translation is often said to
serve as a bridge connecting two or more separate, independent and different
legal systems, each with its own legal tradition and conceptual resources. The

bridge metaphor suggests that successful legal translation enables undistorted *conversations* and at the same time facilitates *conversions* of legal concepts between legal systems. Without questioning the importance of these claims, my argument is that inter-jurisdictional translation is just a part of legal translation practices. Much translation work, indeed the majority of it, is done intra-jurisdictionally, including not just the formulation of multi-lingual law for monistic legal systems but also the harmonisation of laws in pluralistic legal systems.

Legal translation is textual

Legal translation is often perceived to be about the translation of *written* words, be it statutes, case law, opinions and commentaries, or rules and regulations. The textual model of translation views translation as a process that begins with a text (the source) and ends with another (the target). The presumption is that the mode of presentation fixes the meaning of a piece of translated law. The study of legal translation, if translation is defined this way, is the study of the equivalence of conceptual meanings produced by the source text and the target text. As some scholars have pointed out, obsession with a fixed text skews both theoretical and practical understanding about translation (Tymoczko 1990). In my opinion, the textual model of legal translation unnecessarily excludes interpretive practices that would otherwise qualify as translation. One example is the common use of court interpreting in many legal systems. As already indicated, my own opinion is that court interpreting and textual translation are better seen as different options of a repertoire of institutional practices to overcome the problem of the language barrier. Furthermore, in some legally pluralistic systems, translation does not start with a palpable 'source text'. Translation in these systems is more a practice that textualises what is originally unwritten and oral (see below).

Equivalence is the ultimate ideal in translation

As mentioned, under the textual model, the goal of translation is to achieve equivalence between the source and target texts. Of course, what qualifies as equivalence is the subject of much heated debate among translation scholars. Which is the most surefire method of achieving equivalence? Should it be a kind of relentless literalism? Should it be a form of cultural, hermeneutical understanding? Or, to ask a more fundamental question, what kind of equivalence does legal translation aim to achieve? Is it semantic equivalence (the traditional concern of terminological incongruence, whether one term in language A is the same as another in language B)? Is it stylistic equivalence (for example, is a statute is to be written in a more rigid or loosely structured style)? Is it formal equivalence (for instance, should the one-sentence rule form, whereby each section of a statute is to be written in one sentence, be preserved in translation)? Or is it legal equivalence (are two terms in different languages the same in meaning and effect)? The last point, of course, makes legal translation even more technical and impossible

pes of translation. Legal translation is not just about creating equal
languages, but formulating equal concepts that can be applied in the
ithin two different legal systems. And that, of course, never seems
quite possible to achieve.

Diversity in translation practices

It has become commonplace among comparative legal scholars to say that
national legal systems nowadays borrow from other legal systems or traditions.
And because all laws borrow, they are, in a sense, all translated. The idea of a
folk law that sustains a homogeneous conception of the relation between law
and society, in the form of one country, one culture, one language and one law,
is clearly impossible to sustain in reality. Existing legal systems borrow and copy
extensively from each other, both as regards broad legal concepts or principles
and with respect to specific legal instruments such as statutes and codes.

Arguably, in some areas of law translation practices feature in a more prominent role. Common examples include admiralty law, constitutional law and
international commercial law (Gotti 2009). Multilateral treaties, for example,
cannot be promulgated without the service of legal translators. Transnational or
regional law is another obvious terrain where the role of translation can hardly
be overemphasised. European Union law itself is a thoroughly multilingual project (McAuliffe 2009). And then there are the legal systems of plurilingual and
multilingual societies in which works of translation form an integral part. Heavily
translated systems include those of Finland, Belgium, Switzerland and others in
Europe, as well as Canada. I deliberately left out many multilingual societies in
Africa and Asia. I did so for the important reason that many of these societies
share a colonial past, which in various ways has very much shaped their response
to the language challenge. I would venture also to suggest that this is particularly
the case with countries within the common law tradition.

Why is colonialism as a historical legacy important for understanding legal
translation? For these systems, translation was first done in the colonial era to
allow the old imperial languages to be used as the exclusive or primary language
of the law. Two things usually happened. First, court interpreting was extensively
offered to provide what in contemporary terms would be called access to justice.
Secondly, local law was incorporated as part of the colonial law through translation. For example, in both the cases of colonial Hong Kong and Singapore,
some members of the local Chinese populations wanted to have their cases
tried by Chinese customary law. And the colonial governments' response was
to find experts to identify, systematise and, in some cases, codify customary laws
by translating them into English. This form of 'translation practice' allowed an
English judge, as the frontline administrator for a distant ruling power, to apply
local customary law so as to resolve social disputes. Such application would
take place within the institutional framework of a common law adversarial trial
and be subject to the same procedural requirements and evidentiary standards.

Jurisdictional rules and conflicts of law rules were also developed to address the relations between these systems (Evans 1971).

The same can be said about colonial India. When British administrators and judges were faced with the task of applying Hindu law for settling and adjudicating disputes among Hindus, they started to systematise an oral legal tradition. They translated, but at the same time created, new legal materials for the colonial legal system. Beginning in the first half of the 19th century, in order to put the doctrine of *stare decisis* into the practice of Hindu law, they started to publish decisions of the district and provincial courts. By the end of the 19th century, Hindu law had become mainly case law in the English language, based on published cases that operated within a metalegal framework of English common law (Cohn 1965: 112–13; Cohn 1989; Merry 1988). Translation in this particular context was not so much making available existing legal materials in a new language; it was more the production of new elements (originally residing in a different linguistic environment) for a legal system. Legal translation was quite literally a process of text production rather than text conversion (Šarčević 1997: 87–119). Today, intra-jurisdictional translation continues to exist in many post-colonial systems in the name of legal hybridity or plurality. I will say more on this later. Suffice it to point out that translation assumes many more variant forms than we thought it did. It features importantly in the constitution of new legal elements in some legal systems.

The colonial/post-colonial scenario is also interesting for another reason. As mentioned previously, most colonial common law systems relied heavily on court interpreters. The fact that most colonies in Africa and Asia were of a non-settler type means that court interpreting was a crucial feature for the common law to be used in these societies where the majority of the population did not speak English well enough for the purposes of the law. The puzzle is this: if we juxtapose these de facto multilingual legal systems with some official multilingual legal systems in other parts of the world, we realise that the functional distinction between court interpreting and legal multilingualism is virtually indistinguishable. Conventional thinking suggests that court interpreting and legal translation are two entirely different species: one is about providing access to justice; the other is about interfacing a legal system in two or more languages. The two are supposedly incompatible. However, court interpreting and legal translation seem to me to be functionally exchangeable in terms of the problem they set out to resolve: that of the language barrier.

For example, to address the language barrier suffered by its French speaking population in Quebec, Canada could have used court interpreters primarily to provide access to justice. Similarly, it seemed cost-effective if a certain version of legal bilingualism of English and Spanish was implemented in some US states including, for example, California and Texas. However, for reasons that are not purely linguistic, the United States adopts the so-called 'access to justice' model in dealing with the language barrier of Spanish-speaking litigants. Canada, by contrast, goes down the route of fully-fledged legal bilingualism (Ng 2009a).

The underlying cause has much to do with the political economy of languages, as well as what some scholars describe as the language ideologies of a society (Woolard 1998). Suffice it to say that the decision about whether a legal system should adopt the 'access to justice' model or the 'legal multilingualism' model to overcome language barriers is often not a linguistic decision. Legal translation is political. How should things be translated? How much should be translated? In what forms should translated materials appear? Above all, what is the relationship between source and target languages?

A practical definition of translation

In the light of the translation practices discussed above, I want to dissociate the meaning of the word 'translation' from the dominant textual model. The textual model presupposes a unified nature of legal translation; a presupposition that I think is not empirically warranted. It is simply too restrictive to understand translation as a textual exercise alone. My institutional account of translation practices plays upon the tension between the more permanent form of textual translation and the more transient form of oral translation. For my purpose, legal translation means *the addition or conversion of elements integral to the judicial process, including conceptual resources such as legal concepts and principles, written documents of different kinds (case reports, statutes, written pleadings, witness statements, etc), oral debates and testimonies, as well as institutional rituals and practices, from one linguistic environment to another.* The definition is arranged in such a way as to include not only the translation of legal texts, such as law codes, case law, statutes and rule books in a new language but also the carrying out of new or existing legal procedures and practices in another linguistic environment.

The remaining part of this chapter is an attempt to justify the use of this broader, more encompassing and admittedly complex definition. I will do so by showing how this practical or practice-oriented definition of translation can resituate four types of translation practices within some larger legal-institutional contexts.

Translation practices and interpretive autonomy

This section attempts to build the practical view of translation into a typology of translation practices. Specifically, I argue that legal translation can be analysed as an institution that varies in terms of two crucial variables – interpretive autonomy and permanency.

Interpretive autonomy

Interpretive autonomy refers to how independently a translated material can stand on its own in the new environment of the target language without referring

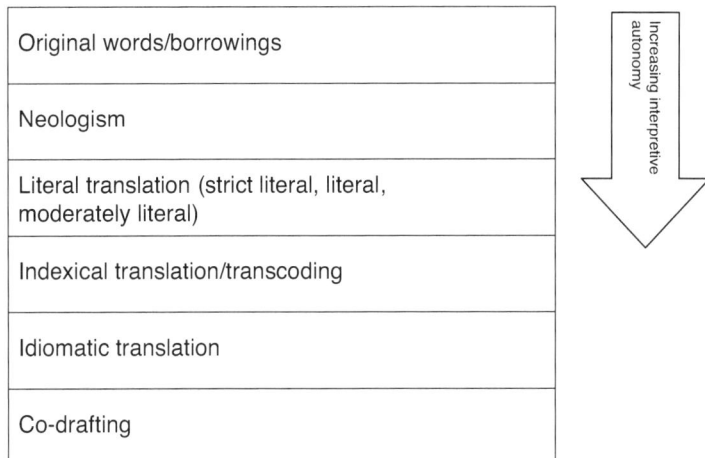

Figure 1 Translation techniques and interpretive autonomy

back to the source language. If we were to consider textual translation alone, a host of related concepts exist, including 'authoritative translation', 'authentic text' or 'parallel texts'; these signal, from a legal point of view, interpretive autonomy. An authenticated translation is one whose interpretive autonomy is, in principle at least, vested with the force of law (Šarčević 1997: 20). It is meant to be a 'stand-alone' legal instrument, that is, its meaning can be understood without resorting to the original text in the source language.

Figure 1 aligns a list of translation techniques along a descending scale of interpretive autonomy. Rather than treating these common techniques as a set of innocuous tools to get meaning across, I see them as ways of imposing some specific criteria of authenticating meaning. Translation is a selective process reflecting institutionally defined goals. Understood in this way, the relations of power between the source language and the target language are implicated by the choice of a certain translation technique.

The most rigid way to retain the original meaning of a term or expression is simply not to translate (or only to transliterate). This technique is otherwise known as 'borrowing' in legal translation. It is a method that basically *throws* a word or expression in the source language into a new linguistic environment. It explicitly expresses a desire to return to the source language in order to get a firmer grip on the law. In the English common law, there are many examples of Latin or French terms that were once borrowings. Even today, *mens rea* is *mens rea*; one does not normally translate the term to 'guilty mind' in English. Of course, the term *mens rea* has acquired new meanings in the common law environment. However, its Latin 'outfit' does carry an illocutionary meaning intended by judges and counsel alike – that *mens rea* is not meant to be understood as an everyday term, and which is not supposed to be interpreted in the linguistic context of everyday English.

A second technique, similar to but not the same as transliteration, is the use of neologisms. It, too, accentuates the primacy of the source language over the target language. But, unlike strict borrowings, translation through the use of neologisms at least attempts to translate. However, this translation is not done with terms already existing in the target language. It is done instead by coining new words for the target language. The use of neologisms is particularly common in the area of international law or in the so-called process of legal transplants, when legal ideas are 'planted' into a cultural environment in which those ideas have no historical roots. By using a newly invented word, the technique differentiates a legal term from other existing words that are organically rooted in the local linguistic environment. Of course, if we take seriously the idea that language is constitutive of the social reality it articulates, then no translated term can render an idea in exactly the same way as the original. However, the use of neologisms is a gesture that signifies non-equivalence between languages. The underlying message is clear – one is not supposed to interpret the meaning of a neologism from within the interpretive framework created by the target language. As such, it is a gesture of 'glancing back' at the original.

The third technique is well known. Until recently, literal translation had been hailed as the gold standard of legal translation. There has been a persistent ideology in the theory and practice of translation to treat literal translation as purer and more accurate (Beaupré 1986). As a method, literal translation is a rather cavalier kind of mechanical glossing. It reduces the complexity of meaning to surface denotational meaning, often with humorous consequences (Ng 2009b). Here, I view literal translation as a technique that leaves elements of the original in the translated text, so much so that a word or expression in its source language is only one short step of back translation away from its translated form. Literalism is a device that limits the interpretive input of the target language.

The awkwardness of literally translated sentences constantly reminds readers of their 'translated' nature. More important, as an institutional practice literalism is an attempt by the source language community to exert control over that of the target language. If we survey the 'letter v spirit' debates of old, it was no coincidence that the source language community almost invariably favoured literalism. The community who used the target language, however, advocated a freer form of spirit translation. The history of the development of bilingual law in Canada is a good example. Literalism was favoured by English-speaking legal professionals when English law was translated into the French language in Canada in the 19th century (Beaupré 1986; Parkin and Turcotte 2004). More recently, the same source language (English)/target language (French) schism over literalism was replayed when the federal law of Canada was to be translated into French after the passage of Canada's Official Languages Act of 1969.

The fourth technique is indexical translation. Some translation scholars describe this practice as legal transcoding (Snell-Hornby 1990, 2006). Others describe it as a form of linguistic engineering (Sin and Roebuck 1996). However, I prefer the words 'indexical translation' to designate the actions taken by translators to ascertain the superiority of the original over the translated text in jurisdictions that are purportedly multilingual (eg when a jurisdiction has an 'equal authenticity rule' in place). This expression requires some explanation. Indexical translation features in the practice of limiting the significance of the target language. Let me use the contemporary bilingual common law system of Hong Kong as an example. When a judge in Hong Kong interprets a Chinese legal term, he approaches it not so much as an ordinary Chinese term but as a token for the original English term with which it bears a corresponding relationship. I call this form of linguistic tokenism 'indexical'.

One can loosely compare this to the difference between the intensional theory and the extensional theory of meaning in the philosophy of language literature. Intensional theory of meaning suggests that words have 'intensions', in the form of concepts associated with the words (for example, a legal term in Chinese has an intension of a legal concept in Chinese). Extensional theory glosses the idea of meaning differently. Meaning is understood as indexical in the sense that it derives its content by pointing to (hence indexical) a certain thing that serves as a paradigm. I have already mentioned borrowings, neologisms and literal translation. In a sense, these can be viewed as techniques emphasising the 'indexical' nature of a translated term. However, indexical translation plays a prominent role in statutory interpretation. In the case of Hong Kong, even though it is officially a fully bilingual system, that is, Chinese statutes are as authentic as English statutes, indexical translation confers on Chinese laws a derivative status.[1] Judges in Hong Kong have argued that in order to understand the true legal meaning of a Chinese term, it is necessary to refer back to the indexed English term (Cao 2010).[2]

Beyond Hong Kong, the use of indexical translation can be found in other aspiring post-colonial common law jurisdictions, where a clear disconnect exists between the political will to assert state sovereignty through the symbolic elevation of the national language and the institutional or professional desire to stick with English as the language of the law.[3] To put it bluntly, translatability is a popular agenda that post-colonial states endorse but which is nonetheless greeted by the legal elites of these societies with sublime indifference, sometimes even downright resistance. Historically, such resistance has been most notable among the elites of former British colonies.

Some see the influx of national languages into the legal sphere as a threat to their vested interests (even today, many lawyers in these countries practise law exclusively in English). Others believe that the growth of national languages in law threatens the status of English and that in turn undermines the rule of law. To cite the case of Hong Kong again, it features arguably the most elaborate system of bilingual law in Asia. Towards the end of colonial rule, the then colonial administration embarked on a massive project to translate all statutes and subsidiary legislation into Chinese. The court system was also reorganised to allow for bilingual capability. But how did this come about? Who pushed for the policy? The lawyers and the judges certainly did not push for it. In fact, barristers there expressed concern about the use of Chinese in courts. Their priority was to preserve the purity of the English common law in the Chinese linguistic environment. The driver for legal bilingualism was China. Chinese was made an official legal language to symbolise the renewed sovereignty of China over the city.

Indexical translation is facilitated at the expense of communicating meaning. I have discussed in detail elsewhere how indexical translation could be an easy trap for Chinese language users (Ng 2009b). Suffice it to say that for a layman in Hong Kong who knows Chinese and only knows Chinese, it is difficult, even mis-leading, to try to understand what a legal Chinese term means. The term looks like a Chinese term but is not meant to be understood in the Chinese semantic universe. It is extension over intension. To understand what it means requires tracing and then reconnecting the term back to its English form. In other words, unless one knows the original English term indexed by the Chinese term, it is impossible to understand its legal meaning.

It is easy to see why this form of translation appeals to legal professionals who do not want to have their law translated into a new language. Translation can shape a legal system by the capacity that it gives to a language to elaborate the principles and concepts of the law within its own environment. Translation means granting a new language (the target language) interpretive autonomy in law. Indexical translation to a significant extent neutralises this autonomy by placing constraints on the interpretive process. It discourages conceptualisation within the meaning universe of the target language. If one asks a lawyer in Hong Kong: 'What does the Chinese term 合同 mean?' he will probably reply that it means 'contract' in English. The method of explaining a Chinese legal term is to find its English original. This method takes on the following form: 'This term in Chinese means that term in English'. By constantly suturing a Chinese term to its English 'original', the practice itself discourages a Chinese user from reflecting in Chinese upon the Chinese legal terms that he uses.

The practice of indexical translation is indicative of the complex nature of legal translation in the post-colonial context. As mentioned, in many post-colonial societies legal bilingualism or multilingualism is not primarily driven by legal interests. Political interests are the main driving force. This tension between political will and legal professionalism is, I believe, a recurrent theme found in many former British colonies. The tension often causes a gap between official language policies and practices – in theory, a national language is often accorded equal or even superior status to English; in practice, English continues to remain the high language of the law.

The fifth common technique is idiomatic translation. Idiomatic translation is often referred as 'free' translation in common parlance. Idiomatic translation offers the target language greater latitude in interpreting the law. In an important sense, idiomatic translation is itself already a reading of the law given in a new language. From the standpoint of the source language, it is an act of ceding a substantial share of interpretive control to the target language. Idiomatic translation is tolerated more in societies where a greater degree of linguistic equality exists, for example, in multilingual societies without a dominant language of power. I think of the example of Switzerland and the relative equal status of its legal languages. It is also practised in international law, where linguistic equality is more often prescribed as a ground rule of exchange.

Finally, by way of sixth technique, co-drafting provides an even more explicit approach to the fracturing of the monopoly over interpretive control assumed by one language. In its pure form, meaning is co-derived from the two or more languages involved in the 'translation' process. Again, this technique is commonly used in societies that actively embrace a multilingual identity, such as Canada and Switzerland.

Permanency

The second variable crucial for developing an institutional theory of translation practices is permanency (figure 2). I use the term to refer to the possibility for future users to retrieve the material translated. The influence of translation on a legal system over time is conditioned upon the state of permanency of the translated material. Different translation practices can be located on an axis between the analytical poles of most fleeting and most permanent. Permanency determines if the translated material, be it books, codes, knowledge and its interpretations or practices and procedures, can become a material part of the legal system for a long time.

Translation is most ephemeral in the so-called 'access to justice' model. A jurisdiction that subscribes institutionally to 'access to justice' acknowledges the presence of a language barrier without acknowledging the status of the target language that constitutes the barrier. I used the example of Spanish in California earlier. Spanish has no permanency in either the US federal or state legal systems. It is translated on a 'need-to-know' basis and the means that facilitates this

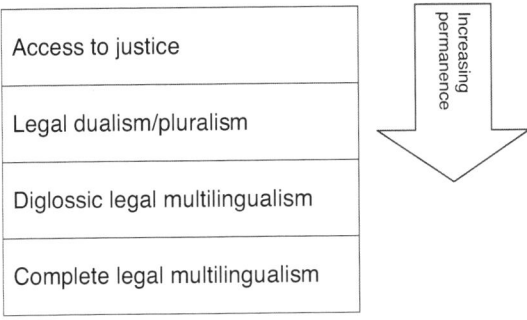

Figure 2 Model of incorporation and permanence

evanescent form of translation is court interpreting, which entails that translation of Spanish is conducted primarily orally. It leaves no textual record. Indeed, it disappears as quickly as it appears.

Dualistic or pluralistic legal systems, particularly those developed from colonial rule, are also systems in which legal translation is conducted in a rather transient manner. In many cases, the initial approach of the colonial power was to import a new legal system for the important purposes of the law and to leave indigenous institutions to function as they would, especially in the hinterlands, where colonisers had limited interests and little power. Often a colonial government would allow the creation or recognition of informal or 'customary' courts run by local leaders (Tamanaha 1989, 2008; Benton 2012). A dual or pluralistic system of law was developed where local customary or religious law was practised in the lower courts and common or civil law was practised in the higher courts.

There was also no systematic translation of customary law into these systems. The customary law officially recognised by the system was often limited to family law issues, minor crimes, issues unique to customary or religious law and minor disputes. Often repugnancy or supremacy clauses were enacted that invalidated particularly offensive (by the coloniser's standards) local laws or practices. The process of interpenetration of parallel legal systems has been insightfully explored in studies of the co-evolution of plural legal systems in Asia and Africa (Daniels, Trebilcock and Carson 2011: 124). In many locations, what resulted was a dual legal system with various complex mixtures and combinations, and mutual influences (Menski 2006; Horowitz 1994; Joireman 2006). Both sides of this dual system influenced one another in various ways, including exchanging or recognising the other's norms (Mamdani 1996; Tamanaha 2008: 383–84).

In terms of language policy, these systems often implement a 'tiered' policy for the purposes of dualistic law. In other words, they allow for the use of local language(s) in lower-tier courts, most of them regional and community courts. However, in the higher courts, it is the principal language, be it English, French, Spanish or another major language that dominates. When compared with the 'access to justice' model, these systems accord a more permanent status to the non-principal language(s) of a society, in the sense that the weaker language(s) has a continuous presence in the lower courts. However, if a case ever reaches the appellate courts, the weaker language steps aside and the principal language takes over. Evidence given in the weaker language, both written and oral, has to be translated. Furthermore, the eventual decisions, both on factual and legal matters, are given in the dominant language. Some systems will translate decisions or legal commentaries into the minority language(s), but this is often only done when requested by litigants and then only for reference purposes.

Diglossic legal multilingualism is in principle a full version of legal multilingualism. Legal systems that practise diglossic legal multilingualism do not adopt a tiered language policy. Instead, they officially use two or more languages as the official languages of the law. However, in practice only the principal language is practised at the top-tier courts of these systems, because of practical constraints such as the linguistic abilities of senior judges, or other material and resource constraints, for example a lack of legal reference books in the local language. So while these systems do not implement a tiered language policy in theory, they do implement it in practice. When compared with the legally pluralistic systems mentioned above, diglossic multilingual legal systems tend to produce a more substantial body of translated law, either in the form of selective case law or bilingual statutes.

The most complete form of legal multilingualism is found in the plurilingual societies in Europe, including Switzerland, Belgium and Finland. As mentioned above, this form of legal multilingualism can also be found in international or transnational law. I want to stress again the relative power parity that promotes legal multilingualism in international law. The legal notion of authenticity means little without some institutionalised authentication mechanism (Rosenne 1983; Šarčević 1997: 206). It is in the area of international law, both private and public, that transnational institutions such as the International Institute for the Unification of Private Law (UNIDROIT) and the Hague Conference on Private International Law (HCCH) are created to promote uniformity.

International law is also the area where legal translation intersects most directly with comparative law. Translation entails not just a matter of sorting out linguistic differences, but a matter of sorting out legal differences as well (Galdia 2003). The ideal of legal uniformity is often challenged by the reality that different national courts produce contrasting legal interpretations by drawing from the legal resources of their own traditions. As a result, the most comprehensive way to institutionalise uniformity is to set up specialised courts with exclusive jurisdiction for the settlement of certain types of international or transnational legal disputes (Teubner 1997). This is the area where the European Union is a major player. The European Court of Human Rights, for example, is an important specialised court of this kind.

Synthesis – a typology of translation practices

It is time to take stock of the discussion so far. Figure 3 presents a picture of four types of translation practices based on the legal systems in which they are carried out. I classify these institutional types by means of the two criteria examined above, permanency and interpretive autonomy.

The first type is court interpreting. It is the predominant mode of translation in monolingual legal systems with a dominant common language. In my view, court interpreting belongs to a type of translation that is low in both permanency and interpretive input. As suggested, it is used to provide 'access to justice'. It does not offer legal recognition of the role of the language translated.

The second type is selective translation or, more precisely, selective production of new elements through translation in pluralistic legal systems. This type of translation practice is most often found in post-colonial legal systems that mix together various legal traditions. The use of translation, while selective and

Permanency of translated material		
	lo	hi
Interpretive autonomy of translated material — lo	(1) *Court interpreting* – found in monolingual legal systems with a dominant common language	(3) *Indexical translation* – found in post-colonial systems with a strong, outward-looking legal professional sector
Interpretive autonomy of translated material — hi	(2) *Selective translation or incorporation* – found in colonial/post-colonial legally pluralistic systems	(4) *Co-drafting and equal authenticity* – found in international/transnational law; legal multilingualism in societies without a single dominant language

Figure 3 A typology of translation practices

thereby limited, has been and remains one of the key contributing factors to the hybridity found in these systems. Furthermore, a reflection of the meaning of translation in this context challenges the narrow idea of translation as conversion of texts from one language to another. Legal translation here is often about creation of texts from oral sources. In other words, translation brings into being new elements to an otherwise common law or civilian legal culture. Despite its limited scope, the interpretive input produced by translation is often high.

The third type is indexical translation. As suggested, it is found in post-colonial legal systems with a strong, outward-looking legal professional sector. Ironically, legal translation of this type is usually not triggered by legal demands. It is instead fuelled by political demands, such as the need to assert political sovereignty by adopting a national language as the language of law. By political decree, a multilingual policy is introduced to allow the national language to be used alongside the dominant language of law. In practice, however, the interpretive autonomy of the new target language is curtailed by the use of indexical translation that favours the legitimacy of the source language through the gesture of pointing back (hence indexical).

The fourth and final type is translation that emphasises equal interpretive input over equivalence between languages. In its strongest form, it very much undermines the distinction between the source language and the target language, as in the case of co-drafting. This type of translation is sometimes found in international/transnational law. It underlines equal authenticity and is also found in multilingual societies without a clear dominant language. The permanency of the new language and its interpretive input to the system are both high.

Conclusion

As noted at the beginning of the chapter, I use the term heteroglossia to highlight the 'otherlanguagedness' found in many state laws today. The co-presence of several languages within a single jurisdiction is a common phenomenon. For many of these systems, legal translation can be understood as encompassing a multitude of institutional practices that at once enable and control the coexistence of languages within the terrain of law. The long-standing approach of treating translation as solely textual, coupled with the concomitant ideal of equivalence, clearly fails adequately to capture what is happening on the ground. My analysis suggests that the ideal of equivalence or exactitude that is basic to any linguistically oriented translation theory is a rather limited concept for understanding the institutional goals of actually existing legal translation practices.

In fact, the notion of equivalence can be justifiably argued as a view interested in preserving the supremacy of the source language. By bringing in the concept of interpretive autonomy, I intend to highlight a neglected reality of legal translation – translation is a power play between the source language (the language from which a text or an oral practice is translated) and the target language (the language into which the material is translated). Some translation techniques insist on retaining the original; others hark back to the original in direct or roundabout ways. However, there are also translation practices that anticipate the possibilities opened up by a new linguistic environment. Legal translation is always potentially subversive. It is the medium through which legal power and social power are at play. On this basis, an institutional account of legal translation is inseparable from its sociology.

As an institutional practice, legal translation varies in terms of its degree of permanency. My typology attempts to capture some important variants – for example, interlingual oral translations of oral legal materials (court interpreting) and interlingual written translations of oral legal tradition (colonial law). Finally, understanding legal translation institutionally offers the potential to produce general insights about the globalisation of law at a microscopic level. Globalisation of law happens both macroscopically and microscopically. At the macro level, we have witnessed in the past few decades the growth of transnational law, conventions and treaties. However, at the micro level, legal translation has turned state laws into a more globalised system. National legal systems are constantly updating (and globalising) themselves by translating new elements into their law. The varieties of intra-jurisdictional translation practices described in this chapter are not minor phenomena. Understanding these practices should produce insights not just into how law works but also into how it interacts with society.

Notes

1 Section 3 of the Official Languages Ordinance states that English and Chinese possess equal status as official languages. Section 10B(1) of the Interpretation and General Clauses Ordinance states that the Chinese language text and the English language text are equally authentic.
2 The principle was established by the Hong Kong Court of Appeal in *The HKSAR v Tam Yuk-ha* [1997] 2 Hong Kong Cases 531.
3 Another example is Malaysia. A cursory survey of judgments produced by its federal courts suggests that English remains the dominant language (Ng unpublished).

Bibliography

Bakhtin, M.M. (1981) *The Dialogic Imagination: Four Essays*, trans. C. Emerson and M. Holquist, Austin: University of Texas Press.
Bassnett, S. and A. Lefevere (eds) (1990) *Translation, History and Culture*, London: Pinter.
Beaupré, R.M. (1986) *Interpreting Bilingual Legislation*, 2nd edn, Toronto: Carswell.
Benton, L. (2012) 'Historical Perspectives on Legal Pluralism', in B. Tamanaha, C. Sage and M. Woolcock (eds) *Legal Pluralism and Development*, Cambridge: Cambridge University Press.
Cao, D. (2010) 'Judicial Interpretation of Bilingual and Multilingual Laws: A European and Hong Kong Comparison', in J. Jemielniak and P. Miklaszewicz (eds) *Interpretation of Law in the Global World: From Particularism to a Universal Approach*, Berlin: Springer.
Cohn, B. (1965) 'Anthropological Notes on Disputes and Law in India', *American Anthropologist*, 67: 82–122.
—— (1989) 'Law and the Colonial State in India', in J. Starr and J.F. Collier (eds) *History and Power in the Study of Law*, Ithaca, NY: Cornell University Press.
Daniels, R.J., Trebilcock, M.J. and Carson, L.D. (2011) 'The Legacy of Empire: The Common Law Inheritance and Commitments to Legality in Former British Colonies', *American Journal of Comparative Law*, 59: 111–78.
Evans, D.M.E. (1971) 'Common Law in a Chinese Setting: The Kernel or the Nut?', *Hong Kong Law Journal*, 1: 9–32.
Galdia, M. (2003) 'Comparative Law and Legal Translation', *The European Legal Forum*, 1: 1–4 http://www.simons-law.com/library/pdf/e/355.pdf (accessed 1 October 2013).

Gotti, M. (2009) 'Globalizing Trends in Legal Discourse', in F. Olsen, R.A. Lorz and D. Stein (eds) *Translation Issues in Language and Law*, New York: Palgrave Macmillan.

Horowitz, D.L. (1994) 'The Qur'an and the Common Law: Islamic Law Reform and the Theory of Legal Change', *American Journal of Comparative Law*, 42: 543–80.

Joireman, S.F. (2006) 'The Evolution of the Common Law: Legal Development in Kenya and India', *Commonwealth and Comparative Politics*, 44: 190–210.

Mamdani, M. (1996) *Citizen and Subject: Contemporary Africa and the Legacy of Late Colonialism*, Princeton, NJ: Princeton University Press.

McAuliffe, K. (2009) 'Translation at the Court of Justice of the European Communities', in F. Olsen, R.A. Lorz and D. Stein (eds) *Translation Issues in Language and Law*, New York: Palgrave Macmillan.

Menski, W. (2006) *Comparative Law in a Global Context*, 2nd edn, Cambridge: Cambridge University Press.

Merry, S.E. (1988) 'Legal Pluralism', *Law and Society Review*, 22: 869–96.

Ng, K.H. (2009a) 'Beyond Court Interpreters: Exploring the Idea of Designated Spanish-Speaking Courtrooms to Address Language Barriers to Justice in the US', in R.L. Sandefur (ed.) *Access to Justice*, Bingley: Emerald.

—— (2009b) *The Common Law in Two Voices*, Stanford, CA: Stanford University Press.

—— (Unpublished) 'Legal Globalization From Within: A Comparative Study of the Postcolonial Legal Systems of Hong Kong, India, Malaysia, and Singapore'.

Parkin, A. and Turcotte, A. (2004) 'Bilingualism: Part of Our Past or Part of Our Future?', Ottawa: Centre for Research and Information on Canada http://bc-yk.cpf.ca/wp-content/blogs.dir/1/files/Bilingaulism-Past-or-Future.pdf (accessed 1 October 2013).

Rosenne, S. (1983) 'The Meaning of "Authentic Text" in Modern Treaty Law', in R. Bernhardt and others (eds) *Völkerrecht als Rechtsordnung, Internationale Gerichtsbarkeit, Menschenrechte: Festschrift für Hermann Mosler*, Berlin: Springer.

Šarčević, S. (1997) *New Approach to Legal Translation*, The Hague: Kluwer.

Sin, K.K. and Roebuck, D. (1996) 'Language Engineering for Legal Transplantation: Conceptual Problems in Creating Common Law Chinese', *Language and Communication*, 16: 235–54.

Snell-Hornby, M. (1990) 'Linguistic Transcoding or Cultural Transfer? A Critique of Translation Theory in Germany', in S. Bassnett and A. Lefevere (eds) *Translation, History and Culture*, London: Pinter.

—— (2006) *The Turns of Translation Studies: New Paradigms or Shifting Viewpoints?*, Amsterdam: J. Benjamins.

Tamanaha, B.Z. (1989) 'A Proposal for the Development of a System of Indigenous Jurisprudence in the Federated States of Micronesia', *Hastings International and Comparative Law Review*, 13: 71–114.

—— (2008) 'Understanding Legal Pluralism: Past to Present, Local to Global', *Sydney Law Review*, 30: 375–411.

——, Sage, C. and Woolcock, M. (eds) (2012) *Legal Pluralism and Development*, Cambridge: Cambridge University Press.

Teubner, G. (1997) 'Global Bukowina: Legal Pluralism in the World Society', in G. Teubner (ed.) *Global Law Without a State*, Brookfield, VT: Dartmouth University Press.

Tymoczko, M. (1990) 'Translation in Oral Tradition as a Touchstone for Translation Theory and Practice', in S. Bassnett and A. Lefevere (eds) *Translation, History and Culture*, London: Pinter.

Woolard, K.A. (1998) 'Introduction: Language Ideology as a Field of Inquiry', in B.B. Schieffelin, K.A. Woolard and P.V. Kroskrity (eds) *Language Ideologies*, Oxford: Oxford University Press.

Chapter 5

Catching the spirit of the law: from translation to co-drafting

*Jean-Claude Gémar**

Introduction

For all their many achievements, translators have yet to dissipate the doubts society entertains about their work. The proverb *traduttore traditore* continues to undermine the very idea of translation in the eyes of many. From the beginning, however, one critical issue has challenged translators: should they translate literally or freely in order best to achieve 'equivalence'? Whichever way they choose, will the source text and the target text ultimately be 'equivalent'? Ought they to be equivalent? When the field of translation is law, the issue of equivalence becomes particularly crucial.

Translators, philosophers and, more recently, linguists and other translation studies scholars have attempted to find ways to extract the meaning from the source text in order to transform it into a target text achieving the desired equivalence. Whether they have been successful or not is a matter of judgment. 'Ninety per cent, no doubt, of all translation since Babel is inadequate and will continue to be so' is George Steiner's pessimistic view (1998: 417). The translator is also faced with the problem of conceptual incongruity between languages. According to many linguistic scholars, the congruity of words between languages is arbitrary. Such statements suggest that *untranslatability* is inevitable. In view of the particular constraints of legal translation, especially when texts of national, international or world importance are involved, the question arises whether legal translation is feasible at all. The great number of translations – whether legal, general or specialised – actually produced throughout the world seems to provide a reassuring answer. However, if the target text does not faithfully mirror the letter and spirit of the source text, that is, in its content (the law) and its form (language), is there any real translation being done?[1]

All those involved in translation, including organisations and states, have long been seeking a way to ensure the elusive equivalence. In trying to achieve this goal, Canadians in particular have followed a long and difficult path, painfully testing several methods and approaches, from extremely literal translation of statutes and other legal documents to much freer ways of achieving the desired textual equivalence, and eventually to co-drafting of laws, thus by-passing translation altogether. Yet it is open to doubt if Canada has finally resolved the issue of interpreting its bilingual statutes, whether translated or co-drafted. Canadians have at least acquired pioneering experience that has resulted in the field called jurilinguistics. This fact demonstrates the rare and natural ability translation possesses to cross-pollinate the disciplines with which it is associated: legal translation + linguistics = 'jurilinguistics' (or 'legal linguistics' in the European Union). Jurilinguistics challenges the status of translation as a discipline. It asks if translation should be looked upon as a science, as an art, or as sheer practical know-how.

From legal translation to jurilinguistics

Montesquieu (1748: XXXI, 2) believed that the laws of a country clarify its history. In the case of Canada, this involves both the letter and the spirit of its laws. Over three centuries, from 1763 to the present, translation in Canada went through three successive stages. From the British conquest (1759–60) to the 20th century, translations were literal, clumsy and unidiomatic (Gémar 1983: 22–24). That situation changed radically early in the second half of the 20th century with the language policies adopted by the Government of Canada under the 1969 Official Languages Act.[2]

Pursuant to Article 5 of the Act, judgments 'issued by any judicial or quasi-judicial body established by or pursuant to an Act of the Parliament of Canada shall be issued in both official languages'. The Supreme Court of Canada's approach to the translation of its judgments, thanks to the remarkable command of both languages by a majority of justices, followed Eugene Nida's basic concept of 'functional equivalence', which is widely accepted in the legal world and elsewhere. It was adopted – and restricted to legal translation – by Louis-Philippe Pigeon, a former judge of the Supreme Court of Canada (1982: 271).

Finally, in the 1970s, the federal Justice Ministry, hoping to get better results, switched to co-drafting the bills and statutes of Canada. Two teams of legal experts, one French and one English, were formed. Unlike translators, who usually worked in isolation from the legal draftsmen, the two teams worked closely together to draft bills in the two official languages of Canada (Covacs 1982: 83; Labelle 2000: 269). This is how jurilinguistics came of age (Gémar 1982; Gémar and Kasirer 2005; Poirier 2010). The result of the solid, impressive linguistic knowledge and experience acquired by translators over three centuries was a new approach to dealing with the language of law and its various means of expression. Since then, the Canadian model has spread to other countries around the world where bilingualism and bijuralism coexist (Mattila 2013).

Whatever the translation method or approach to translating adopted, transferring the meaning of a message contained in a source text into a target text is a complex and difficult task to perform. In the legal field, interpretation of bilingual texts – not to mention multilingual situations – poses a real challenge. Can we rise to the challenge of translating a legal text, a statute for instance, given that law is a field where culture is the dominant feature (*locus regit actum*)? All states that need to provide themselves with bilingual or multilingual laws face more or less the same difficulties as Canada. However, the Canadian situation is exceptional. Its legislative bilingualism and bijuralism make it a unique country for various reasons (Allard 2001; Gaudreault 2012), the structure of statutes not being the least (Bastarache and others 2008). Jurilinguistics, in providing ways to help draft better legal texts, address these difficulties (Gémar and Kasirer 2005). The interpretation of legal texts is not limited to language issues but extends to values and traditions, in other words, to socio-cultural matters, which of course makes things even more complicated (Gémar 2011: 129).

Four decades later and after much trial and error, one may wonder whether Canada has succeeded in achieving its tricky goal of making the law more readable and comprehensible, both to lawyers and citizens, in two languages. One may wonder, too, whether translation failed so utterly that co-drafting had to be substituted for it. Which method is more likely to yield the expected 'equivalence' or, more correctly, equivalences? Does the elusive nature of language, always subject to interpretation, allow of a sure and unique meaning for every word? Last but not least, in order to determine the meaning of a legal message, whether translated or co-drafted, is interpretation the only legitimate method for assigning objective meaning to a legal text?

Translation – a necessary evil?

Since Biblical times, mankind has been asking itself the same question: should one translate a message, a 'text' (de Beaugrande and Dressler 1981) according to the letter or the spirit? There is no easy answer to that question (Steiner 1998). Many wise and learned thinkers have addressed the issue and proposed solutions, methods and approaches, even sophisticated systems, all supposed to make translators' work easier for them. Every translator, however, whether experienced or not, knows for sure that translating is a 'performing art', not an exact science. You do not translate with the help of equations, ready-made formulae and grids that can be expected to yield the best or the 'right' solution systematically. The difficulties AI and machine translation have met with in their attempts to construe and reproduce human language bear eloquent testimony to the fact that translating is still a human privilege, and that translation aids, whatever the tools used, are just that – aids, albeit useful and worthwhile, especially for translating technical texts.

Hence, whenever legal translation is involved, a wise thing to do is to look for what jurists, comparatists in particular, say and think about it. Specialists in comparative law are best placed to deal not only with the problems posed by the language of law and its vocabulary, but also with the concepts that vocabulary conveys when transferred from one legal system to another. These concepts are sometimes so abstract and yet so culturally specific, so much bound to a local system, its traditions and customs, that many lawyers and linguists alike question the translatability of law (David and Jauffret-Spinosi 2002; Didier 1990; Fletcher

1999; Glanert 2011: 202; Legrand 2005: 30). If translation is thought to be a word-for-word operation, an uncompromising search for a lexical equivalent to a source language term in the target language, then, since linguists claim that no word possesses an exact equivalent in another language, one may seriously doubt the feasibility of translating human languages.

Now, is this what translation is all about? The answer is no. Translating does not consist of finding matching equivalents that can be assembled into a chain of words making phrases and sentences and, eventually, a text conveying a meaning of sorts. Let us consider an example of what a simple, legal English sentence literally translated into French would produce:

Adjudication implies for a judge to decide in a dispute that has been brought, through one means or another, by the parties before the bar of justice. (27 words)	*Juger implique qu'un juge décide un litige que les parties ont porté devant la barre de justice d'une façon ou d'une autre.* (22 words)

This translation does make sense in French. However, it does not convey what is effectively expressed in the English source sentence, where every word tells; it is awkward, to say the least.

Now, let us compare this version with a translation made according to the *spirit* of the target language. Using this approach, one can arrive at a more idiomatic text, like this:

Adjudication implies for a judge to decide in a dispute that has been brought, through one means or another, by the parties before the bar of justice. (27 words)	*Rendre un jugement consiste, pour un juge, à dire le droit dans le litige que les parties ont soumis à la justice.* (22 words)

Here, too, every word tells. Have we ever heard anyone complain that laws were too short? Contrary to conventional wisdom, it is possible to express an idea, a concept or a message, in French in as few, if not fewer words than in English. Even the law can be wrestled into understandable prose, and yes, a target text (translated text), a legal text in particular, can be shorter than the source text (Gémar 1989: 599). This is not an absolute necessity, of course, as long as the entirety of the message is transferred.

Danica Seleskovitch, one of the most renowned translation specialists of the second half of the 20th century, defined translation thus: 'translating means transmitting the meaning of messages embedded in a text, not converting into another language the language in which it is formulated' (Seleskovitch 1979: 7). This definition applies to all provinces of human activity, law and its wide diversity of texts included, since there is not one 'language of law' but many of them, depending on who is using it: legislators, judges, law professors, legal scholars, lawyers, (public) authorities, governments, NGOs, national and international organisations, and so on. These, in turn, produce different categories of texts as part of their varied activities. Each category of text possesses its own stylistic specificity, a phraseology that is unique, a particular way of drafting and presenting (form) a legal message (substance). Since this wide variety of texts can fulfil several functions (eg argumentative, informative, normative or referential) at once, and even different ones as between source text and target text, one must again acknowledge that these features do not simplify the translator's already difficult task.

Translation does not simply consist in translating words, terms and phrases (and the ideas they represent). This would be the easy way, and a misleading one. Translators must not underestimate the way in which legislation is drafted, given that the style of drafting can vary, sometimes considerably, from one language to another. This is the case, among many other pairs of languages, with English and French: their writing styles differ dramatically, and particularly in the development of legal texts. These styles were developed over the course of centuries by great jurists, writers and philosophers, who have left their mark on the drafting of legislation; examples would include George Coode (1845), who 'laid down for the first time some important rules of drafting that have formed the basis for modern principles of drafting' (Garner 2011: 535), and Montesquieu, who wrote that '[t]he style [of laws] ought to be concise. [...] The style [of laws] should also be plain and simple' (1748: XXIX, 16). English jurists tend to juxtapose clauses and put the conditions at the head of sentences, while their French counterparts tend to state a general principle, which implies things supposedly known. English is rooted in the real, whereas French is situated in a world 'both real and cerebral' (Edwards 2008). Two different languages, two different styles, two different spirits, which could be summed up in two words: English is 'centrifugal', whereas French is 'centripetal'.

Given such conditions, to say that translators experience difficulty in reformulating legal messages from English into French, and vice versa, is an understatement. They succeed daily, nonetheless, whatever the length of the sentences and their complexity. Translating legal texts is not fundamentally different from translating general ones. However, a legal text differs significantly from a general text and also from other technical texts in two essential aspects: not only is legal language a specialised sub-language used by lawyers, but the rules (or standards) laid down in legal texts are enforceable by law. Translators must consider these constraints whenever they are dealing with legal texts, regardless of the languages and the systems involved.

Translating law: ways and means

Translating law is thought to be difficult – for valid and invalid reasons. When English and French are the languages involved, we are also dealing with the two major legal systems in the Western world: common law and civil law (see http://www.juriglobe.ca/fra/index.php). Bilingualism added to bijuralism puts a country at the highest level of complexity (Cornu 1995: 13), which is the case with my country, Canada. Canadian translators have to deal with two legal systems and law families operating very differently from each other in many ways. Whereas, in common law, remedies precede rights, in civil law rights precede remedies.

Consequently, before starting to translate a legal text and looking for possible equivalents between languages, the translator must consider whether and how equivalence can be achieved.

In search of equivalence

Throughout history, translators have sometimes opted for a literal form of translation, sometimes for a freer approach to translating, without neglecting opportunities to combine these (Delisle and Woodsworth 2012). Each method and approach has its supporters and opponents, and doctrinal disputes have been frequent. Over time, most great translators have raised the same, but variously worded, question: how can we produce a text that best reflects the message of the original text? More often than not, they provided original answers to most of the major problems posed by translation (Ballard 2007). In this quest for equivalence, jurists and lawyers, too, from Cicero to the present day, have mulled over the question and proposed solutions to the problems posed by the translation of law. The persistent attention paid by comparatists to lexical as well as conceptual difficulties posed by translating is of great interest for translators. This is not without reason: translating texts of a legal nature or significance amounts to performing an act of comparative law, but coupled with a translation process. That is the translator's daunting task (Beaupré 1987; Fletcher 1999; Sacco 1999; Legrand 2005; Moréteau 2009).

Legal comparatists and translators have much in common. In particular, they both 'interpret' texts, although for different purposes and by way of different methods. Thus, for Rodolfo Sacco, one of the leading comparatists of recent decades, the interpretation of terms conveying legal concepts is one of the major problems of comparative law (1999: 168).

Finding equivalence

Translators live with a permanent obsession: how best to achieve equivalence? Is the target text, once translated, equivalent – which does not mean identical – to the source text? A comparative analysis of the concepts denoted by any two legal terms belonging to two different systems of law shows that perfect equivalence is never achieved. The common-law 'contract' is not equivalent to the *contrat* in French law, any more than the German *bewegliche Sachen* is equivalent to the French *biens meubles*. Similarly, the Spanish *el fiscal* is not equivalent to the US 'district attorney' or to the French *procureur (général)*. Should they nonetheless be considered equivalent, this commonality would have to operate at a functional level only, which would entail a linguistic fiction. Examples like these lead us to the conclusion, not quite that law is untranslatable but, at least, that we cannot achieve perfect equivalence between terms designating concepts which differ in their shades of meaning. So much for terms and concepts.

What about 'texts'? Concepts differ, argues Sacco; however, the rule is the same in both cases, and legal interpretation 'is made on the basis of how the interpreter evaluates the possible solutions, and not on the basis of lexicon' (2002: 238). When translating law, as in any 'soft' field, it is pointless to try and search for perfect equivalence. What matters is not conceptual but textual equivalence. This is the translator's goal. Equivalence is a matter of degree, since it may be more or less complete; partial, or, in some cases, impossible. As Justice Pigeon said: '[o]ne can see why it is simply impossible to translate into French with perfect precision the technical terms of the common law vocabulary' (1982: 275).

In fact, it is not so much the term and its associated concept as much as the scope and legal effects of equivalence that trouble translators. Are the scope and effects the same in the target text as those implied by the source text? Such is one of the critical issues involved whenever the equivalence of two legal texts (or of several texts, as in the European Union) is being considered. This problem, and not merely the matter of readability, has prompted jurists to reflect on the optimal way to achieve equivalence in statutes and laws across languages. Thus arose the idea that co-drafting laws rather than translating them would produce texts both idiomatic and readable and, at the same time, facilitate their interpretation.

Equivalence: a four-part approach

In the quest for equivalence, it is the spirit of the law, not the letter, that is sought. This is part of a general trend in modern communication – writing more concise, plainer and simpler texts – that is reaching even the legal world, where 'it appears that form (language) is increasingly governing substance (law)' (Vogt and Drolshammer 2007: 230). The trend is particularly visible in English and French with the emergence of jurilinguistics (Mattila 2013). In Canada, the prevailing process has been 'translation by equivalence' (Pigeon 1982: 276). In the late 1950s, Canadian translation scholars Jean-Paul Vinay and Jean Darbelnet introduced 'equivalence' among the seven *procédés* (processes) they identified as possible approaches to translating (1967: 52). Since then, the search for equivalence has been considered as a translation method; but equivalence is generally specified with a qualifying adjective, varying according to the school of translation theory involved: dynamic, formal, functional, natural, semantic, textual and so on.

In law, the principle of equivalence should not be an issue since, whatever the legal system, similar problems and cases are met with everywhere, calling for similar solutions. However, in each case different means are used in different places to determine these problems and cases, judicial proceedings not being the least. Furthermore, according to the comparatist Olivier Moréteau: 'an equivalent institution or technique is not always available' (2005: 419–20). For all these reasons, 'functional' equivalence is generally held among comparatists to be the preferred solution for translating when comparable systems and situations are involved. It is no panacea but, given the absence of a satisfying all-inclusive solution, it is the practical solution the comparatists adopted decades ago. In the absence of a neutral or universal terminology, it is a reasonable solution that has proved to be effective, in Canada at least.

The term 'equivalence' in the scientific sense has a specific meaning. It may have uncertain, often vague, meaning(s) in the social sciences, but its significance in the field of mathematics ($P \Leftrightarrow Q$), for instance, is indisputable. However, when the term equivalence is used in translation, whether it is applied to law, philosophy or poetry, one does not always see clearly what it means for the translation of any particular text. Precision, however, is of the essence of law, particularly in legal instruments (legislation, judgments, deeds, contracts).

A text is unique, one of a kind. The message depends on the principle or concepts conveyed by the language of law, which is composed of numerous terms and phrases. Depending on the person who is dealing with a legal text and their purpose in doing so, the typology and register of the text will vary, thus affecting translation (Trosborg 1997). The vocabulary of law can be broken down into different categories, for example for lexicographic purposes. For (legal) translation purposes (English $\Leftrightarrow$ French), according to Jean Kerby, law terms can be classified into three main categories: (i) English terms having a French semantic equivalent (offer = *offre*); (ii) English terms without any exact French equivalent, but likely to have a functional equivalent, such as mortgage and *hypothèque*; reasonable and *raisonnable*; and (iii) terms totally untranslatable (eg 'common law', 'equity') (1982: 9).

Although I concur, basically, with Kerby on this categorisation of legal terms for translation purposes, I believe it needs to be developed further. Jurilinguistic considerations lead me to break the approach to equivalence into four parts. This four-part approach will take account of language variation and its consequences: the semantic and morphological development of words and the variability of the concepts they designate. The meaning of a word, its *signifié* (signified) in Saussurean terms, varies over time, as does its *signifiant* (signifier), in the field of law as in any other. Examples abound both in the English and French legal languages. A well known example refers to 'jurisprudence' as the word is used by the English-speaking community in Quebec, where the term has gradually been shifting from its original meaning of 'philosophy of law'[3] to that of 'case law'. French has some difficulty in following the pace with which the English language, principally in the United States, creates neologisms. There are other terms (and their associated concepts) that do not vary much over time in one system, but do change in another, which creates a time lag for translation.

Exploring terms and concepts

Each legal term present in a text is a significant part of the distinctive history of the local language of law concentrated within a synchronic set of signs. It summarises the complex history of a legal institution or concept. Following a diachronic path, which is at the same time an ethnographic one, the translator should then return to the source of the concept in order to grasp its various shades of meaning before endeavouring to transfer them into the target text. Armed with this vital information, the translator will more easily go to the next step: comparison of these features with those of the potentially equivalent term in the other language and system.

The main difficulty, however, lies in the details of the concept denoted by a term. A few examples will show how complex the process of comparing concepts can be, suggesting that there is more to comparative analysis than a mere exercise in rhetoric. Let us start with an example given by George Fletcher about 'fair/fairness' and 'reasonable/reasonableness' (1999). The notion of fairness has little to do with its French pseudo-equivalent: *(procès) juste/équitable*. Fletcher argues, rightly I think, that the concept of fairness, associated with a distinct language and culture, is untranslatable (ibid: 61), not only into French but into any other language. This also applies to the notion of 'reasonableness'. Although continental countries such as Belgium, France and Germany share with England the concept of 'reason' (from the Enlightenment era), the core idea, its origin and meaning, are basically British (ibid: 66). Equivalents in other languages, owing to and despite the omnipresence of this term in English legal language and texts, are but 'a parrot's screech' (Nabokov 1955: 34).

Now for a more complex example: the case of 'property', a term which designates one of the long-established institutions of private law. Article 2 of the Canadian Criminal Code (RSC 1985 ch C-46) lists the English and French definitions of the key words and terms appearing in the code, including 'property'. The French equivalent of 'property' is *bien* or *propriété*, which means the English word has two possible equivalences in French – not an infrequent situation, in law or in any other field. When we compare the definitions of 'property' in French[4] and in English,[5] the difference is obvious.

In contrast to the civil law, the common law concept of 'property' is not precisely defined, so that the two definitions do not overlap. Words are powerless to express the entirety of the notion, leaving it to the context to sort out the real meaning for the translator: is it *bien* or *propriété* that is meant? This odd situation, characterising Quebec's system of law, where some common law and much civil law coexist on the same territory, accounts for the differences between how Quebec (and Canadian) common law lawyers understand the notion of 'property' (within a *jus non scriptum*, an unwritten, feudal law originating in custom) and how civil law lawyers understand both *un bien* and *la propriété* (within a *jus scriptum*, a written law). These differences may profoundly affect the meaning of the law's essential concepts and the terms denoting them: are 'ownership' and *propriété* truly equivalent? Or, to be more specific, are these words merely functionally equivalent? One could continue almost indefinitely with such examples. They show the importance of a minimum of comparative legal analysis that anyone engaged in translation of a legal text should undertake, regardless of the legal systems and languages involved.

Legal terms can be classified into at least three main categories for translation purposes from English into French, and vice versa. Terms for which equivalence in the other language is obvious, established or accepted (eg damages = *dommages-intérêts*) are in the first category. Terms the equivalence of which is only partial, not total (eg tort = *délit*) fall into the second category. Terms belonging to the third category are terms which, for various reasons (eg proper nouns, concepts or institutions existing in only one system), cannot be translated into another language (eg 'common law'). The first two groups can be sorted into the 'functional equivalence' category (Pigeon 1982: 271). The terms of the third group correspond in most cases to loan words and borrowings. Unable to find an equivalent term in their own language, translators have to borrow the foreign word.

For want of correspondence

Is equivalence a second-best solution for translators when all other translation approaches have been tried and have failed? In translation, one deals with two languages, that is, two different cultures and ways of expressing ideas, concepts and notions – legal ones included. When the language of law has to be re-expressed in another language, legal complexity adds to the linguistic sophistication required. Linguists have taught us a basic principle: the concept denoted by a linguistic sign or signs – a word or words, to keep it simple – and the mental image they convey, being specific to a particular language, are not easily transferred from one sign system into another (Hagège 1985: 47). And when they are, through elaborate translating processes, the resulting text is no more than a 'reasonable compromise' achieving an unlikely result: functional equivalence.

Unlike literary translation, where the author's style and creativity matter a great deal, in specialised translation terms take precedence because they denote the technical concepts and messages of the field concerned. In law, where terms must have a fixed legal meaning, this principle is critical. Culture-bound terms such as 'due process', 'rule of law' or 'tort' exemplify the difficulties confronting translators. Seemingly simple, innocent terms such as 'constitution' can be deceptive (Cern, Juchacz and Wojciechowski 2012: 455). They epitomise the difficulties the translator of a legal text is likely to encounter. Everybody knows (or at least, everybody thinks they know) what a constitution is: a set of fundamental laws and principles governing a country. But how many people know the difference between written and unwritten constitutions, or between codified and uncodified constitutions, and how many people know where to classify, for example, the Canadian and US constitutions, or France's and the United Kingdom's? It is in the way laws are implemented, as well as how court proceedings work, that differences emerge (Moréteau 2009: 708). Given these differences, equivalence can then be properly described as 'functional'. This is the case with a major culture-bound term such as the 'rule of law' and its supposedly equivalent terms in French (*règle de droit/primauté du droit*), German (*Rechtsstaat*) and Spanish (*estado de Derecho*). Terms sometimes hide very different *realia* under apparently similar or comparable concepts.

Partial equivalence

In the vast majority of cases, if not in all cases, the equivalence achieved is only partial. Identity,[6] which is absolute sameness of linguistic signs making up words, terms and phrases, and of the concepts denoted by them, is considered impossible by modern linguists. For Ferdinand de Saussure, among many others, each language possesses its own signs to denote things; so different languages have different signs for denoting. All the more so with legal language, which is a specialised sub-language. Specialised languages tend to be univocal; so is the language of law. With few exceptions, legal terms can have only one meaning.

However, when we compare common law and civil law, a 'contract' is not exactly *un contrat*; a 'crime' is not always *un crime*; a 'mortgage' not exactly *une hypothèque*, and so on. In order to compare terms and concepts, an ideal solution would be to have at one's disposal a range of levels and degrees of equivalence so as to determine with relative precision the 'conceptual gap' separating terms (Gémar 2007: 196). A concept may include more elements than the foreign law term, and vice versa. Regarding the law of contracts, to take one example, the 'consideration' condition in common law, which is 'of the essence of the contract', does not exist in civil law. Without consideration, the contract is not valid under common law, and French translators must find a way to express this essential condition in the target text, a linguistic crutch of sorts to restore the balance of laws (eg *en contrepartie de la somme de* …). This kind of equivalence is only a fiction, but it allows for the functional equality of source text and target text.

One could rightly underline that the differences between the two groups of terms tend to be fairly trivial. They are nevertheless real. In the first case, the difference is conceptual[7] in nature. However, it is a matter of subjective interpretation in the second.

To translate or not to translate?

I now turn to the last feature of my four-part approach to equivalence, which concerns a very small group of terms. Here, the issue of translatability resurfaces.

All languages have words, variable in number depending on the language concerned, which denote a concept, a notion or *realia* specific to a linguistic community, a culture, and for which there are no known equivalents in other languages. Language and culture are inextricably linked. Inuktitut, in Canada's North, is a language that defines things with precision, snow for instance (a dozen words).

In Argentina, the *gauchos* (no English equivalent!) are said to use more than 100 words to describe the different colours of coats of their *criollo* horses. This linguistic specificity affects all sectors of human activity, including law and its language. Common law and civil law are not immune to the phenomenon, although the number of such terms is limited and not as great as some ill-informed people believe.

Terms such as 'common law' or 'equity' are invariant proper nouns, which do not have equivalents of any kind in any other language and thus are untranslatable. Translating them would, in many cases, lead to doubtful results and false, even absurd, solutions. A literal translation of 'common law' into French is *droit commun*, but this would mislead French readers, as it means something else in the civil law. 'Common law' must not be confused with the Roman law term *jus commune* (*droit commun*), although 'common law' originates from the Norman French *commune ley*. The case of 'equity' is somewhat similar; literally translated into French (*équité*), it does not convey the source-term meaning at all, and would distort the concept involved.

This four-part approach to equivalence, although extensive, does not exhaust the matter. It deals with terms, phrases and concepts only, that is, micro-contexts. The written language of law goes far beyond words as it includes the sentences, paragraphs and, eventually, the entire text of the law, which conveys the whole legal message. The text may be composed of a few words ('I plead guilty, your Honour') or of many pages (a Supreme Court of Canada judgment). Translators generally need a macro-context to interpret the text to be translated. The message is expressed in a certain way, words and phrases being organised according to a particular genre of legal writing (statute, contract, judgment, testament, and so on) with its own conventions. Each legal tradition has developed a particular organisation of words and phrases, a way of drafting laws – a style. This style, because it expresses a specific, deeply-embedded legal culture, in itself conveys a certain amount of meaning. In common law and civil law, conventions used in drafting texts are, for better or for worse, the stylistic templates that have influenced most, if not all, subsequent legal discourse.

Canada is a bilingual, bijural and multicultural state. This 'natural-born translators' country' has evolved from the stage of a servile, heavy and awkward way of translating to co-drafting, a radical post-translational way of producing bilingual legislative texts. In the course of this evolution, in the mid-20th century, legal translation went through numerous institutional reforms, freeing itself from some of its old demons – of which literal translation was one – to embrace freer and more idiomatic ways of translating federal legislation and Canadian judicial decisions (Gémar 2013: 155).

From a translated society to a society of free expression

By 1934, when a Canadian Translation Bureau was established, merging all ministerial translation services within one single unit, two centuries of bad practice and poor translating habits had seriously corrupted the French language of law and government, whether written or spoken, on account of the predominance of English source texts (Gémar 1982: 127). Public opinion continues to hold translators largely responsible for this situation, although the media, institutions and politicians share a significant part of this liability. Government bilingualism did not come into force until 1969, when the Official Languages Act was passed. The status and quality of the French language became a political issue (Deschênes 1980), and French-Canadians, then more language-conscious, started paying greater attention to the quality of the legal texts produced by their political institutions. All these actions contributed notably to the improvement and standardisation of French legal language (see http://www.btb.gc.ca). Translation seemed to have fulfilled its historic function just as serious questioning regarding the part it played in the preparation of legislation began to make itself heard. In short order, governments were starting to think about alternative reader-oriented methods for producing legislative texts in more idiomatic French (Gémar 2013).

This is how the concept of co-drafting Canadian laws was developed and implemented by the end of the 1970s (Covacs 1982: 83; Labelle 2000: 269). Co-drafting, in Canada, means writing a text at the same time in the two official languages, English and French, without resorting to translation, thus avoiding the 'commanding language' issue. It confers an equal status on the two versions of the law, generally a statute. It also confers on the legal message the natural idiom and style of a text that embodies the *esprit des lois* of the language concerned. The concept of co-drafting has since spread throughout the world, inspired other countries and revealed that solutions exist to solve some of the problems posed by the translation of legal texts into French or English (Šarčević 2005: 279; Mattila 2013: 245; Glanert 2011: 209). Nowadays, more emphasis is placed on the readability of texts. According to Swiss jurists, in the legal world, 'form (language) is increasingly governing substance (law)' (Vogt and Drolshammer 2007: 230), and legal translation must be idiomatic, and not strictly literal (Flückiger 2005: 356).

Compared with the previous translation method, the results obtained with co-drafting are remarkable. The best way to assess these results is to examine two co-drafted texts that have been adopted and promulgated, displayed here side by side, and to judge for oneself. Here is Article 7 of The Interpretation Act (RSC 1985 ch I-21):

| 7. Where an enactment is not in force and it contains provisions conferring power to make regulations or do any other thing, that power may, for the purpose of making the enactment effective on its commencement, be exercised at any time before its commencement, but a regulation so made or a thing so done | 7. *Le pouvoir d'agir, notamment de prendre un règlement, peut s'exercer avant l'entrée en vigueur du texte habilitant; dans l'intervalle, il n'est toutefois opérant que dans la mesure nécessaire pour permettre au texte de produire ses effets dès l'entrée en vigueur.* (40 words) |

| has no effect until the commencement of the enactment, except in so far as may be necessary to make the enactment effective on its commencement. (78 words) | |

This demonstrates what writing in the spirit of a language and its culture can convey. Note the brevity of the French text, compared with the English, which suggests that an idea, a principle or a statement can be expressed in French as concisely as in English, if not more so. The ultimate goal of co-drafting bilingual (or multilingual) statutes is to produce two or more 'separate but equal' texts, each being written according to the linguistic and cultural standards of the language involved. The challenge facing drafters when they generate a text in a co-drafting situation is to avoid creating a text that is too distinct and one-of-a-kind for the two versions to be comparable, thus distorting the message of the law and making its interpretation all the more difficult. In this instance one must ask: do the texts really comply with the legislator's intent? And where is the limit of free expression? Information transfer in general causes problems and difficulties that must be solved case by case.

Both methods, translating and co-drafting, have their merits and limitations. But co-drafting has demonstrated that legal writers can produce a text meeting a linguistic community's socio-cultural and linguistic aspirations. Given that co-drafting places the two texts on an equal footing, it meets people's longing for free expression and contributes to strengthening the democratic life of society.

Whatever the method, the only limit lies in the courts' interpretation, which seeks to understand bilingual and multilingual legislation by basing itself on the law's plain meaning (Côté 1984). Although translators and jurists both engage in textual interpretation, they do not resort to a common method. Similarly, lawyers from the two legal families use neither the same approach (for example, as regards the *travaux préparatoires*) nor similar techniques in the construction process. Ultimately, the version that will be retained by the court, whatever the language (English or French), is the one conveying what seems to be the intended meaning (Bastarache 2005: 107). Such is the view of the Supreme Court of Canada as it criticises the use of English and French dictionaries 'as if just one language was to be considered'.[8] This judicial approach contributes to bringing the two systems closer to each other.

The difference between law and translation, however, is that a system such as the Canadian one confers on its translated statutes an objective status of equality, whereas translation scholars recognise only a relative equivalence of pairs of texts. Translated legal texts have been interpreted by courts for centuries, so translation is presently well ahead of co-drafting. Translation possesses a strong case law corpus while co-drafting has just started developing its own. It remains to be seen whether co-drafting will stand the test of time.

Law and equivalence

To translate is to seek truth without the expectation of resolution. Translation and truth can sometimes meet in an unexpected way. As Heraclitus put it: '[men] do not understand how, while differing from [...], (it) is in agreement with itself. [There is] a back-turning connection, like [that] of a bow or lyre' (circa 475 BCE: 51, 37). Language signs, to borrow a phrase from the astrophysicist Martin Rees: 'embody intricate structures that render them far more mysterious than atoms or stars' (2011). Like any language act, a translation is but an approximation, the result of a compromise or of a 'negotiation' of sorts (Eco 2003). As Claude Hagège argues: 'any passage in another language is at best an equivalent' (1985: 49).

The systematic, total and precise interpretation of the source text is one of the essential steps in the translation process, over which it takes precedence. Translators are natural interpreters of language as such. Translators, especially legal translators, employ a highly complex sense-reading and sense-giving process to construe the meaning of the source text they have to transfer and re-express in a target text. In Canada, the difficulty of this task is aggravated by the fact that the translator is working in a bilingual and bijural environment, which reaches the highest level of complexity (Cornu 1995: 13). This situation confers some advantages; however, without both versions, the text of a statute would be incomplete (Lavoie 2003: 123) or uncertain (Bastarache 2005: 116).

The search for equivalence is the holy grail of translation. Zealous messengers between systems of law and languages, translators are natural construers of texts who, through the process of interpreting the source document, can shed new light on the meaning of its message, thus even contributing to its clarification.

Notes

* I gratefully acknowledge Dr Terence Macnamee's helpful comments and editorial assistance in the preparation of the manuscript. Translations are mine.
1 In this chapter, the 'spirit' (of a language) is understood according to the French essayist and historian Marc Fumaroli's definition: 'We speak of the "spirit" of a text, as opposed to the "letter": the letter "kills" because it sticks blindly to the matter of words; the "spirit" gives life because it is the result of a penetrating synthesis that captures the essence of deep meaning and intent' (2008: 7).
2 RSC 1985 ch 31 (4th Supp). The Official Languages Act came into force on 9 September 1969.
3 'Jurisprudence': 'philosophy of law'. *Oxford English Dictionary* http://www.oed.com (accessed 1 October 2013).
4 '*La propriété est le droit d'user, de jouir et de disposer librement et complètement d'un bien, sous réserve des limites et des conditions d'exercice fixées par la loi*' (Article 947 of the Code civil du Québec). The English version reads as follows: 'Ownership is the right to use, enjoy and dispose of property fully and freely, subject to the limits and conditions for doing so determined by law'.
5 'Property': 'A (usually material) thing belonging to a person, group of persons'. *Oxford English Dictionary* http://www.oed.com (accessed 1 October 2013).

6 'Identity' is 'absolute sameness'. This concept that is different from 'equiva-lence', an essential linguistic distinction for translators, meaning 'equality of value, force, importance, significance'. *Oxford English Dictionary* http://www.oed.com (accessed 1 October 2013).
7 'Concept': 'an idea of a class of objects, a general notion or idea'. *Oxford English Dictionary* http://www.oed.com (accessed 1 October 2013).
8 See *Pfizer Co Ltd v Deputy Minister of National Revenue* [1977] 1 SCR 456, 464–65.

Bibliography

Allard, F. (2001) 'The Supreme Court of Canada and Its Impact on the Expression of Bijuralism', Department of Justice Canada http://www.justice.gc.ca/eng/rp-pr/csj-sjc/harmonization/hfl-hlf/b3-f3/toc-tdm.html (accessed 1 October 2013).

Ballard, M. (2007) *De Cicéron à Benjamin: traducteurs, traductions, réflexions*, 3rd edn, Lille: Presses Universitaires du Septentrion.

Bastarache, M. (2005) 'Les difficultés relatives à la détermination de l'intention législative dans le contexte du bijuridisme et du bilinguisme législatif canadien', in J.-C. Gémar and N. Kasirer (eds) *Jurilinguistics: Between Law and Language*, Montreal: Thémis.

—— and others (2008) *The Law of Bilingual Interpretation*, Montreal: LexisNexis Canada.

Beaugrande, R.-A. de and Dressler, W.U. (1981) *Introduction to Text Linguistics*, London: Longman.

Beaupré, M. (1987) 'La traduction juridique', *Cahiers de droit*, 28: 735–45.

Cern, K.M., Juchacz, P.W. and Wojciechowski, B. (2012) 'Whose Reason or Reasons Speak Through the Constitution?', *International Journal for the Semiotics of Law*, 25: 455–63.

Coode, G. (1845) *On Legislative Expression*, London: W. Benning.

Cornu, G. (1995) 'Français juridique et science du droit', in G. Snow and J. Vanderlinden (eds) *Français juridique et science du droit*, Bruxelles: Bruylant.

Côté, P.-A. (1984) *The Interpretation of Legislation in Canada*, 1st edn, Cowansville: Y. Blais.

Covacs, A. (1982) 'La réalisation de la version française des lois fédérales du Canada', in J.-C. Gémar (ed.) *The Language of the Law and Translation: Essays on Jurilinguistics*, Québec: Éditeur officiel du Québec.

Crépeau, P.-A. (1993) 'L'affaire *Daigle* et la Cour suprême du Canada ou la mécon-naissance de la tradition civiliste', in E. Caparros (ed.) *Mélanges Germain Brière* Montreal: Wilson & Lafleur.

David, R. and Jauffret-Spinosi, C. (2002) *Les Grands systèmes de droit contemporains*, 11th edn, Paris: Dalloz.

Delisle, J. and Woodsworth, J. (eds) (2012) *Translators Through History*, 2nd edn, Amsterdam: J. Benjamins.

Deschênes, J. (1980) *Ainsi parlèrent les tribunaux: conflits linguistiques au Canada, 1968–1980*, Montreal: Wilson & Lafleur.

Didier, E. (1990) *Langues et langages du droit*, Montreal: Wilson & Lafleur.

Eco, U. (2003) *Mouse or Rat? Translation as Negotiation*, London: Weidenfeld & Nicolson.

Edwards, M. (2008) 'A Wonderful World' http://bibliobs.nouvelobs.com/actual ites/20080814.BIB1847/a-wonderful-world-par-michael-edwards.html (accessed 1 October 2013).

Fletcher, G. (1999) 'Fair and Reasonable: A Linguistic Glimpse into the American Legal Mind', in R. Sacco and L. Castellani (eds) *Les Multiples langues du droit européen uniforme*, Turin: L'Harmattan.

Flückiger, A. (2005): 'Le multilinguisme de l'Union européenne: un défi pour la qualité de la législation', in J.-C. Gémar et N. Kasirer (eds) *Jurilinguistics: Between Law and Language*, Montreal: Thémis.

Fumaroli, M. (2008) 'Qu'est-ce que l'esprit français?', *Le Point*, Hors-série, 20: 7.

Garner, B.A. (2011) *Dictionary of Modern Legal Usage*, 3rd edn, Oxford: Oxford University Press.

Gaudreault, M.-C. (2012) 'Legislative Bijuralism: Its Foundations and Its Application', Department of Justice http://www.justice.gc.ca/eng/csj-sjc/harmonization/bijurilex/aboutb-aproposb.html (accessed 1 October 2013).

Gémar, J.-C. (ed.) (1982) *The Language of the Law and Translation: Essays on Jurilinguistics*, Quebec: Éditeur officiel du Québec.

—— (1983) *Les Trois états de la politique linguistique du Québec*, Québec: Éditeur officiel du Québec.

—— (1989) 'La longueur des textes en traduction juridique: domaine anglais-français', in P. Pupier and J. Woehrling (eds) *Language and Law*, Montreal: Wilson & Lafleur.

—— (2007) 'Style et sens du texte juridique en traduction', in *'Un paysage choisi': mélanges de linguistique française offerts à Leo Schena*, Turin: L'Harmattan.

—— (2011) 'Traduire le droit. Lettre, espirit et équivalence', in M. Cornu and M. Moreau (eds) *Traduction du droit et droit de la traduction*, Paris: Dalloz.

—— (2013) 'Translating vs Co-drafting Law in Multilingual Countries: Beyond the Canadian Odyssey', in A. Borja Albi and F. Prieto Ramos (eds) *Legal Language in Context*, Bern: P. Lang.

—— and Kasirer, N. (eds) (2005) *Jurilinguistics: Between Law and Language*, Montreal: Thémis.

Glanert, S. (2011) *De la traductibilité du droit*, Paris: Dalloz.

Hagège, C. (1985) *L'Homme de paroles*, Paris: Fayard.

Heraclitus (circa 475 BCE) *Fragments*, T.M. Robinson (ed. and trans.), Toronto: University of Toronto Press, 1987.

Kerby, J. (1982) 'La traduction juridique, un cas d'espèce', in J.-C. Gémar (ed.) *The Language of the Law and Translation: Essays on Jurilinguistics*, Quebec: Éditeur officiel du Québec.

Labelle, A. (2000) 'La corédaction des lois fédérales au Canada vingt ans après: quelques réflexions', in GREJUT (ed.) *La Traduction juridique: histoire, théorie(s) et pratique*, Geneva: ASTTI.

Lavoie, J. (2003) 'Le bilinguisme législatif et la place de la traduction', *Meta: Translators' Journal*, 16: 121–39.

Legrand, P. (2005) 'Issues in the Translatability of Law', in S. Bermann and M. Wood (eds) *Nation, Language, and the Ethics of Translation*, Princeton, NJ: Princeton University Press.

Mattila, H.E.S. (2013) *Comparative Legal Linguistics*, trans. C. Goddard, 2nd edn, Farnham: Ashgate.

Montesquieu (1748) *De l'esprit des lois*, in *Œuvres complètes*, R. Caillois (ed.), vol II, Paris: Gallimard, 1951.

Moréteau, O. (2005) 'Premiers pas dans la comparaison des droits', in J.-C. Gémar and N. Kasirer (eds) *Jurilinguistics: Between Law and Language*, Montreal: Thémis.

—— (2009) 'Les frontières de la langue et du droit: vers une méthodologie de la traduction juridique', *Revue internationale de droit comparé*, 4: 695–713.

Nabokov, V. (1955) 'On Translating "Eugene Onegin"', *The New Yorker*, 8 January: 34.

Perelman, C. (1977) *L'Empire rhétorique: rhétorique et argumentation*, Paris: Vrin.

Pigeon, L.-P. (1982) 'La traduction juridique: l'équivalence fonctionnelle', in J.-C. Gémar (ed.) *The Language of the Law and Translation: Essays on Jurilinguistics*, Quebec: Éditeur officiel du Québec.

Poirier, L. (2010) 'Whose Law Is It? A Jurilinguistic View from the Trenches' http://www.opc.gov.au/calc/docs/Loophole_papers/Poirier_Jan2010.pdf (accessed 1 October 2013).

Rees, M. (2011) 'Higgs Boson Might Yield Origins of Universe But Questions Remain', Newsweek Magazine, 19 December http://www.thedailybeast.com/newsweek/2011/12/18/higgs-boson-might-yield-origins-of-universe-but-questions-remain.html (accessed 1 October 2013).

Sacco, R. (1999) 'Langue et droit', in R. Sacco and L. Castellani (eds) *Les Multiples langues du droit européen uniforme*, Turin: L'Harmattan.

—— (2002) 'L'interprète et la règle de droit européene', in R. Sacco (ed.) *L'Interprétation des textes juridiques dans plus d'une langue*, Turin: L'Harmatton.

Šarčević, S. (2005) 'The Quest for Legislative Bilingualism and Multilingualism: Co-drafting in Canada and Switzerland', in J.-C. Gémar and N. Kasirer (eds) *Jurilinguistics: Between Law and Language*, Montreal: Thémis.

Seleskovitch, D. (1979) 'Traduction et mécanismes du langage', *Parallèles*, 2: 7–12.

Steiner, G. (1998) *After Babel*, 3rd edn, Oxford: Oxford University Press.

Terral, F. (2004) 'L'empreinte culturelle des termes juridiques', *Meta: Translators' Journal*, 49: 876–90.

Trosborg, A. (ed.) (1997) *Text Typology and Translation*, Amsterdam: J. Benjamins.

Vinay, J.-P. and Darbelnet, J. (1967) *Stylistique comparée du français et de l'anglais*, Paris: Didier.

Vogt, N.P. and Drolshammer, J. (2007) 'English as the Language of Law', *LeGes*, 18: 229–38.

Part II

The specificity of comparative law

Chapter 6

Legal comparison and the (im)possibility of legal translation

*Jennifer Hendry**

> 'Translation [...] is thus the art of facing the impossible, of confronting unbridgeable discontinuities between texts, between languages, and between people. [...] [T]o attempt to "translate" is to experience a failure at once radical and felicitous'
>
> James Boyd White (1990: 257)

> 'Translating is not a simple act: it is not enough to substitute the space traversed for the movement; a series of rich and complex operations is necessary'
>
> Gilles Deleuze and Félix Guattari (1980: 486)

Introduction

In a 1951 article, the US comparatist Ferdinand Stone observed that the 'encouragement [...] given to "translations of basic legal works"' and the 'increasing attention given by many universities to building up libraries in "foreign law"' were an 'indispensable first step' in comparative law (1951: 327). According to Stone, these two considerations naturally went hand in hand for, in order to compare a feature of domestic law with a foreign version of it, not only must the scholar have access to the relevant materials but those must also be rendered in a form understandable to her. However, this *linguistic* translation of foreign legal texts is merely the starting point of the process of comparison; although nothing effective can be accomplished up to this point, once a scholar is able to read and comprehend the materials she is still only at the very beginning of the comparative enterprise. Indeed, as Stone emphasises, while 'it may be enough [for the librarian] to collect and catalogue in substantial volumes translations of all the legal materials, [...] for the "comparative" lawyer these are but the tools, the means, and not the end' (ibid).

Although scholars have long been engaged with the conundrum of translation, a distinction must be drawn between the linguistic translation of foreign legal texts, such as those discussed by Stone, and the more contested notion of translation as employed by contemporary 'comparative law and comparative legal studies'. (To be clear, any mention of 'comparative law and comparative legal studies' refers to the research field since its inception, inclusive of all the permutations it has undergone over time. For its part, 'comparative law' means the traditional, once mainstream, process of comparison, while 'comparative legal studies' indicates those post-positivist approaches that are more sensitive to the importance of context.) To the layperson, legal translation may appear simply to be the rendering of legal terminology in different languages, an exercise that would be undertaken for the purposes of comparing and contrasting selected legal features, processes or functions. However, one should be wary of restricting any analysis of legal translation to the merely linguistic, interpretive or phraseological. Despite the language of the law arguably being of a particular, technical and complex nature, regardless of the tongue in which it is expressed, these issues pale into relative insignificance when those of context, *locus*, meaning and understanding are also brought into the frame.

In this chapter, I propose that translation be conceptualised as both a lens and a frame for the critique of legal comparison. As such, the focus does not rest upon the technical/linguistic aspect of translation (Harvey 2002), important as it is, but rather upon considerations of context and meaning. It engages with (what I style) 'comparative legal studies', which is to say, the legal comparatist's more interpretive endeavour.

'Comparative law and comparative legal studies': ends and means

To have any hope of understanding the complex issue of translation within such a diverse research field as 'comparative law and comparative legal studies',[1] it is vital first to establish what are the 'ends' of comparison, generally speaking. As Rodolfo Sacco has observed: '[t]hose who compare legal systems are always asked about the purpose of such comparisons' (1991: 1), an interrogation which seems to suggest that a comparative perspective is somehow questionable. Although the rise in supranational processes and global jurisprudential approaches (Twining 2009) over the past two decades has arguably resulted in a gradual lessening of this pressure, 'comparative law and comparative legal studies' – perhaps more than any other field of legal research – must still shoulder the burden of proving its own legitimacy and, indeed, of justifying its own existence. A sceptic could argue, of course, that the fact that such inquiries are (even now) so often repeated rather suggests that the answers have remained somewhat inadequate. But this claim does not withstand scrutiny. In fact, there tends to be a broad acceptance of the view that the 'gathering of knowledge obtained through comparative law can be a vital portal to a foreign culture' (Eberle 2009: 452).

The point is that the answers provided by contemporary comparatists pertain more to the somewhat abstract 'ends' of increased knowledge of foreign legal orders, with a view to an improved understanding of how legal features, institutions and processes operate. This has led to these responses being seen as having fallen short, or as being somewhat unsatisfactory when juxtaposed against the more concrete outcomes of either domestic legal reform (one recalls how Sacco famously took umbrage with the idea that 'the study of foreign legal systems is a legitimate enterprise only if it results in proposals for the reform of the domestic law' (1991: 1)) or the uniformisation of legal systems (one thinks of the instrumentalist approach often used in legal integration and harmonisation debates within the European Union).

Much of the difficulty faced by comparatists can be seen as a direct consequence of the very character of 'comparative law and comparative legal studies', namely its cross-jurisdictional, multi-linguistic, often interdisciplinary-leaning features, not to mention the way in which it has developed.[2] For example, in their influential book, *An Introduction to Comparative Law*, Konrad Zweigert and Hein Kötz argue that 'the primary aim of comparative law, as of all sciences, is knowledge' (1996: 15). The authors also list the following four additional *practical* objectives in addition to their original epistemological goal. First, comparison affords resources for legislators; secondly, it operates as an instrument of interpretation; thirdly, it contributes to methodology (specifically concerning university legal instruction); and, fourthly, it has implications for supranational legal unification (ibid: 16).

While the last of these purposes is so loosely formulated as to be of questionable value, not to mention ranking perhaps as the most controversial of the list as shown by contemporary debates within the field (Legrand 1996a; 2010), it illustrates how the shifting of poles and parameters within the discipline can have an effect upon the pursuits of comparatists employing a (traditional) method. More generally, these four overtly practical objectives suggest that even comparative law's leading exponents are not wholly comfortable dealing with questions of effects and utility. By including these practical aims under the umbrella of the stated primordial claim of legal comparison, Zweigert and Kötz *de facto* provide a justification for both their discipline and method by highlighting its expediency. In effect, the process of translation within the traditional comparative approach is harnessed to the task of ascertaining functional equivalence. According to Zweigert and Kötz: '[t]he basic methodological principle of all comparative law is that of *functionality*' (1996: 34, original emphasis). Translation is thus reduced to an interim step whereby the *otherness* is 'removed' from the foreign legal text, feature or practice.

In this chapter, I neither attempt to prove the legitimacy of 'comparative law and comparative legal studies' nor to justify its existence. Rather, I focus my investigation and critique on how comparatists understand translation and, moreover, on how translation is employed within their processes and methodologies. In addition to being a key issue in terms of the focus and content of comparative law, I argue that translation informs and frames the debate at second-order level by permeating both the world view and the method of its proponents. As I proceed, I draw attention to this first- and second-order distinction and to the subsequent polarisation of second-order approaches. I also analyse how translation and its (im)possibility inadvertently became the defining criterion within this schism, and I discuss the effects this situation has had upon the discipline and methodology of contemporary 'comparative law and comparative legal studies'.

Translation: metaphrase and paraphrase

What is the meaning of the word 'translation'? Translation studies scholars remind us that: '[t]ranslation is, etymologically, a "carrying across" or "bringing across": the Latin *translatio* derives from *transferre* (*trans*, "across" + *ferre*, "to carry" or "to bring")' (Kasparek 1983: 83).[3] Both Latin terms connote a movement from one position or context to another, although arguably the verb employed is less important than the prefix in this regard; it is indeed the prefix 'trans-' that suggests a passage 'across' space, a threshold or boundary. Translation, transfer, transplantation, transformation and transposition – all of these terms feature a basic definitional commonality that indicates a change in state, status or location. As a result, many have been employed within legal comparison, often to the extent of representing different theoretical approaches (Frankenberg 2010: 566).

In general, however, *translation* is the term used when the discussion concerns issues of language, interpretation, communication and understanding. For example, some legal comparatists critically assess the possibilities and limits of legal translation (Glanert 2011). They mobilise the concept of translation to engage with the question of whether or not it is possible to assert that a legal term, feature or process used in one legal language or locus has an equivalent in another. They also analyse the extent to which legal features specific to one legal setting, system, culture or *mentalité*[4] can be 'understood' by individuals situated or educated in a different one. Much turns upon this issue of understanding, for this is the measure by which the fruitfulness of a given translation is judged.

It is not unusual, of course, for understanding to be used as a gauge of communicative success. Then, the focus is ordinarily on *reception*, which is to say on whether or not the information communicated has been received and, vitally, whether it has been received in the specific form in which it was transmitted. Framed in this way, communication and understanding fall into a binary construction of either 'wholly efficacious' or 'completely unsuccessful', which is, on further reflection, an overly rigid and misleading way to think about (mis)understanding. If understanding is rather conceptualised as a matter of degrees, the relevant spectrum can then range from 'full understanding' to 'utter misunderstanding', while at the same time including within these extremes the possibilities of qualification, approximation, parity and equivalence. Indeed, this is the case even leaving aside for the moment the issue of constructive misunderstanding specific to autopoietic theory (Bankowski 1994). These options give greater flexibility to the process, while at the same time providing for more instances of *partially* successful communication.

Although its designation in terms of the distinction between metaphrase and paraphrase may sound rather abstract, the observation I discuss is one with which many of us are readily familiar. Frequently employed in translation terminology, the former term denotes a literal or exact translation while the latter, arguably the more commonly and colloquially used, means to restate in other words. By contrast to the formal equivalence (between the original and the new version) postulated by metaphrase, paraphrase offers a 'gist' translation, that is, a rearticulation of meaning, if not of form. Along the way, it provides for an equivalence of *spirit* and possibly even function, although much will depend on circumstances (Kasparek 1983). The delineation between metaphrase and paraphrase in translation can be equated for present purposes to that between full and partial understanding of communication, which I outlined above.

In essence, understanding can be said to occur when there is a degree of equivalence between the information sent and received. Anyone who enjoys competence in a second language will appreciate how a direct literal translation of the specific words employed can often lead to an unclear outcome, whereas a restated version can better approximate the original meaning despite a different phrasing. This situation manifests itself most clearly in the linguistic translation of idiomatic language. For instance, if a traveller were to encounter the Italian expression '*in bocca al lupo*', she might be surprised to find that its literal translation into English is 'in the mouth of the wolf', while its 'gist' translation can be given as 'good luck'. In turn, it is perhaps idiomatically closer to the English phrase 'break a leg'. Alternatively, good wishes could be expressed in English by saying that you are 'keeping your fingers crossed' on behalf of someone, while Germans prefer to 'squeeze their thumbs'.[5] In each case, it is evident that the paraphrased translation favours the spirit of the original meaning over any literal accuracy. These examples well illustrate the situatedness of language. They also show language's deep structures. Moreover, they draw attention to the translator's task.

It should be acknowledged at this stage that while there are similarities between communication and translation, the two activities remain fundamentally different in terms of character and objective. I can clarify this point by turning to the *process* of communication. Instead of communication featuring strictly a communicator and a recipient, the *message* communicated can be considered, in and of itself, to form a constituent part of the process, which therefore effectively boasts a tripartite structure.

In this regard, the scenario I discuss reminds one of Niklas Luhmann's structuring of communication in his theory of autopoietic social systems, where he refers to information, message and understanding (1984). The separation drawn between these three components renders the message component as neutral, that is, as something unconditioned by either its original form or its final received form. The neutral quality of the message entails that its reception can be undertaken on the receiver's terms rather than on the sender's. The message can therefore be *recontextualised* within the parameters constructed by the receiver.

If the matter is framed in terms of *understanding*, it can be said that the burden is shouldered by the communication's recipient, for it is she who must 'understand' the message to the best of her ability. In addition, this 'understanding' must occur under circumstances where the recipient is 'blind' to the original, which finds itself inevitably decontextualised along the way. Thus, she must remain unaware of the extent to which her understanding is either complete or accurate.

Following this reasoning, therefore, translation can be viewed as a particular *mediated* type of communication, in other words, as an active, additional step that overlies the basic communicative process and thus alters its character. Translation adds another dimension to the communicative process, because the very 'bringing across' implicit to it 'requires the active and constructive input of a translator' (Hendry 2013: 167). The translating subject thus mediates between the two legal texts or legal spaces.

To return to the metaphrase/paraphrase distinction, it could be said that the selection between formal or dynamic ('gist') equivalence is one that is *taken by the translator*. Regardless of which goal is chosen, however, this intervention by the translating subject has an effect upon that which is translated – the message – a fact serving to undermine its neutral quality. This loaded intercession constitutes translation's own 'observer effect', that is, an unavoidable influence upon the communication through mediation, which is at once determinate of aims or parameters and innately creative.

It is here that the great task of the translator is shown in sharp relief for, while the aim of the endeavour is invariably to recreate as accurately as possible a facsimile of the original information in a new tongue or setting, the very process of translation requires that someone should undertake the 'bringing across'. And it is in this *conveying*, this steering, this reimagining, this process of operations, that the hand of the translator is noticeable. This is what James Boyd White means when he describes translation as 'the art of facing the impossible, of confronting unbridgeable discontinuities between texts, between languages, and between people' (1990: 257). The point is that a translation attempt must necessarily be doomed to failure, as it is impossible that it should succeed.

The idiomatic examples I discuss above demonstrate this aporia: even if a translation boasts contextual accuracy when expressed in the receiving language's own idiom, it lacks linguistic or literal accuracy, and vice versa. And this *impasse* begs the question, therefore, as to which of these approaches to translation – metaphrase (literal equivalence) or paraphrase ('gist' equivalence) – is preferable, especially when neither can make a genuine claim to accuracy. In the next section, I propose to explain how 'comparative law and comparative legal studies' has attempted not only to deal with this impossible task of translation, but to involve it as a central component within its own processes and methods.

Comparative law and comparative legal studies: translation as lens and frame

For the sake of clarity, I have thus far focused on linguistic translation. However, if the line of reasoning I have developed is applied not simply to language but to a cultural and social construct such as law (which, of course, also comprises a linguistic aspect), the issues I have emphasised become even more salient. This is owing to the increase both in the number of variables and in their complexity. Indeed, in a comparative analysis of law, attention must be paid not only to the linguistic aspect, but also to legal tradition, legal family, legal history and the intriguing legal *mentalité* (Legrand 1996a). Moreover, the specific legal order and its practitioners both have to be considered. It is simply not enough merely to examine and compare written legal texts, for law is situated within a wider culturally determined context. Legal meaning cannot be usefully detached from this context, such that there is a need to interpret legal texts in conjunction with the cultural context, and vice versa. Indeed, the 'situatedness' of law within a spatial, jurisdictional, temporal or conceptual *locus* lies at the very heart of legal comparison. It should also be borne in mind that, in terms of complexity, translation is rarely a stand-alone event. More often than not, translation is an ongoing process whereby communications are relied upon in stabilised interactive situations of reciprocity and dialogue; this remains the case, despite the issues I have outlined above.

However, translation in the dialogic sense that I have explained is very different from the translation undertaken or critiqued by the legal comparatist, whatever her aim or intent may be. For a start, in comparative law the translation process must be recognised as dualistic in character, the two separate but interrelated aspects roughly approximating the familiar distinction between 'law in books' (legal language or legal proscription) and 'law in action' (social practice or legal life) (Pound 1910; Nelken 1984).[6] The treatment of each feature of the process is necessarily different, with the latter being more overtly embedded in social practice than the former, while the former requires more active linguistic interpretation on the part of the comparatist before the law itself can be observed.

Also, instead of being on one or other side of the translation process (either as sender or receiver), the comparatist has a choice of two positions. She can act either as the mediator or author at the heart of the process or as a meta-commentator, wholly separate from the translation yet interested in its operation and engaged with its results in a more 'macro' and methodological sense. In terms of the former, the first-order position, translation is used as an instrument, a lens through which comparison is undertaken. The latter, the second-order position, employs translation more as a methodological frame; this stance is less technical, more self-aware, more epistemological in both its character and aims, and it also attempts to transcend the simple identification of functional equivalence across legal and normative orders. I argue that this distinction between first- and second-order approaches provides a specific insight into the schism at the heart of 'comparative law and comparative legal studies', particularly in relation to the polarisation that has occurred at second-order level. This opposition, and the role of the (im)possibility of translation within it, will be the focus of my conclusion.

Before I turn to the next stage of my argument it seems to me, however, that it would be helpful to mention the discipline/method distinction, which I have avoided thus far. But I have proceeded deliberately. Up until this point, it has been more straightforward to refer to 'comparative law and comparative legal studies' as a 'research field', mainly for clarity but also to avoid becoming entangled in what is, on the face of it, a complicated and also rather frivolous debate. The quibbling over the pigeon-holing of the work of comparatists often comes across as something of a nuisance – after all, what does it really matter whether the discipline is restricted to the analysis of foreign law and legal systems or is expanded to include second-order examinations of epistemology and methodology? Is it of any real importance whether comparison is understood to be 'a central element of "legal method"' (Twining 2007: 84) or whether 'comparative law and comparative legal studies' is considered to be a discipline in its own right?

Somewhat infuriatingly, the answer here is both yes and no. Of course, it does not really matter which niche 'comparative law and comparative legal studies' fits into, or what is included within its ambit (these arguments have a tendency to come across as territorial disputes rather than as informed academic debate). What is certainly required, however, is a form of consensus concerning the terminology used and the boundaries drawn, so that the debate can once again become meaningful and allow the research field a way out of its current situation of entrenchment and *impasse*.

Until now, the net result of all of the equivocation over the research field's disciplinary and methodological identity has been the emergence of two distinct second-order approaches, which to all intents and purposes serve to contradict each other entirely. I argue that it is in fact different understandings of *translation* that both create and perpetuate this schism at both first- and second-order level, although most importantly in terms of the latter. At the risk of essentialising these two second-order approaches, I will refer to them as functionalist or contextualist. My discussion shows how over the past 35 years of comparative legal undertakings, translation has always been at the heart of the matter.

Methods of legal comparison and critique: a brief overview

In this section, I provide a brief summary of the (development of the) main contours of 'comparative law and comparative legal studies', a process which can, I claim, be organised into three discrete stages. Despite the fact that some commentators (Siems 2007) have recently argued that the discipline has already reached its peak and is now falling into a period of decline, it is undeniable that over the past 30 years there has been a genuine explosion in both the quantity and scope of comparative legal research. This development can be mapped into rough chronological periods (although the timeline is arguably of less importance than the specific protagonists, most of whom have maintained discernible internal consistency). The approaches I address can be styled: (i) descriptive-positivist; (ii) legal-sociological; and (iii) legal-cultural.

The first of these perspectives, perhaps the most familiar to comparative scholars, is the descriptive-positivist approach favoured, most notably, by Zweigert and Kötz, whom I discussed above.[7] Having initially come to prominence in the 1970s, this approach boasts an endeavour to identify similar legal features and operations across legal orders as its defining characteristics. This correlates clearly to the stated objectives of comparative law given earlier, the most prominent of which is the pursuit of knowledge, followed by additional practical goals such as the provision of resources for law-makers, the facilitation of interpretation or methodological guidance within legal education and legal training. This first-order, descriptive, translation-based approach to comparative legal research, although nowadays somewhat old-fashioned, is still in evidence within the field.

The reason for this situation – which may admittedly bring to bear rather a harsh appreciation – is that this positivist approach tends to be the ready methodology employed by 'dabblers' in comparative analysis. Whether or not we are in fact 'all comparatists now' (Twining 2000, 2011), the rise of globalisation, Europeanisation and governance processes certainly has caused a broadening of the research field. While such an expansion is to be welcomed and encouraged, it should not be allowed to manifest itself at the expense of either methodological rigour or scholastic expertise nor should additional information about something be confused with an improved understanding of it.

The descriptive approach is most easily observed in comparative analyses of French and German contract law undertaken since 1970. Of late, it has also seemed to feature in encyclopaedic-type collaborative collections, where national experts provide a detail-rich account of a given legal feature followed by a kind of contextualisation which is offered in contradistinction to an alleged equivalent featuring in one or more neighbouring legal orders (Zweigert and Kötz 1996; Smits 2006). The descriptive approach has, in essence, been a victim of its own popularity: perceived as being straightforward and as giving a maximum return on one's investment, it has been stretched, co-opted and misapplied by enthusiastic comparatists whose analyses remain squarely mired in the first order.

Possibly the best known recent example of a descriptive-positivist project is the 2010 publication of the *Draft Common Frame of Reference* (DCFR) (von Bar and Clive 2010). While it is perhaps too unkind to say that this £900 six-volume collection has basically been sitting in a drawer since its release, it is unfortunately neither unfair nor an exaggeration to observe that the DCFR undertaking has had very little impact on the understanding or practice of European private law.[8] Considering that this was, after all, its stated aim, this observation suggests that 'the detailed description of commonalities and differences in comparative law, coupled with the explicit rejection of any evaluation, has not been a great success story' (Michaels 2009: 780). It is specifically the lack of any genuine critical and methodological self-reflection that restricts this formerly mainstream descriptive approach to the first order. Indeed, when this shortcoming is twinned with its questionable utility, the continued use of a descriptive-positivist approach to comparison today seems increasingly inexplicable.

However, these criticisms concerning the self-awareness and critical capabilities of a descriptive-positivist perspective are not new. As far back as the mid-1980s, it was possible to identify a number of comparatists who had started to inveigh against the lack of epistemological and critical engagement offered by such a mere translation-based undertaking. Despite having markedly different starting points, these scholars all recognised the value of a comparative method that was combined with a more legal-sociological approach, to wit, one that was no longer 'wedded to the "method of detail"' (Cotterrell 2006: 17, quoting Twining 1974).

For some comparatists, notably Günter Frankenberg, the aim was to draw attention to the 'fictitious neutrality' of the comparatist's own perspective (1985: 425) and to emphasise the importance of context within both the method and the process of legal comparison.[9] In this regard, Frankenberg's specific concern was with the comparatist's awareness, at second-order level, of how one's perspective was necessarily ethnocentric. For other scholars such as Roger Cotterrell, who came to comparative legal studies via the sociology of law later in his career, the focus was less on the comparative method per se and more on how legal ideas can only be properly understood if they are informed by a consideration of the 'social' (1983, 2012).

What is noticeable in each of these markedly different approaches is how the notion of simply 'translating' and describing first-order legal features rather languished, to be progressively replaced by a more critical second-order awareness of what was required if the aim was to have a better understanding of how law comes into being and operates within society. While translation remained a vital component of the newly expanded comparative process, proponents of comparative law were for the first time presented with alternatives to a mere first-order examination of 'foreign' law and were invited to include within their strictly black-letter analyses considerations of perspective, context and even culture.

What manifests itself very strongly at this juncture is the extent to which the consideration of culture and context began to shape the field of comparative legal studies. Indeed, it is at this point that 'comparative legal studies' emerged as a discrete term of reference (Legrand 1995). The third stage, what I call the legal-cultural approach, represents yet another step towards the inclusion of contextual and cultural features within comparative analysis. This stage developed throughout the late 1990s and early 2000s, and two clusters of reasons can be mentioned to account for this fact.

First, as a field begins to get more crowded, scholars tend to cling to their own territory and in doing so become more attached to their own particular perspective and arguments. Positivists, then, were not moving. Secondly, the complexities, conflicts and fragmentations borne of globalisation, Europeanisation and transnational governance processes, as I mentioned earlier, combined to place more emphasis and even pressure on (the outcomes of) legal comparison. For example, the classic Westphalian state and the attendant modern liberal ideology of state centrism came under challenge in the form of legal pluralism (Griffiths 1986; Tamanaha 2000; Delmas-Marty 2006; Melissaris 2009), while the Soviet bloc democratic turn in Central and Eastern Europe engendered an increase in constitutional borrowing (Tushnet 1998; Osiatynski 2003; Slaughter 2004; Nickel 2010), drawing unprecedented attention to how law and legal features move, are transferred (Frankenberg 2010) or disseminated (Twining 2011) from one *locus*, jurisdiction or context to another.[10]

This legal-cultural stage can be exemplified by making brief reference to two scholars in the field, namely David Nelken on legal culture (2002, 2004) and Pierre Legrand on legal *mentalité* (1996a). The standpoints adopted and the arguments submitted by Nelken and Legrand have been chosen for inclusion here because they provide the greatest insight into this particular stage, although at the same time it should be noted that, with such a wealth of scholarship to draw upon (Friedman 1994; Cotterrell 1997; Van Hoecke and Warrington 1998; Silbey 2001; Smits 2007), any selection must fail to mention many names. It is not even possible to do full credit to either Nelken or Legrand in this short space. My account must therefore necessarily confine itself to a brief report on their main insights as regards the cultural specificity of law. In passing, it should be noted that I do not attempt to define 'legal culture' but rather aim to explain what is involved in a comparative legal method that is culturally informed.

For Nelken, who rather like Cotterrell can be said to have come to comparative law via the sociology of law, the idea of 'legal culture' concerns itself with how 'aspects of law are themselves embedded in larger frameworks of social structure and culture which constitute and reveal the place of law in society' (2002: 333). Perhaps of most interest is the way Nelken sees the notion of 'legal culture' as a way of avoiding and, indeed, superseding the 'tired categories', such as legal families, that have traditionally been central features of comparative law (2004: 2). His main approach has been to draw on the sociological insights of the previous stage, while placing more emphasis on law-related behaviour within society. As such, Nelken's work adopts an approach that is clearly of the second order; it can be said that he is interested in '*finding* law-in-context' (2007: 109–32).

Legrand, for his part, introduces the idea of 'legal *mentalité*' alongside that of legal culture, making the argument that the laws of a legal culture cannot be unpicked or disentangled from the meanings that arise as a result of the distinct cognitive structure prevailing within it (1996a). Further, Legrand claims that place plays an essential role in the creation of legal meaning. In his view: '[p]lace [...] is not a mere static backdrop to legal meaning: it is a dynamic constituent of it' (2009: 215). Therefore, comparative legal analysis must necessarily include considerations both of *mentalité* and of social context (place). Such an analysis takes the form of an epistemological undertaking – indeed, he often refers to legal cultures as *epistemes* – but Legrand is always conscious of the frontiers of the enterprise, namely what he sees as the unsurpassable limits of translation. This causes him to critique agenda-driven 'strategies of simplification' that 'purport to show that the problem of understanding across cultures and traditions is a false one' (2002: 63). Legrand's targets in this regard are often the proponents of instrumentalist approaches to European legal integration who 'wish to efface difference, to erase it' (ibid); indeed, for Legrand the issue of *unknowability* is very real.

This legal-cultural stage differs from the legal-sociological stage that immediately preceded it, owing to the fact that it engages specifically with the compound nature of law, which is to say, with the social norms, socio-political constellations, historical underpinnings, institutional arrangements, societal practices and population dynamics within a jurisdiction or legal 'space' that inform the law's social context. The extent to which different approaches within comparative legal studies consider such analysis to be possible, with particular reference to the role of translation within the debate, is the focus of my final section.

Functionalist v contextualist approaches

There is a common thread running through each of the three stages I have outlined – the descriptive-positivist, the legal-sociological and the legal-cultural – and that is, of course, a functionalist methodology. As Ralf Michaels has indicated in his excellent text on the functionalist method within comparative law, what is actually meant by the term 'functionalist' is not readily identifiable since many different scholars and approaches make use of it in a variety of ways (2006). For example, functionalism could be equated with the traditional positivistic descriptive method of comparative law discussed earlier (which is indeed often referred to as *the* functionalist approach) or it could be understood as having an evaluative, universalising role for the agenda-driven identification of the 'best law'.[11] Alternatively, a functional approach to comparative law could be more sociological in character, that is, it could be concerned with social patterns and operations, while a further reading could be of functionalism as an interpretive endeavour, premised upon a methodologically aware employment of equivalence functionalism (ibid: 343–63).

Difficult as it is to generalise across these different understandings of what a functional approach involves or seeks to accomplish, one common aspect that can be identified concerns the way in which functionalism allows for degrees of understanding to occur across legal orders and normative boundaries, both in a first- and (importantly) a second-order sense. In terms of the former, the comparatist-as-translator is authorised uncritically to occupy a space of privilege between the original and the translated, a sort of mediator's no man's land. More importantly, however, at second-order level the comparatist is altogether more aware of both her own 'fictitious neutrality' (Frankenberg 1985) and of the impossibility of 'pure' translation from one legal context to another. Nevertheless, she *does not consider* this incompleteness as being necessarily indicative of failure. Indeed, if anything, translation is viewed as being an essential step within the process, in spite of all the issues it raises in terms of metaphrase, paraphrase and innate participatory bias on the part of the comparatist.

By contrast, however, the contextualist approach to comparative legal studies finds translation far more problematic. The defining feature for those adopting a second-order contextualist view is that the deep structures of law in a specific context cannot be and will never be, fully understood by outsiders – whether we are talking of a legal order, a legal culture or a legal *mentalité*. Indeed, Legrand's standpoint on the epistemic legal-cultural approach, which considers law's deep structures to be innately untranslatable, could be regarded as paradigmatic in this regard. These are, in essence, the limits of legal translation: for a meta-observer schooled in an alternative legal culture, a foreign legal feature remains *unknowable* in its entirety, and this is something that simply has to be accepted.

When the contextualist approach is juxtaposed against the (broad) function-alist one, the *impasse* becomes immediately apparent. While the contextual-comparatist privileges the embedded and innate quality of law and the specific legal features of a legal order, functional-comparatists disagree that these deep structures even exist and, if they do, that they represent insurmountable obstacles to understanding. These counterclaims even go so far as to include charges of relativism (Peters and Schwenke 2000: 811–13). From the other perspective, proponents of the contextualist approach object to the way in which those employing a functional method downplay the importance of these epistemic structures and differences, alleging methodological cherry-picking and a privi-leging of aim over method (Legrand 1996b: 234–36). The research field of contemporary comparative legal studies, therefore, currently exists in a situation of second-order polarisation.

Conclusion: translation's (im)possibility

I have attempted to show how translation is a core consideration in terms of how legal comparison is both conceptualised and undertaken and how translation has come to assume a definitive role within the debate at both first-order and, more importantly, second-order level. But what does this mean for 'comparative law and comparative legal studies'?

In a way, this methodological polarisation within 'comparative law and com-parative legal studies' reflects the broader lack of consensus concerning transla-tion and the extent to which it is at all possible, that is, whether metaphrase or paraphrase counts as being translation in the purest sense of the term. As discussed earlier, translation is different from communication in as much as it is mediated: it could very well be that even after a 'series of rich and complex operations' (Deleuze and Guattari 1980: 486) has been conducted, the translator is still left with 'unbridgeable discontinuities' (White 1990: 257). If this is the case, then the question ceases to be whether or not translation is possible but, rather, considering the restrictions under which it necessarily has to take place, how can translation be satisfactorily operationalised. Within 'comparative law and comparative legal studies' it appears that one must admit that certain deep structures are untranslatable, while recognising that partial understanding is preferable to no understanding at all.

To be sure, there will be some who argue that the issue I have addressed can be reduced to semantics and nothing more and that translation is, by its very nature, a flawed process and one which can never create a facsimile but only an approximation. This line of thinking, however, gives little more purchase than that offered by a conclusion to the effect that translation is impossible, for the possibility of a flawed process appears to be equivalent to the operation of an impossible one.

Notes

* I wish to express my gratitude to the *Legal Theory Seminar Series* group at the University of Edinburgh for their valuable feedback on the presentation of an earlier version of this chapter, and to Günter Frankenberg and Mathias Siems for their comments. Any errors remain my own.

1 'Research field' is used specifically here, for at this stage the term's neutrality is convenient in precluding the selection either of 'discipline' or 'method', a somewhat sticky issue for many proponents (Hendry 2008).

2 'Comparative law and comparative legal studies' has perhaps suffered somewhat owing to its all-encompassing 'umbrella approach', which has seen the inclusion, among others, of legal anthropology, legal sociology, comparative politics, legal history and even linguistics within its broad disciplinary church.

3 In Latin, *latum* is the supine form of *fero*, meaning 'to bring' or 'to carry', and 'across' is added by means of the preposition *trans-* to form both *transfero* and *translatio*.

4 In relation to legal comparison, the term *mentalité* was coined by Pierre Legrand to convey the distinct structure and epistemological foundation of the law, specific to its social and temporal context (1996a: 60–64).

5 The German idiom is *[jemandem] die Daumen drücken*.

6 The 'legal proscription' versus 'legal life' distinction is Eugene Ehrlich's version of this famous opposition (Ziegert 1979: 233).

7 Michaels refers to this (early) Zweigert and Kötz approach as functionalist rather than positivist, although he draws attention to the way its usage (as in so much of comparative law) is more in the form of an umbrella term: 'for supporters and opponents alike, "functional method" merely serves as shorthand for traditional comparative law' (2006: 341). Here, although I note Zweigert and Kötz's overt methodological pragmatism, I use 'positivism' to signify the descriptive aspect of this traditional approach and also, for the sake of clarity, in contradistinction to the specifically functionalist method discussed later in this section.

8 This is, of course, the retail price, not the project cost!

9 Frankenberg rejects the standpoint adopted by Zweigert and Kötz, who claim that 'the basic methodological principle of all comparative law is that of *functionality*' (1996: 34; original emphasis) and that 'the solutions we find in the different jurisdictions must be cut loose from their conceptual context and stripped of their national doctrinal overtones so that they may be seen purely in the light of their function' (ibid: 44). For Frankenberg, the functionalist method in comparative law only serves to reify 'function' as a 'principle of reality [instead of it being] taken as an analytical principle that orders the real world' (1985: 440).

10 At any rate, this is unprecedented since Alan Watson's seminal work on legal transplants (1993).
11 This comparative law approach to functional equivalence in terms of 'better law' does not withstand examination, as Michaels outlines: 'The specific function itself cannot serve as a yardstick, for functionally equivalent institutions are by definition of equal value with respect to that function – equivalence means, literally, of equal value. Once a specific function has been used to determine relative similarity, the same function cannot determine superiority, for this would require a relative difference. It is impossible first to isolate the function of a legal institution from its doctrinal formulation and to measure this remaining functional element against some ideal function, for no such ideal function exists beyond the mundane reality of the legal order. In this strict sense, better-law theory is not compatible with functionalist comparative law' (2006: 374).

Bibliography

Bankowski, Z. (1994) 'How Does It Feel to Be on Your Own? The Person in Sight of Autopoiesis', *Ratio Juris*, 7: 254–66.

Bar, C. von and Clive, E. (eds) (2010) *Principles, Definitions and Model Rules of European Private Law: Draft Common Frame of Reference (DCFR)*, 6 vols, Oxford: Oxford University Press.

Cotterrell, R. (1983) 'The Sociological Concept of Law', *Journal of Law and Society*, 10: 241–55.

—— (1997) 'The Concept of Legal Culture', in D. Nelken (ed.) *Comparing Legal Cultures*, Aldershot: Dartmouth.

—— (2006) *Law, Culture and Society: Legal Ideas in the Mirror of Social Theory*, Aldershot: Ashgate.

—— (2012) 'Comparative Sociology of Law' in D.S. Clark (ed.) *Comparative Law and Society*, Cheltenham: E. Elgar.

Deleuze, G. and Guattari, F. (1980) *A Thousand Plateaus*, trans. B. Massumi, New York: Continuum, 1987.

Delmas-Marty, M. (2006) *Ordering Pluralism: A Conceptual Framework for Understanding the Transnational Legal World*, trans. N. Norberg, Oxford: Hart, 2009.

Eberle, E.J. (2009) 'The Method and Role of Comparative Law', *Washington University Global Studies Law Review*, 8: 451–86.

Frankenberg, G. (1985) 'Critical Comparisons: Re-thinking Comparative Law', *Harvard International Law Journal*, 26: 411–55.

—— (2010) 'Constitutional Transfer: The IKEA Theory Revisited', *International Journal of Constitutional Law*, 8: 563–79.

Friedman, L.M. (1994) 'Is There a Modern Legal Culture?', *Ratio Juris*, 7: 117–31.

Glanert, S. (2011) *De la traductibilité du droit*, Paris: Dalloz.

Griffiths, J. (1986) 'What is Legal Pluralism?', *Journal of Legal Pluralism and Unofficial Law*, 24: 1–55.

Harvey, M. (2002) 'What's so Special about Legal Translation?', *Meta: Translators' Journal*, 47: 177–85.

Hendry, J. (2008) 'Contemporary Comparative Law: Between Theory and Practice

– Review of Esin Örücü and David Nelken's *Comparative Law: A Handbook*', *German Law Journal*, 9: 2253–62.

—— (2013) 'Legal Pluralism and Normative Transfer', in G. Frankenberg (ed.) *Order from Transfer: Comparative Constitutional Design and Legal Culture*, Cheltenham: E. Elgar.

Hoecke, M. Van and Warrington, M. (1998) 'Legal Cultures, Legal Paradigms and Legal Doctrine: Towards A New Model for Comparative Law', *International and Comparative Law Quarterly*, 47: 495–536.

Kasparek, C. (1983) 'The Translator's Endless Toil', *The Polish Review*, 28: 83–87.

Legrand, P. (1995) 'Comparative Legal Studies and Commitment to Theory [Review of P. de Cruz, *A Modern Approach to Comparative Law*, Deventer: Kluwer, 1993]', *Modern Law Review*, 58: 262–73.

—— (1996a) 'European Legal Systems Are Not Converging', *International and Comparative Law Quarterly*, 45: 52–81.

—— (1996b) 'How To Compare Now', *Legal Studies*, 16: 232–42.

—— (2002) 'On the Unbearable Localness of the Law', *European Review of Private Law*, 10: 61–76.

—— (2009) 'Econocentrism', *University of Toronto Law Journal*, 59: 215–22.

—— (2010) 'Antivonbar', *Journal of Comparative Law*, 1: 13–40.

Luhmann, N. (1984) *Social Systems*, trans. J. Bednarz and D. Baecker, Stanford, CA: Stanford University Press, 1995.

Melissaris, E. (2009) *Ubiquitous Law*, Aldershot: Ashgate.

Michaels, R. (2006) 'The Functional Method of Comparative Law', in M. Reimann and R. Zimmermann (eds) *The Oxford Handbook of Comparative Law*, Oxford: Oxford University Press.

—— (2009) 'Comparative Law by Numbers? Legal Origins Thesis, *Doing Business* Reports, and the Silence of Traditional Comparative Law', *American Journal of Comparative Law*, 57: 765–95.

Nelken, D. (1984) 'Law in Action or Living Law? Back to the Beginning in Sociology of Law', *Legal Studies*, 4: 157–74.

—— (2002) 'Comparative Sociology of Law', in R. Banakar and M. Travers (eds) *An Introduction to Law and Social Theory*, Oxford: Hart.

—— (2004) 'Using the Concept of Legal Culture', *Australian Journal of Legal Philosophy*, 29: 1–26.

—— (2007) 'Defining and Using the Concept of Legal Culture', in E. Örücü and D. Nelken (eds) *Comparative Law: A Handbook*, Oxford: Hart.

Nickel, R. (2010) 'Transnational Borrowing Among Judges: Towards a Common Core of European and Global Constitutional Law?', in R. Nickel (ed.) *Conflict of Laws and Laws of Conflict in Europe and Beyond*, Cambridge: Intersentia.

Peters, A. and Schwenke, H. (2000) 'Comparative Law Beyond Post-Modernism', *International and Comparative Law Quarterly*, 49: 800–34.

Pound, R. (1910) 'Law in Books and Law in Action', *American Law Review*, 44: 12–36.

Osiatynski, W. (2003) 'Paradoxes of Constitutional Borrowing', *International Journal of Constitutional Law*, 1: 244–68.

Sacco, R. (1991) 'Legal Formants: A Dynamic Approach to Comparative Law', *American Journal of Comparative Law*, 39: 1–34.

Siems, M.M. (2007) 'The End of Comparative Law', *Journal of Comparative Law*, 2: 133–50.

Silbey, S.S. (2001) 'Legal Culture and Legal Consciousness', in N.J. Smelser and P.B. Baltes (eds) *International Encyclopaedia of the Social & Behavioural Sciences*, Oxford: Elsevier.

Slaughter, A.-M. (2004) *A New World Order*, Princeton, NJ: Princeton University Press.

Smits, J.M. (ed.) (2006) *Elgar Encyclopedia of Comparative Law*, Cheltenham: E. Elgar.

—— (2007) 'Legal Culture as Mental Software, Or: How to Overcome National Legal Culture?', in T. Wilhelmsson, E. Paunio and A. Pohjolainen (eds) *Private Law and the Many Cultures of Europe*, The Hague: Kluwer.

Stone, F.F. (1951) 'The End to be Served by Comparative Law', *Tulane Law Review*, 25: 325–35.

Tamanaha, B.Z. (2000) 'A Non-Essentialist Version of Legal Pluralism', *Journal of Law and Society*, 27: 296–321.

Tushnet, M. (1998) 'Returning with Interest: Observations on Some Putative Benefits of Studying Comparative Constitutional Law', *University of Pennsylvania Journal of Constitutional Law*, 1: 325–49.

Twining, W. (1974) 'Law and Social Science: The Method of Detail', *New Science*, 27 June: 758–61.

—— (2000) *Globalisation and Legal Theory*, Cambridge: Cambridge University Press.

—— (2007) 'Globalisation and Comparative Law', in E. Örücü and D. Nelken (eds) *Comparative Law: A Handbook*, Oxford: Hart.

—— (2009) *General Jurisprudence: Understanding Law from a Global Perspective*, Cambridge: Cambridge University Press.

—— (2011) *Globalisation and Legal Scholarship*, Nijmegen: Wolf.

Watson, A. (1993) *Legal Transplants: An Approach to Comparative Law*, 2nd edn, Athens: University of Georgia Press.

White, J.B. (1990) *Justice As Translation*, Chicago: University of Chicago Press.

Ziegert, K.A. (1979) 'The Sociology Behind Eugene Ehrlich's Sociology of Law', *International Journal of the Sociology of Law*, 7: 225–73.

Zweigert, K. and Kötz, H. (1996) *An Introduction to Comparative Law*, trans. T. Weir, 3rd edn, Oxford: Oxford University Press, 1998.

Chapter 7

Translation and the 'contamination' of comparative legal research

C.J.W. (Jaap) Baaij*

Introduction

This chapter asks how a legal translator should approach the translation of authoritative legal texts for the purpose of subsequent comparative legal research. Comparative legal research may serve many purposes, one of which is to gain knowledge of a foreign legal system and to inform a domestic audience about it (Sacco 1991: 4; Zweigert and Kötz 1996: 15; Gordley 1995: 566–67; Curran 2002: 47; Samuel 2003: 15). Authoritative legal texts, such as statutes and judicial decisions, will probably be amongst the primary sources of information in most comparative legal research. This is the case if the comparatist chooses to compare the abstract content of formal legal rules (Schulte-Nölke, Twigg-Flesner and Ebers 2008), but also when focusing on extra-legal elements in the foreign society or culture that may affect judicial decision-making in that legal system (Van Hoecke 2002: 7; Gerber 1998: 720–24; Frankenberg 1985: 421). After all, even the US legal realist Karl Llewellyn writes that ascertaining what 'officials are going to [...] do about disputes', will involve a study of the 'so-called *rules of law* which judges say they are bound by, which judges say they have to apply' (1960: 6–7; original emphasis).

Comparative legal research entails translation of foreign legal texts as soon as the legal systems included in the comparison use different general languages. Take a comparatist who wishes to compare, for example, a legal rule expressed in a decision by a Portuguese court and a rule stipulated in a provision of Czech legislation. The comparatist cannot avoid expressing at least one of these legal texts in a language that is different from the language in which it is written, whether it is the Czech text in Portuguese, the Portuguese text in Czech or both in a third language. In such cases, whether the comparatist translates in person, or instead relies on existing translations, at some point translation will become an element of the comparative legal research. One could indeed say that translation of legal information is a core question of comparative law (de Groot 1998: 22, 2006: 423).

In this chapter, I argue that when legal systems use different general languages, no intelligible comparison of legal comparanda is possible without bridging the different languages involved. I examine the basic tenets of the receiver-oriented approach to legal translation and the consequent tendency towards relatively free or otherwise adaptive translation methods. Owing to the level of comparative legal analysis required by this approach, I claim that use of literal translation methods is to be preferred instead, on the basis of the hermeneutic, source-oriented approach in literary translation.

The entanglement of legal translation and comparative legal research

In theory, legal translation and comparative legal research involve distinct disciplines. Whereas the comparatist requires 'legal knowledge' in order to analyse alternative legal phenomena, the legal translator requires 'legal literacy' so as to choose the most equivalent term (Chromá 2004: 50, 2012: 113). Similarly, in the words of Jaakko Husa, whereas a legal linguist operates at the 'surface level' of a legal text, the lawyer deals with the 'legal-epistemic level' of the text (2012: 163). However, some believe that comparative legal analysis and legal translation are nevertheless caught up in a methodological vicious cycle. As Geoffrey Samuel wonders, must one first compare the specific legal phenomena before one can adequately translate a legal text, or must one first translate the general language in which the legal text is written before comparing the legal phenomena? (1998: 825). It seems impossible to imagine comparative legal research without prior translation and vice versa, not unlike asking whether the egg or the chicken comes first (Sefton-Green 2008; Lindroos-Hovinheimo 2007: 367).

If it is true that legal translation necessarily entails a substantial degree of comparative legal analysis, the translated text is less useful for the comparatist. The reason is that if translations of legal materials are already the outcome of a preceding comparative legal analysis, the legal translator has beaten the comparatist to the post, so to speak. The comparatist will then have recourse to the translator's rendition rather than getting to the original legal sources themselves. In fact, the comparatist would not be in a position to vouch for his own findings, since he would not be able to discern or critically assess the comparative legal analysis conducted by the legal translator. That is, the comparatist who is capable of critically evaluating the translator's work does not require translation in the first place.

It must be noted here that the question of circularity of legal translation and comparative legal research is not one of *who* comes first: the translator or the comparatist. The question also applies when a single individual acts as both legal translator and comparatist. In fact, whether or not advisable, in many instances a comparatist may rely on his own language skills while conducting comparative legal research.

However, the problem of 'contamination' of comparative legal research by legal translation is avoidable; it is not necessarily the case that legal translation is caught in a vicious methodological cycle with comparative legal research. In fact,

I argue that the relationship is linear, rather than circular, because translating in the linguistic sense necessarily precedes 'translating' in the legal sense, that is, comparative legal analysis (contrary to Heutger 2003: 5–6, 2004: 2). Imagine the existence of what you assume is a language, but a language of which you have no mastery at all. Each of what you assume to be its characters is utterly unrecognisable to you. It would then be impossible to say whether a particular text is a legal text, a novel or someone's shopping list. In fact, you would not be able to ascertain whether any of the marks on the paper in front of you actually amount to an instance of language to begin with. Hence, without prior translation in the most linguistic sense, there is no start to discerning and thus comparing legal concepts, rules, systems or other legal comparanda. Translation comes before legal comparative analysis. Moreover, in the event that both are carried out by a single individual, legal comparative analysis logically follows, and is therefore analytically distinguishable from, translation. One will *first* need linguistically to translate the general language in which the foreign legal text is written – in order to distinguish a shopping list from a legal text, so to speak – before embarking on a comparative legal analysis.

The methodological succession of comparative legal analysis and legal translation does not work in both directions; legal translation does not necessarily require prior comparative legal knowledge. It is true that most lawyers would agree that mere linguistic knowledge of the general language used by a foreign legal system is not sufficient for understanding the niceties and complexities of legal language. In this view, being able to translate linguistically is not enough for adequate or proper legal translation (de Groot 1996: 159). Nonetheless, bad legal translation is still legal translation. Consequently, legal translation and comparative legal research do not relate to each other as do the proverbial chicken and egg. Whereas translation *precedes* comparative legal analysis, legal translation 'merely' risks being inadequate without prior comparative legal analysis.

In sum, to avoid 'contamination' by subsequent comparative legal research, legal translation should be as linguistic as possible, leaving as much as possible of the comparative legal analysis to comparative legal research. Nonetheless, this creates a new challenge: how is the translator to do this without translating inadequately? The following sections demonstrate that the answer to this challenge lies in what should be regarded as 'adequate'. This touches upon rudimentary assumptions about the nature of language that underlie thinking about legal translation. Two opposing translation strategies are considered: the receiver-oriented approach on the one hand and the source-oriented approach on the other. It is then demonstrated why, at least for the purpose of comparative legal research, a source-oriented approach and the resulting preference for literal methods of legal translation are to be favoured over the receiver-oriented approach and its leaning towards freer legal translation methods.

The receiver-oriented approach to legal translation

The degree of comparative legal analysis required in legal translation is particularly high in so-called 'receiver-oriented translation'. Receiver-oriented translation aims to observe the specific circumstances in which its intended recipients receive the translation. Translation equivalence is not sought at word or sentence level, but primarily at the level of the *message* (Nida 1964: 123). Various receiver-oriented translation theories dominate contemporary translation studies, with notable proponents such as Eugene Nida (1964), Katharina Reiß and Hans Vermeer (1984), and Mary Snell-Hornby (1988). As Lawrence Venuti points out, common to these receiver-oriented strategies is a commitment to a pragmatic notion of language (2012: 5–6). In contemporary language philosophy, this notion is put forward for instance by Paul Grice (1989) and John Searle (1969). In this tradition, language is understood primarily as a vehicle for communicating or exchanging information, intentions and other mental contents between speakers and listeners (Stokhof 2000: 29). Similarly, translation theorists have made the case that translation itself must be understood as an act of communication (Catford 1965: 20; Dewey 1879).

When *legal* translation, too, is seen as an act of communication, the situational context in which this communication takes place becomes vital for determining the appropriate translation method (Šarčević 1997: 7, 55; Chromá 2004: 38–39; Trosborg 1997: 153). Merely copying the words and sentences of the source legal text is not satisfactory. As Nida argued in the field of Bible translation, the language chosen for the target text should ideally have the same effect on its recipient as the source text itself had on its recipient (1964: 159). He identified the problem of texts producing different responses in different cultural contexts. According to Nida, translators should therefore satisfy the intended recipient's specific linguistic needs and cultural expectations (ibid: 241–45). In other words, instead of formal equivalence, that is, equivalence at the level of words and syntax, Nida proposed that the translator should seek 'dynamic equivalence' (ibid: 166; Nida and Taber 1969: 12). Nida's dynamic equivalence entails an equivalence of the relation between, on the one side, the source text and its recipient and, on the other side, the target text and its recipient (Nida 1964: 159). In Nida's view, a target text is dynamically equivalent to the source text if the response of the recipient of the target text in the target context or culture is equivalent to the response of the recipient of the source text in the source context or culture (Nida and Taber 1969: 202).

Equivalence in receiver-oriented legal translation here involves equivalence between the legal consequences of, on the one hand, the source text on recipients in the source legal system or culture and, on the other hand, the legal consequences on recipients of the translation in the target legal system or culture (Šarčević 1997: 48, 73, 234–35). The shift from formal to dynamic equivalence in legal translation therefore requires from legal translators far more than mere linguistic skills. Receiver-oriented legal translation broadens the emphasis from mere linguistic aspects to include cultural and other extra-lingual factors (Šarčević 1997: 18; Gentzler 2001: 70, 73; Obenaus 1995: 249; Snell-Hornby 1988: 34).

Free methods of receiver-oriented legal translation

The need to accommodate the receiver of the target text in receiver-oriented legal translation may call for free or adaptive methods of legal translation. Such is the case because, in order to have the target text accommodate the communicative context of the target legal culture, the legal translator might need to adapt grammar, lexicon and cultural references (Nida 1964: 159, 166–68; Nida and Taber 1969: 12). The reason governing the translator's strategy is as follows: for the purpose of effective and fluent cross-lingual communication, the target text should appear as natural and comprehensible as it would be if it were an original text (Varó and Hughes 2002: 179; Chromá 2004: 29). The legal translator achieves his goal by applying a 'cultural filter', to quote from Juliane House (1997: 69, 114). This means that the legal translator should filter out any idiosyncrasies pertaining to the source language that would make the target text less intelligible for its recipients in the target legal culture. Whenever necessary, the legal translator should modify the cultural elements to make them fit the target culture.

Consider a simple example to illustrate the gist of this point. Article 107 subsection 1 of the Dutch Burgerlijk Wetboek (BW) reads as follows:

(1) *Bezit is het houden van een goed voor zichzelf.*

The currently leading published English translation of the Dutch BW, the Civil Code of the Netherlands (Warendorf, Thomas and Curry-Sumner 2009), offers a suitable example of receiver-oriented English translation of (1):

(2) Possession is the detention of property for oneself.

The resulting translation may be classified as receiver-oriented as it uses legal terms that suggest to an English speaking comparatist that *bezit* must be understood to be the legal equivalent of 'possession', and *goed* of 'property'. Here, the translator's approach is to adapt the Dutch legal lexicon by replacing Dutch legal terms with common law legal terms. In that fashion, this translation thus suggests to the recipient that certain Dutch legal concepts are akin to particular common law legal concepts.

Another receiver-oriented, English translation of (1) is provided by a Dutch organisation called Dutch Civil Law (DCL),[1] a non-profit project that offers online translations of the Dutch BW:

(3) Possession is the legal status in which a person holds an asset for himself.

As does example (2), this translation adapts the legal lexicon; it translates *bezit* as 'possession' and instead of 'property' chooses the legal term 'asset' in English for the Dutch legal term *goed*. However, this example takes the receiver-oriented approach slightly further than (2). It also adapts the grammatical structure of the original text (1) by adding an English predicate of 'legal status' to *bezit*. As demonstrated below under (5), this diverges from the original Dutch sentence (1) from a linguistic point of view. Translation (3) thus offers its recipient a legal explanation in the English language of *bezit* that suggests to the recipient that this Dutch legal term is readily intelligible in terms of the legal language of the common law.

One should not conclude, however, that a relatively free translation method is the sole method allowed for within receiver-oriented legal translation. As discussed further in the next section, the decision of choosing which method is the most appropriate hinges on the purpose that a particular translation serves (Chromá 2004: 40; Gentzler 2001: 71; Vermeer 1989: 198–201). Nonetheless, in order to obtain the best results in this view, a legal translator must have extensive legal knowledge of all legal systems involved, in order to draft a translation that transmits the purported message of the text in a fully intelligible manner to the receiving audience. One can therefore at least generally conclude that the greater the cultural or contextual differences involved, the more the receiver-oriented legal translator needs to depart from the linguistic structures and legal-cultural references of the source legal text. In those cases, therefore, a relatively free method of translation will probably be preferred.

Receiver-oriented legal translation and comparative legal knowledge

Use of free or adaptive methods of legal translation, which receiver-oriented legal translation might call for, requires the legal translator to have legal knowledge of both source and target legal systems, as well as the skills to compare what he knows of these systems (de Groot 1998: 13–14, 2006: 423–24). The reason is that in order to establish the equivalent legal effects of both source and target text, the legal translator must observe the specific communicative situations in which the judiciary would interpret the source and target text respectively. For example, in their introduction to the English translation of the Dutch BW, Hans Warendorf, Richard Thomas and Ian Curry-Sumner (2009: xxiii) explicitly announce that they want to make their translation understandable to readers familiar with the common law. Susan Šarčević (1997: 72, 229) explicates that receiver-orientation requires the legal translator to predict how courts in the target legal culture would interpret and apply the terms of the particular texts to concrete fact situations. In other words, the legal translator should go about it as if he were a judge in the target legal system solving a legal problem (Šarčević 1997: 235–36). Legal translation is in this sense as much a linguistic endeavour as it is a legal one (Chromá 2004: 50; Šarčević 1997: 236–37). Translations (2) and

(3) exemplify the importance of the legal dimension of receiver-oriented legal translation, tailoring the source text to the English reading audience.

Obviously, this type of receiver-oriented bridging of linguistic and legal differences begs the question how the legal translator should go about his legal comparisons. Proponents of receiver-oriented translation have emphasised the societal *function* of legal texts, rules, terms and concepts (Šarčević 1997: 236; Chromá 2004: 53). The emphasis on function has been inspired, on the one hand, by Katharina Reiß and Hans Vermeer, who established the importance of function – or *skopos* – in translation studies (Reiß 1971; Reiß and Vermeer 1984: 96; Vermeer 1989: 192). The appropriate method of translation in each case depends on the *skopos* of the target text, as Vermeer explains (1989: 198). Thus, similarly, the legal translator needs to take account of the *reasons* why the original legal text in question is translated in the first place (Gentzler 2001: 70–73; Šarčević 1997: 2, 18, 65; Cao 2007: 10; Vermeer 1989: 192). In this light, when translation of foreign authoritative legal texts is conducted for the purpose of comparative legal research, the target text can be said to have the function of *informing* the recipient, that is, the comparatist, about the foreign legal system (Munday 2012: 112–114; Sager 1990: 102; Šarčević 1997: 7–8, 17).

The significance of the function of source and target texts in legal translation studies is further inspired by certain movements in comparative law. Šarčević proposes that, when searching for equivalent terms in the target legal system, the legal translator should use a functional comparative legal strategy, most notably advocated by Konrad Zweigert and Hein Kötz, two influential German comparatists (1997: 13, 2012: 96). Since Zweigert and Kötz maintain that legal concepts are incomparable (1996: 34), the best strategy in comparative legal research is to find what legal systems have in common, namely, social problems (ibid: 39). According to this view, laws are only comparable if they perform the same task or fulfil the same function (ibid: 34–35, 43–44). As a result, the required comparative legal knowledge in receiver-oriented legal translation involves a combination of both legal texts *and* the social, political, historical and cultural contexts in which the text exists (Curran 2006: 8; Grossfeld 2005: 91, 98).

As argued above, legal translation of authoritative legal texts involving a high level of comparative legal analysis, contaminates comparative legal research which makes use of translations. If we accept receiver-oriented legal translation, such contamination appears an unavoidable aspect of legal translation. Hence, solely based on the standards of receiver-oriented legal translation, it is tempting to conclude that legal translation and comparative legal analysis are intrinsically and unavoidably inseparable. In the light of the previously discussed entanglement of comparative legal analysis and legal translation, receiver-oriented legal translation thus clearly poses problems for the comparatist who relies on translated foreign legal texts. The degree of comparative legal analysis needed for receiver-oriented legal translation and its inclined preference for adaptive translation methods, risks contaminating the data of subsequent comparative legal research. The next sections, therefore, make the case that an alternative approach is called for; one that requires substantially less comparative legal analysis. These sections provide arguments in favour of source-oriented legal translation and use of literal translation methods.

Receiver-oriented arguments against literal legal translation

In legal literature, proponents of literal legal translation are like needles in a haystack. True, occasionally one might find positive remarks about literal translation in legal literature, but these hardly amount to a genuine movement or school of thought advocating literal legal translation. For example, James Boyd White takes a liking to literal *literary* translation but merely discusses it in developing his theory of legal discourse, not of legal translation specifically (1990: 252–53, 300, n 18). Further, Peter Schroth argues that the translator should offer the reader a strict-literal translation alongside a 'clear, readable translation' of a foreign legal text (1986: 17). Contrary to these modest tokens of support, literal legal translation is generally discarded. In particular, proponents of receiver-oriented legal translation often express a strong distaste for a literal method of legal translation. These authors derogatorily rebuff literal legal translation as 'traditional' and 'primitive' (Chromá 2004: 47; Šarčević 1997: 16–18, 25; Gentzler 2001: 75; Trosborg 1997: 153; Lindroos-Hovinheimo 2007: 367). Enrique Alcaraz Varó and Brian Hughes argue that the preference for literal legal translation is a position 'often held by legal practitioners with no knowledge of the linguistic niceties involved' (2002: 179).

However, some of the conventional arguments against literal legal translation ultimately provide something of a man of straw; it merely attacks a rather easy-to-defeat support for literal legal translation that we find in, for example, Gerhard Obenaus (1995: 247–48) and David Mellinkoff (1963: 25). One argument against literal legal translation is that it adheres to the principle of fidelity, which requires legal translators to stay as closely as possible to the wording and syntax of the original legal text. Consequently, literal legal translation would be reduced to some sort of mechanical *transcoding*. Such automatic conversion of a string of words from one text into an equivalent string of words in the target language is usually found to be objectionable nowadays (Šarčević 1997: 5, 18, 55; Gémar 1995: 12; but see Obenaus 1995: 248). However, this condemnation of literal legal translation can be traced back to the pragmatic's take on language that underlies receiver-oriented legal translation. Indeed, merely seeking formal equivalence does not amount to much if the meaning of a text is understood to consist not in its literal meaning but primarily in the context in which communication of the text takes place (Varó and Hughes 2002: 23).

Another argument against literal legal translation is directed at the issue of intelligibility of the target text. In the receiver-oriented view, the success of an act of translation generally depends on the degree to which the translator is able to transmit the 'message' of the source text to the recipient of the translation. For those who depict translation as an act of communication, literal legal translation is considered to fail if the language of the target text turns out to be awkward and less than fluently intelligible (Obenaus 1995: 248). Making specific reference to literary translation, translation studies scholars show that this stance echoes the Roman poet Horace, who in his *Ars Poetica* (circa 10 BCE) argued that an unduly literal translation risks obstructing the rendering of the source text's message (Venuti 2008: 4; Munday 2012: 30).

In themselves, these lines of attack against literal legal translation seem convincing. However, they are mostly persuasive if one adheres to a pragmatic take on the nature of language and a consequent portrayal of legal translation as an act of communication. Literal translation or, more broadly, the quest for formal equivalence, indeed seems a flawed technique if one aims for the utmost uninterrupted transmission of a particular message from one legal culture to another. However, the next section demonstrates that as soon as one departs from such a pragmatic, instrumental view of language and translation, the criticism discussed here does not succeed in refuting the case for literal legal translation once and for all.

Source-oriented arguments in favour of literal (literary) translation

As discussed above, a receiver-oriented approach to legal translation leans strongly towards the use of free and adaptive methods of legal translation. Literal translation methods are often considered 'naïve' or simply inadequate. However, throughout the centuries, numerous authors in literary translation studies and the philosophy of language offer reasons to think otherwise. In the 19th and early 20th centuries, Friedrich Schleiermacher (1813) and Walter Benjamin (1923) famously advocated a literal method in literary translation. In contemporary translation studies this view has found support with George Steiner (1998: 318, 341), Antoine Berman (1995: 17, 94) and Venuti (2008: 101). These authors share a so-called 'source-oriented' approach to literary translation and provide strong arguments in favour of the literal method of legal translation. According to this approach, the translator will want to stay as close as possible to the linguistic peculiarities of the source text and expose the very fact that this text is indeed foreign to the target language and culture (Venuti 2012: 4).

At first glance, this source-oriented preference for literal translation methods may appear suspicious. Surely, translating a text literally, let alone *verbatim*, and purposely having the target text appear 'strange', risks failing to convey the intention of the author or the message of the source text. However, recall that such concerns stem from a pragmatic concept of language as an instrument by which we communicate information. Equivalence is then sought at the level of the message conveyed by the source and target text to their respective recipients. In contrast, the source-oriented approach to translation is inspired by an alternative, hermeneutic take on the nature of language; namely, of language as primarily *creative* and *constitutive* of the very world in which we find ourselves (Venuti 2008: 92, 2012: 5–6).

In the philosophy of language, Martin Heidegger and Hans-Georg Gadamer must be regarded as two of the most influential contemporary proponents of this constitutive notion of language. Although Heidegger and Gadamer do not fully reject the instrumental understanding of language, they find it inadequate. In their view, the instrumental understanding of language misses the essence of language, in that language above all brings entities *as* entities into the open (Heidegger 1971b; Lafont 2000: 91–92). In other words, anything understood *as* what it is, is constituted by something we grasp in advance, something which Heidegger calls *Vorgriff* or 'fore-conception' (Heidegger 1927: 191; Lafont 2000: 188, 2002: 185) and Gadamer *Vorverständnis* or 'fore-understanding' (Gadamer 1986: 269–72; Malpas 2009).

From the view in which language constitutes intelligibility, both Heidegger and Gadamer explain that we are in the world because we are 'in' language (Lafont 2000: 89–90); we always find ourselves within a situation (Gadamer 1986: 301). To Heidegger, language sets the world in motion (*die Welt-bewegende Sage*) (Heidegger 1971a: 107). If the language that we use indeed precedes the very world in which we find ourselves, as Heidegger and Gadamer contend, then *different* languages are radically irreconcilable. The reason is that an ontological common denominator, or an ontological common frame of reference, is lacking. Consequently, no message could journey from one language to another, as there is no bridge to cross, so to speak. In this light, the search for dynamic equivalence that proponents of receiver-oriented translation advocate is futile.

Nonetheless, within this constitutive perception of language, the essential divide between languages does not necessarily preclude translation. Likewise, in the source-oriented approach to translation, some sort of *relation* between languages is acknowledged. However, by the lights of a constitutive notion of language, bringing together two ontologically separated languages is not about seeking sameness but about exposing difference (Benjamin 1923: 81–82). Translation should consequently render as precisely as possible the *resistance* of the barriers at the heart of understanding (Steiner 1998: 338, 381; Venuti 2008: 308–09).

Recall that from a receiver-oriented point of view, translation is directed at tailoring the target text to the linguistic and cultural needs and expectations of the intended recipients. Source-oriented translation points in the opposite direction, as Schleiermacher proposes: rather than moving the author of the source text toward the reader of the target text, the translator should leave the author alone and move the reader towards him (Schleiermacher 1813: 49). Rather than drafting the target text as the author of the source text would have done in the target language, the translator should give the reader the impression that the reader would have received if reading the source text in its original language (ibid: 50). Consequently, instead of applying a 'cultural filter' so as to *eliminate* cultural, social and historical differences between source and target languages; source-oriented translation aims exactly to *illuminate* those differences (Venuti 2008: 15, 72–73). In the words of Venuti, the translator should send the reader 'abroad' (ibid: 15).

Literal literary translation would in most cases be the appropriate method by which the source-oriented translator relates insulated languages. Benjamin, for example, explains that a genuine translation is transparent and does not 'block the light' of the original text. Translation, he argues, must release the 'pure language' of the source text and let it shine through in the target language (Benjamin 1923: 81). For him, literal translation is the way to preserve and reveal the foreignness of the source text (Benjamin 1923: 77; Berman 1995: 17, 94). As Steiner argues, the translator should intentionally and deliberately establish an elucidating 'strangeness' (1998: 336, 413). The awkwardness of a literally translated text is not a defect, but a ploy by which to tell the intended recipient of the target text that the latter is dealing with a translation (Venuti 2008: 120). According to Venuti, the artificial fluency of receiver-oriented translations merely gives the false impression that the target text is not a translation but the original; that the linguistic or stylistic peculiarities chosen by the translator reflect the personality or intention of the author of the source text (idem: 1, 5–6).

For these reasons, by exposing the resistance between languages, literal literary translation helps bridge what Gadamer calls the 'gulf' between them (1986: 387). Instead of adapting grammar, lexicon and cultural references in order to give the recipient of the target text an easy read, the translator should intentionally give the reader a hard time.

Comparative legal knowledge in source-oriented legal translation

The source-oriented approach to literary translation, inspired by hermeneutics' constitutive depiction of language, demonstrates that favouring literal methods of translation is not necessarily a naïve stance. Applied to the field of legal translation, one may infer from the hermeneutic tradition in literary or general translation studies that support for literal translation methods does not demonstrate a lack of 'knowledge of linguistic niceties' or commitment to a 'primitive' principle of fidelity to the letter of the law. On the contrary, literal translation helps the intended recipient of the target text to understand the original authoritative legal source in its most original make-up. Given the notion of language as constitutive of the world in which we find ourselves, source-oriented translation brings legal languages closer by revealing what sets them apart.

The question remains whether source-oriented legal translation, and its preference for more literal methods of translation, indeed requires considerably less comparative legal analysis. As pointed out, freer, adaptive methods of legal translation requires from the legal translator excellent knowledge of both the source and the target legal systems. Further, the more comparative legal analysis is necessary for translating an authoritative legal text, the more the translation steers the outcome of comparative legal research that uses this translation. In fact, as the receiver-oriented legal translator aims to make the target text appear as natural and thus as domestic as possible, the target text will carry a bias of sameness.

The legal translator then gives the comparatist, whose research leans on the translation, the impression that the foreign legal text is more related to the latter's domestic legal system than he might have concluded if only capable of reading the foreign text in its original language. By contrast, a source-oriented legal translation registers rather than filters out any deep-seated incongruence. It illuminates the 'out-of-placeness' of the original legal text in the target legal culture, rather than creating an illusion of effortless constancy. In principle, a source-oriented legal translation thus leaves it as much as possible to the comparatist to draw his own comparative conclusions from translated legal texts. Consequently, this would lower the risk of contaminating the target text with a covert comparative legal analysis.

Nonetheless, source-oriented legal translation will still require some degree of comparative legal analysis, in that without it the legal translator would not be able to register the foreignness of the source legal text in the target legal language to begin with. As Venuti points out, foreignising translation still involves some degree of 'domestication'. He explains that because one translates a source text *intended for* a target culture, the translated text does *depend* to an extent on that culture's dominant values, in order for the translation to become visible as foreign (2008: 28, 40).

As to the need for comparative legal knowledge in literal legal translation, take for example a possible literal translation of (1), the previously discussed Dutch provision Article 107 subsection 1 BW:

(4) Possession is the keeping of a good for oneself.

A translator without any knowledge of either common law or Dutch law could argue that 'possession' is the appropriate translation of *bezit*, if only because in everyday use a native English speaker would use 'possession' where a Dutch native speaker would use *bezit*. However, a source-oriented legal translator having some acquaintance with both Dutch law and common law might want to avoid translating *bezit* by 'possession', simply because 'possession' is a specific common law legal term. Use of that term therefore risks giving the recipient comparatist the impression that Article 107 subsection 1 BW applies to the same or a similar legal phenomenon as possession in common law. True, a comparatist reading the translation might come to the very conclusion that these phenomena are indeed similar. The point here is that this conclusion should come as much as possible from his own comparative legal analysis; not accidentally because the legal translator who translated the Dutch text thought so. Hence, instead of opting for translation (4), the source-oriented legal translator might choose to translate (1) in the following manner:

(5) Having is the keeping of a worthable for oneself.

A source-oriented legal translator will aim to circumvent use of 'possession'. Even if convinced that these terms have the same meaning or relate to the same or similar legal phenomena, he would aim to avoid imposing his legal conclusion on the target text. After all, as this chapter argues, legal translation of authoritative legal texts for the purpose of subsequent comparative legal research should leave it to the recipient-comparatist to undertake his own analysis. Admittedly, a translator with no legal awareness whatsoever might argue that, linguistically, the gerund 'having' is a less appropriate translation of the noun *bezit* than the noun 'possession'. However, unlike 'possession', from a legal perspective 'having' lacks a specific common law connotation – regardless of what specific legal connotation that might be. Additionally, the source-oriented legal translator might opt to translate the distinct Dutch legal term *goed* with a neologism such as 'worthable', which hints at things of worth. Even though 'worthable' might appear inelegant and perhaps even comical to the recipient, it signals the foreignness of the Dutch term *bezit* to the common law.

This example demonstrates that the source-oriented legal translator needs at least a rudimentary level of comparative knowledge of the legal systems involved; just enough to avoid accidentally hitting on legally loaded words. Put differently, the legal translator needs at least to know how to avoid influencing comparative legal analysis by recipients of their translation. Obviously, there may be more than one way for a source-oriented legal translator to disclose that the original text is *not* domestic. In particular, one could opt for neologisms, for example translate *bezit* as 'apprehentment' or 'havement', or choose simply to keep the original term. Here, there is no absolute right or wrong. Both receiver and source-oriented translations are exactly that: *orientations*, not end points.

The level of literalism

The final question that this chapter addresses is exactly *how* literal does literal legal translation need to be? The answer is that a source-oriented approach to legal translation does not necessitate a strict-literal, *verbatim* or word-for-word translation as advocated by Schleiermacher and Benjamin in the field of literary translation. Translating a legal text is a different matter from translating a poem. A source-oriented *literary* translator probably aims to preserve the linguistic idiosyncrasies of the foreign general language in order to register the specific qualities of this foreign piece of written art. A source-oriented *legal* translator, by contrast, would primarily aim to register the peculiarities of the foreign *legal* language.

Let us take as an example Article 107 BW again, but now subsection 2:

(6) *Bezit is onmiddellijk, wanneer iemand bezit zonder dat een ander het goed voor hem houdt.*

A strict-literal, word-for-word or *verbatim* translation might look something like this:

(7) Possession is immediate, when someone possesses without that an other the good for him keeps.

Besides the unwelcome use of the term 'possession', as discussed above, there is no reason to translate (6) in this strict fashion. Such a level of literalism might reveal the syntactic structure of the Dutch sentence and thus register in the English language the foreignness of the Dutch language. However, that in itself does not tell the recipient anything about the foreignness of Dutch law in common law legal culture. In fact, registering with mechanistic rigidity the peculiarities of general language that the foreign legal text uses may even fail to register the foreign nature of the law that it expresses. In ancient times, for example, Roman constitutions were transcribed *et verbatim* (word-for-word) or even transliterated *et literatim* (letter-for-letter) into Greek – the translations would serve as authoritative legal texts in the Greek regions of the Roman Empire. Reportedly, this translation method led to translations that were fully incomprehensible to their Greek recipients (Plisecka 2012). This shows that, in order for literal legal translation to succeed in laying bare a foreign law in its purest form, the language of the target text should at least be sufficiently comprehensible as such. Additionally, the word 'good' might be a perfectly literal translation of the Dutch legal term *goed*. However, as said, it implies a degree of equivalence in legal connotation that a comparative lawyer might very well conclude to be unwarranted.

Legislative provision (6) is therefore better translated as follows:

> (8) Having is immediate, when someone is having without someone else keeping the worthable for him.

Besides use of the word 'having', as discussed, the legally knowledgeable source-oriented legal translator will allow himself grammatically to adapt the syntax of the original, as long as this does not create a level of naturalness that might suggest to the recipient of the target text that the foreign *legal* language is equivalent to his domestic legal language. Nevertheless, the source-oriented legal translator should be cautious here. He should not fear rendering the target text less than fully comprehensible. The idea that a translation of a foreign legal text *must* appear natural, be fully understandable and read like an original, stems from a pragmatic notion of language as an instrument for communication. As discussed, based on this notion, successful translation is measured by the level at which a presumptive stable message is transmitted across different languages to a recipient in a different context. However, as demonstrated, this is not the only defensible position. From a constitutive view of language, one should actually be wary of a translation that appears all too natural or domestic.

Let us take as a further example yet another part of Article 107 BW, namely subsection 4:

> (9) *Houderschap is op overeenkomstige wijze onmiddellijk of middellijk.*

A source-oriented translation of this sentence might read as follows:

(10) Keepership is in corresponding ways immediate or mediate.

Translating *houderschap* by 'keepership' may puzzle the common law lawyer-reader of the target text. However, for a source-oriented legal translator, such bewilderment is exactly the desired response. After all, *houderschap* is a Dutch legal phenomenon, not a common law one. The translation offered by Warendorf, Thomas and Curry-Sumner (2009) falls short of creating that level of foreignising awkwardness:

(11) Detention is direct or indirect, mutatis mutandis.

Again, use of the word 'detention' suggests to the recipient a fully intelligible similitude that the recipient comparatist should be allowed to decide for himself. As Schroth notes, using legal terms that are all too familiar to the target legal culture 'may lead the audience to assume it understands more than it really does' (1986: 17).

Conclusion

This chapter argues that a receiver-oriented approach to legal translation, and its acceptance of freer or more adaptive translation methods, is not conducive to comparative legal research. The adoption of that strategy inevitably prompts the undertaking of a brand of comparative legal analysis that will seek to ascertain similarities with a view to eliciting an equivalence in the target-language that will match the source-word. Therefore, a comparatist who later relies on the translated text would in effect, unbeknownst to him, be using legal terminology that is already 'contaminated' by the legal translator's similarity-based comparative analysis. A source-oriented approach and its preference for literal translation allow to minimise 'contamination' of comparative legal analysis by legal translations.

Proponents of receiver-oriented legal translation may generally criticise literal translation methods, but the potency of this criticism is limited. It ultimately comes down to one's rudimentary ideas on the nature of language. In other words, literal legal translation may be the evil stepmother in one tale, but the knight in shining armour in another. By offering an alternative – the hermeneutic approach to literary translation – I wanted to demonstrate that the philosophical tenets of receiver-oriented theories of translation are not uncontested. I hope to have shown that other, substantial arguments support a literal method for legal translation; a translation method that best serves comparative legal research.

Notes

* The author wishes in particular to thank Jean-Claude Gémar, Geoffrey Samuel and Fabrizio Megale for their most helpful comments on the draft version of this chapter.
1 See http://www.dutchcivillaw.com (accessed 1 October 2013).

Bibliography

Benjamin, W. (1923) 'The Task of the Translator: An Introduction to the Translation of Baudelaire's *Tableaux Parisiens*', trans. H. Zohn, in L. Venuti (ed.) *The Translation Studies Reader*, 3rd edn, London: Routledge, 2012.

Berman, A. (1995) *Pour une critique des traductions: John Donne*, Paris: Gallimard.

Cao, D. (2007) *Translating Law*, Clevedon: Multilingual Matters.

Catford, J.C. (1965) *A Linguistic Theory of Translation: An Essay in Applied Linguistics*, Oxford: Oxford University Press.

Chromá, M. (2004) *Legal Translation and the Dictionary*, Tübingen: M. Niemeyer.

—— (2012) 'A Dictionary for Legal Translation', in C.J.W. Baaij (ed.) *The Role of Legal Translation in Legal Harmonization*, The Hague: Kluwer.

Curran, V.G. (2002) 'Intercultural Immersion', in V.G. Curran (ed.) *Comparative Law: An Introduction*, Durham, NC: Carolina Academic Press.

—— (2006) 'Comparative Law and Language', in R. Zimmerman and M. Reimann (eds) *The Oxford Handbook of Comparative Law*, Oxford: Oxford University Press.

Dewey, J. (1897) 'In My Pedagogic Creed', *School Journal*, 54: 77–80 http://dewey.pragmatism.org/creed.htm (accessed 1 October 2013).

Frankenberg, G. (1985) 'Critical Comparisons: Re-thinking Comparative Law', *Harvard International Law Journal*, 26: 411–55.

Gadamer, H.-G. (1986) *Truth and Method*, trans. J. Weinsheimer and D.G. Marshall, 3rd edn, New York: Continuum, 2004.

Gémar, J.-C. (1995) *Traduire ou l'art d'interpréter*, vol I, Montreal: Presses de l'Université du Québec.

Gentzler, E. (2001) *Contemporary Translation Theories*, 2nd edn, Clevedon: Multilingual Matters.

Gerber, D.J. (1998) 'System Dynamics: Towards a Language of Comparative Law?', *American Journal of Comparative Law*, 46: 719–37.

Gordley, J. (1995) 'Comparative Legal Research: Its Function in the Development of Harmonized Law', *American Journal of Comparative Law*, 43: 555–67.

Graziadei, M. (2003) 'The Functionalist Heritage', in P. Legrand and R. Munday (eds) *Comparative Legal Studies: Traditions and Transitions*, Cambridge: Cambridge University Press.

Grice, P. (1989) *Studies in the Way of Words*, Cambridge, MA: Harvard University Press.

Groot, G.-R. de (1996) 'Law, Legal Language and the Legal System: Reflections on the Problems of Translating Legal Texts', in V. Gessner, A. Hoeland and C. Varga (eds) *European Legal Cultures*, Aldershot: Dartmouth.

—— (1998) 'Language and Law', in *Netherlands Reports to the 15th International Congress of Comparative Law*, Antwerp: Intersentia.

—— (2006) 'Legal Translation', in J.M. Smits (ed.) *Elgar Encyclopedia of Comparative Law*, Cheltenham: E. Elgar.

Grossfeld, B. (2005) *Core Questions of Comparative Law*, trans. V.G. Curran, Durham, NC: Carolina Academic Press.

Heidegger, M. (1927) *Being and Time*, trans. J. Macquarrie and E. Robinson, Oxford: Blackwell, 1962.

—— (1971a) 'The Nature of Language', in *On the Way to Language*, trans. P.D. Hertz, New York: Harper & Row.

—— (1971b) 'The Origin of the Work of Art', in *Poetry, Language, Thought*, trans. A. Hofstadter, New York: Harper & Row.

Herder, J.G. von (1772) 'On the Origin of Language', in M.N. Foster (ed.) *Herder: Philosophical Writings*, Cambridge: Cambridge University Press, 2002.

Heutger, V. (2003) 'Law and Language in the European Union', *Global Jurist Topics*, 3 http://igitur-archive.library.uu.nl/law/2006-1117-200528/heutger_03_lawandlanguage.pdf (accessed 1 October 2013).

—— (2004) 'A More Coherent European Wide Legal Language', *European Integration Online Papers*, 8 http://eiop.or.at/eiop/pdf/2004-002.pdf (accessed 1 October 2013).

Hoecke, M. Van (2002) 'Deep Level Comparative Law', *European University Institute Working Paper LAW*, 13 http://cadmus.eui.eu/bitstream/handle/1814/191/law02-13.pdf?sequence=1 (accessed 1 October 2013).

House, J. (1997) *Translation Quality Assessment: A Model Revisited*, Tübingen: G. Narr.

Husa, J. (2012) 'Understanding Legal Languages: Linguistic Concerns of the Comparative Lawyer', in C.J.W. Baaij (ed.) *The Role of Legal Translation in Legal Harmonization*, The Hague: Kluwer.

Jameson, F. (1972) *The Prison-House of Language: A Critical Account of Structuralism and Russian Formalism*, Princeton, NJ: Princeton University Press.

Kelsen, H. (1979) *Allgemeine Theorie der Normen*, Vienna: Manz.

Kjaer, A.L. (2004) 'A Common Legal Language in Europe?', in M. Van Hoecke (ed.) *Epistemology and Methodology of Comparative Law*, Oxford: Hart.

Lafont, C. (2000) *Heidegger, Language, and World-Disclosure*, trans. G. Harman, Cambridge: Cambridge University Press.

—— (2002) 'Précis of Heidegger, Language, and World-Disclosure', *Inquiry*, 45: 185–90.

Lindroos-Hovinheimo, S. (2007) 'On the Indeterminacy of Legal Translation', in T. Wilhelmsson and others (eds) *Private Law and the Many Cultures of Europe*, The Hague: Kluwer.

Llewellyn, K.N. (1960) *The Bramble Bush: The Classic Lectures on the Law and Law School*, Oxford: Oxford University Press, 2008.

Malpas, J. (2009) 'Hans-Georg Gadamer', in E.N. Zalta (ed.) *The Stanford Encyclopedia of Philosophy* http://plato.stanford.edu/archives/sum2009/entries/gadamer/ (accessed 1 October 2013).

Mellinkoff, D. (1963) *The Language of the Law*, Boston, MA: Little, Brown & Co.

Munday, J. (2012) *Introducing Translation Studies*, 3rd edn, London: Routledge.

Nida, E.A. (1964) *Towards a Science of Translating*, Leiden: E.J. Brill.

—— and Taber, C. (1969) *The Theory and Practice of Translation*, Leiden: E.J. Brill.

Obenaus, G. (1995) 'The Legal Translator as Information Broker', in M. Morris (ed.) *Translation and the Law*, Amsterdam: J. Benjamins.

Plisecka, A. (2012) 'Legal Translation and the Bilingual Publication of Roman Imperial Constitutions', *Language and Law*, 1 http://www.languageandlaw.de/volume-1/3337 (accessed 1 October 2013).

Reiß, K. (1971) *Möglichkeiten und Grenzen der Übersetzungkritik*, Munich: M. Hueber.

—— and Vermeer, H.J. (1984) *Grundlegung einer allgemeinen Translationstheorie*, Tübingen: M. Niemeyer.

Sacco, R. (1991) 'Legal Formants: A Dynamic Approach to Comparative Law (Installment I of II)', *American Journal of Comparative Law*, 39: 1–34.

Sager, J.C. (1990) *A Practical Course in Terminology*, Amsterdam: J. Benjamins.

Samuel, G. (1998) 'Comparative Law and Jurisprudence', *International and Comparative Law Quarterly*, 47: 817–36.

—— (2003) *Epistemology and Method in Law*, Aldershot: Ashgate.

Šarčević, S. (1997) *New Approach to Legal Translation*, The Hague: Kluwer.

—— (2012) 'Coping With the Challenges of Legal Translation in Harmonization', in C.J.W. Baaij (ed.) *The Role of Legal Translation in Legal Harmonization*, The Hague: Kluwer.

Schleiermacher, F. (1813) 'On the Different Methods of Translating', trans. S. Bernofsky, in L. Venuti (ed.) *The Translation Studies Reader*, 3rd edn, London: Routledge, 2012.

Schroth, P.W. (1986) 'Legal Translation', *American Journal of Comparative Law*, 34: 47–65.

Schulte-Nölke, H., Twigg-Flesner, C. and Ebers, M. (2008) *EC Consumer Law Compendium – Comparative Analysis* http://ec.europa.eu/consumers/rights/docs/consumer_law_compendium_comparative_analysis_en_final.pdf (accessed 1 October 2013).

Searle, J. (1969) *Speech Acts: An Essay in the Philosophy of Language*, Cambridge: Cambridge University Press.

Sefton-Green, R. (2008) 'The CFR and the Preservation of Cultural and Linguistic Plurality', paper presented at the SECOLA meeting, University Popeu Fabra, Barcelona, Spain, 6 June.

Snell-Hornby, M. (1988) *Translation Studies: An Integrated Approach*, Amsterdam: J. Benjamins.

Steiner, G. (1998) *After Babel: Aspects of Language and Translation*, 3rd edn, Oxford: Oxford University Press.

Stokhof, M. (2000) *Taal en Betekenis*, Amsterdam: Boom.

Teubner, G. (1998) 'Legal Irritants: Good Faith in British Law or How Unifying Law Ends Up in New Divergences', *Modern Law Review*, 61: 11–32.

Trosborg, A. (ed.) (1997) *Text Typology and Translation*, Amsterdam: J. Benjamins.

Varó, E.A. and Hughes, B. (2002) *Legal Translation Explained*, Manchester: St Jerome.

Venuti, L. (2008) *The Translator's Invisibility: A History of Translation*, 2nd edn, London: Routledge.

—— (ed.) (2012) *The Translation Studies Reader*, 3rd edn, London: Routledge.

Vermeer, H.J. (1989) 'Skopos and Commission in Translational Action', trans. A. Chesterman, in L. Venuti (ed.) *The Translation Studies Reader*, 3rd edn, London: Routledge, 2012.

Warendorf, H.C.S., Thomas, R.L. and Curry-Sumner, I. (2009) *The Civil Code of the Netherlands*, The Hague: Kluwer.

White, J.B. (1990) *Justice as Translation*, Chicago: University of Chicago Press.

—— (2005) 'Translation as a Way of Understanding the Language of Law', in B. Pozzo (ed.) *Ordinary Language and Legal Language*, Milan: Giuffrè.

Zweigert, K. and Kötz, H. (1996) *An Introduction to Comparative Law*, trans. T. Weir, 3rd edn, Oxford: Oxford University Press, 1998.

Chapter 8

Translating civil law 'objectivity' with an adversarial brain: an ethnographic perspective

*Shawn Marie Boyne**

'[A]s factfinders, we embrace a vision of the world in which there is reality beyond language'

Mirjan Damaška (1997: 290)

Introduction: translation in comparative law

Not only does the act of translation encompass the transfer of linguistic sense but it also involves the transportation of larger cultural and epistemological meanings (Wolf 2008). When legal texts are the object of translation, the process further includes the 'mechanism of the law' (Šarčević 2000: 1). However, when it comes to legal texts, the roles of the linguist and of translation theory have been contested (Poirier 1995: 1036–37). Indeed, some legal scholars argue that legal texts possess a unique communicative function that is often overlooked (Šarčević 2012: 189). While legal scholars have therefore questioned the linguists' claims to participate in the law-related interpretation enterprise, I sidestep that debate here (Poirier 1995: 1034). Instead, I address the problems of subjectivity and of interpretation that legal scholars themselves face as they attempt to analyse the role that law plays on unfamiliar turf. Specifically, I identify and detail two challenges embedded in comparative legal jurisprudence. While one stems from the pitfalls that legal scholars encounter when they choose to rely on legal texts as a source of understanding rather than investigate how the law actually functions on the ground, the second arises from the comparative legal scholar's subjectivity.

As a legal scholar who studies the German prosecution service, my knowledge of the matter of 'translatability' has been forged in the field, rather than through theory-building. In my interviews with prosecutors and judges, as I sought to assess whether code provisions structure decision-making, I discovered how malleable normative terms such as 'objectivity' can prove to be in the context of practice. I must emphasise that, from my standpoint, coming to understand the functioning of a prosecution service grounded in the civil law tradition proved to be an iterative process. Indeed, the questions that I posed in my initial round of interviews carried the strong imprint of my own subjectivity as a former US prosecutor. While my past experience opened doors, I relied on humour and self-deprecating remarks to overcome mistaken assumptions and mispronounced words.

I begin with a short summary of the challenges faced by comparative legal scholars. I then detail the early comparative legal scholarship that promoted the German prosecution service's highly-touted objectivity. In particular, I show how scholarly reliance on codes, rather than on a deeper interrogation of legal practices, led many to take for granted the positivistic portraits of prosecutorial decision-making drawn by German academics. By framing statutory texts as reliable descriptors of practice, comparative legal scholars represented German prosecutors as models of dispassionate and scientific decision-making (Schram 1969; Wagner 1974; Langbein 1974; Herrmann 1976). Interestingly, during that same period, US academics, strongly influenced by socio-legal studies of decision-making processes, were heavily criticising US prosecutors on account of their conviction-driven mindset (Kagan 2003; Pizzi 1999). I argue that the willingness of many comparative legal scholars readily to accept the scholarship of German legal 'scientists', who adhered to the civil law tradition's conviction that the law could prescribe practice, even as other academics were eviscerating the normative claims of US prosecutors, may be explained by a failure of translation. In fact, this misunderstanding, quite apart from constituting a failure of translation, must also act as an indictment of the comparative method itself – which I understand as a tool serving both to examine how the law functions in other societies and to challenge the normative claims of a foreign legal system.

Finally, I address the issue of a researcher's subjectivity. As Richard Posner has stated: '[i]n reading the literature of another culture one cannot divest oneself of one's own cultural identity; understanding, like translation, is mediation, not just reconstruction' (1988: 236). Although the matter of subjectivity is often problematic, I observe that knowledge of one's own system may provide the critical distance necessary to contextualise native perceptions of the law. This is particularly true with respect to the German legal system, where traditional legal scholarship has long maintained a reverential positivistic orientation.

The challenge of law and language

Legal language conveys meaning beyond the words on a page. It is a highly structured system of language that reflects the legal culture in which it was born. Because a legal culture represents a distinct way of viewing the role that law plays in organising society, these ways of understanding the law are embedded in the language of the law. The translation of legal terminology requires unique attention because the law 'consists primarily of abstract terms deeply and firmly rooted in the domestic culture and intellectual tradition' (Chroma 2004: 48) and thus entails a transfer between two different legal systems, each with its own unique system of referencing.

A key barrier to producing an 'objective' translation of foreign law is the fact that language is a mere starting point to understanding law's real meaning

(Itzcovich 2012: 479). While law functions as a binding code that regulates community life, linguistic acts may not wholly encompass legal standards (Endicott 2010). The structure of language itself complicates the task of understanding a foreign legal system. As Ginevra Peruginelli notes, languages are 'intended not only as a system of symbols, but also as a means of communication and as a tool for mediating between different cultures' (Peruginelli 2007: 64–65). Although linguists have long recognised the interdependent relationship between language and culture (Yule 2010), comparative legal scholars have been slow to recognise the system-specificity of legal language (de Groot 2006: 423).

Not only does legal language convey a system of meaning: when the law is written in a foreign language, comparatists must uncover the hidden structure of a foreign legal system. As Simone Glanert argues: 'each national language continues to signify according to its own structures and continues to express its legal thought by means of a particular vocabulary' (2008: 164). Comparative legal translation is a non-linear process as comparatists must translate the meaning of the legal text, interpret that text within its particular legal culture, and understand the role that legal actors play. In short, we must understand how the machinery of the law operates as legal translation is 'an act of communication in the mechanism of the law' (Šarčević 1997: 55, 2000: 1).

One example of the complexity of this process and its potential for misunderstanding can be understood by looking at the role of the judge. Although we may think we know what a 'judge' is, our understanding of how a judge may operate in another legal system is filtered through our knowledge of the role that judges play in our legal home. When we examine the role of US and German judges, the judge's role is often framed within a binary comparison between adversarial and inquisitorial forms of justice.[1] In this frame, text-based comparisons with civil law judges often describe the role of adversarial judges in the truth-finding process as a largely passive one (Jolowicz 2000: 220). In comparison, scholars have described the role of judges in inquisitorial systems as more active. In comparative legal terms, judges in the inquisitorial system are described as 'active' since they structure the presentation of evidence in the courtroom, actively question witnesses, and decide the fate of the accused (ibid).

The comparative frame is certainly a useful starting point. Unless a US judge wants to intervene and overturn a jury verdict, the judge plays a subservient role to the jury in adjudicating a suspect's guilt. In that strict sense of the bottom line issue of who decides guilt, a US judge plays a more passive role than a German judge. Yet, the 'active' and 'passive' labels obscure the extent of the power of US judges and underestimate the limits on the decision-making power of German judges. For example, a US judge may in a single stroke eviscerate a prosecutor's case by suppressing evidence obtained in violation of the constitution. Because the standards for exclusion are described with fluid terms such as 'reasonable', 'exigent' and 'undue', and trial judges are often granted a wide range of discretion, in many cases judicial decision-making may decisively impact the outcome of the case. Conversely, decisions of inquisitorial judges are constrained by the contents of the prosecutor's dossier (Hodgson 2002: 229), as well as the prosecutor's analysis of a case (Boyne 2010: 1357). Shallow comparisons of judicial decision-making and use of labels such as 'active' and 'passive' miss capturing the richness of judicial decision-making.

To build this broad picture, comparatists must acknowledge that efforts to construct dichotomies between various characteristics of different legal systems miss capturing the complexity of practice. Hidden in the web of legal practice are ways of knowing and meaning reflecting a legal system's normative assumptions that may be lost in translation. As a result, legal translation cannot be done in isolation, divorced from the practice of law. Ultimately, scholars who engage in comparative legal research must be willing to test their theoretical claims in the world of practice. As Susan Šarčević states: 'the success of an authenticated translation depends on its interpretation and application in practice' (2000: 1).

Unravelling the meaning of the legal rules in a foreign country and discerning how those rules operate requires the comparative legal scholar to engage in an iterative process of engaging both text and practice. Against this backdrop, mere text-to-text translations that focus on a narrow piece of another legal system risk missing the essence of how a foreign legal system functions. First and foremost, because the meaning of the law ultimately resides in the minds of the actors who practise law, the research process must uncover and understand the assumptions about law possessed by legal actors in the system. For example, we cannot discern whether or not the use of efficiency-driven procedures such as plea bargaining undermines the normative assumptions of inquisitorial systems without understanding how legal actors on the front lines of those systems think. In some cases, true understanding of the import of a legal text cannot be achieved without shifting our level of analysis to the ground level of practice.

This text is often hidden as, unlike judicial practice, it is rare that a prosecutor will explain her decision-making process. Sometimes, prosecutors themselves may have difficulty explaining the unarticulated assumptions that guide decision-making. Whereas many comparative criminal law scholars focus on the similarities and differences between national laws as they exist on the books, I prefer to be embedded with the objects that I study – observing and seeking to understand how prosecutors make numerous daily decisions designed to move cases towards dismissal, negotiation or adjudication.

By researching the German criminal law system from the 'bottom up', rather than from the 'top down', I have come face to face with the issue of 'translatability'. In the field, the challenge of translation is larger than the problems inherent in translating the meanings of particular words. Because words are embedded in a particular structure of meaning, the researcher cannot understand the meaning that particular key legal words carry without understanding the underlying normative assumptions of that legal structure. To apprehend the 'translation' challenges that I faced in the field, one must first appreciate how many German legal scholars 'understand' the function of the German prosecution service. To that topic I now turn.

Textual centrism and German legal scholarship

In the past two decades the growing gap between the 'text' of the German Code of Criminal Procedure (Strafprozeßordnung – StPO) and actual practice has created a unique comparative case study regarding the subject of prosecutorial discretion. When I began to research the nature of that gap, my understanding was shaped and constrained not only by my own training as a US lawyer but also by the dominant binary categorisation of adversarial and inquisitorial systems. This section summarises how those categories have shaped the comparative narrative regarding the German and US criminal justice systems. The section is a necessary prelude to understanding how comparatists, in their rush to destroy the 'mythology of objectivity' surrounding the German system, have largely missed how organisational norms, rather than the law, limit discretionary decision-making.

The dividing axis between adversarial and inquisitorial systems has traditionally centred on each system's core assumptions about the structure of the truth-finding process. Although both systems strive to 'find the truth', the roads they take to reach that outcome are on paper decidedly different. Whilst the adversarial model assumes that the truth will emerge out of a contest between two parties, the truth-finding process in Germany's inquisitorial system consists of an objective investigation, completed by the prosecution and the police, with a judicially-managed adjudication process (Weigend 2003). Although judicial panels in German cases may include lay jurors, whatever the size of the panel, it is always chaired by a professional judge who conducts most of the questioning of witnesses during the trial. In the US system, because the prosecutor bears the burden of proving that the defendant is guilty beyond a reasonable doubt, the primary burden of production falls on the prosecutor's table. While the defendant need not present any testimony, criminal defence attorneys in the United States typically play an active role in shaping the jurors' opinion of the evidence when they cross-examine prosecution witnesses seeking to sow doubt in jurors' minds.

Criticism of the fact-finding process in US jury trials, in particular the gamesmanship of the parties, sparked much of the initial comparative interest in the German legal system. While comparatists praised the limited discretion of German prosecutors, scholarship critical of the role of the US prosecutor has continued to flourish. According to some scholars, in the United States a 'conviction mentality' motivates certain prosecutors to place securing convictions above all other goals (Pizzi 1999; Kagan 2003). Scholars such as Kenneth Davis (1976), William Pizzi (1999) and Robert Kagan (2003) have argued that the adversarial nature of the US criminal justice system created norms of behaviour that undermine, rather than further, the system's truth-finding orientation. Critics alleged that the system's underlying normative assumption that the truth will emerge from a battle between parties emboldens prosecutors and defence attorneys to treat trials as contests. According to the eminent legal historian, John Langbein, trials in the United States had become a 'truth-defeating' enterprise (1985: 825).

When comparatists juxtaposed portraits of US justice with positivistic scholarship focused on the German Code of Criminal Procedure, the German system in general and German prosecutors in particular appeared to be the antidote. In hindsight, the quest for an alternative to adversarialism, coupled with the positivistic faith of German legal scholars in the text of the law, coloured scholars' claims about the objectivity of German prosecutors. Although he does not himself endorse this statement, the well known German legal theorist, Claus Roxin, thus recalls how the early 20th-century German prosecutor, Hugo Isenbiel, declared that German prosecutors were the 'most objective civil servants in the world' (1997: 113). While US scholars, who had long since abandoned confidence in the law's prescriptive ability, decried US prosecutors' thirst to 'win' cases, comparative scholarship continued to highlight the neutrality of the German prosecution corps (Herrmann 1976: 18).

Long after German attorneys knew that prosecutors had begun to exercise more and more discretion, comparative scholars continued to point to the existence of the code provisions that mandate prosecution and limit discretion as conclusive proof that discretionary decision-making by German prosecutors was sharply circumscribed (Langbein 1985). Although a few scholars in the early 1990s pointed out that the scope of prosecutorial discretion in Germany was increasing, for a significant period leading scholarship maintained that institutional and legal mechanisms controlled prosecutorial discretion (ibid). While some German scholars contend that discretion has slipped into the legal system only recently, in fact informal plea bargaining practices began to emerge in the German system as far back as the 1970s (Herrmann 1992: 775).

What then accounts for this myopic vision of the German legal system? While translation errors contributed to the gap between scholarship and practice, one cannot attribute this divergence completely to translation errors. Indeed, many of the prominent comparative scholars writing about the German legal system were native German speakers. Instead, a deeper cultural gap was in play – namely that scholarly work on the German criminal justice system focused on statutory law, reflecting 'the "legicentrism" of legal culture generally' (Kasirer 2001: 339). Scholarship that heralded the normative principles of prosecutorial practice as proof of practice on the ground lacked reflexivity. In Nicholas Kasirer's language, the scholars neglected to step out of 'law's empire' and enter 'law's cosmos' (2002: 29). Their attention to the text of the law, rather than to legal culture, led them to cite specific provisions of the Code of Criminal Procedure, rather than observations of practice, as evidence of advantages of the inquisitorial system.

Comparisons of scholarship focused on both the German and the US criminal justice systems overlooked the fact that, although US scholars had long lost their faith in positivism, many German scholars continued to believe that law functioned as a science. This gap in perspectives coloured comparative legal scholarship. While realistic critiques of the law had dominated US legal scholarship for decades, the bulk of German legal scholarship evidenced a blind faith in the code's ability both to structure prosecutorial decision-making and to banish discretion. Perhaps nowhere was this faith more misplaced than in discussions about how code provisions ensured the predictability and apolitical nature of the law. In line with this argument, for decades German legal scholars maintained that the law effectively constrains discretion. This *mantra* has been especially prevalent in the case of so-called major crimes, where pre-trial diversion programmes are not available. For over a decade, many scholars pointed to the existence of the code provisions that mandate prosecution and limit discretion as conclusive proof that German prosecutors possess limited discretion (Schram 1969: 627; Herrmann 1976: 16).

As a case in point, in 1978, John Langbein and Lloyd Weinreb wrote that: 'the Germans have been remarkably successful in eliminating discretion from the prosecution of serious crime' (1978: 1561). The authors referred to section 152(II) of the Code of Criminal Procedure, which mandates that prosecutors file charges in all cases with sufficient evidence to support their argument. Langbein and Weinreb boldly proclaimed that prosecutors lacked the authority 'to offer to reduce the charge in return for a concession of guilt' (ibid: 1562). One year later, this claim was reiterated by Klaus Sessar, who argued that 'dismissal of felony cases was (and is) not permitted by law' (1979: 257). At this time, leading comparative scholars were content to rely on code provisions as conclusive evidence of legal practice:

> The prosecutor is under a duty to investigate thoroughly and impartially, and the dossier contains exculpatory as well as inculpatory evidence. It is made available in advance of the trial to the accused and his defense counsel, who can by motion require the prosecutor to investigate defensive claims and evidence that he has overlooked on his own.
>
> (Langbein and Weinreb 1978: 1562–63)

In hindsight it is difficult to comprehend such faith in the law on the books. It only begins to make sense when viewed through the prism of the civil law tradition, which is founded on the conviction that the 'substantive truth' exists and that prosecutors and judges can dispassionately find it. The Code of Criminal Procedure was conceived as a road map for procedures designed to ensure that the process produced the truth. For a time, comparative scholars declared that German prosecutors functioned objectively because the code directed prosecutors to investigate the facts both for and against the accused. To be sure, the content of the code is not meaningless. In most cases German prosecutors do not function as interested parties but as civil bureaucrats. However, by relying on code provisions as the template of practice, comparative scholars remained oblivious to the gap between the law and practice.

One of the first challenges to the 'myth' of limited discretion was authored by two US scholars, Abraham Goldstein and Martin Marcus, who suggested that pronouncements about limited prosecutorial discretion in civil law systems were more myth than reality (1977: 279–83). Importantly, in another article, Goldstein (1974: 1021) argued that it was necessary to understand not only the law's normative standards but also how organisational factors affect delivery of justice in any system:

> The operation of any model and of the procedure reflecting it will depend on the interaction of many factors: the normative content of the standards to be applied in making decisions, how the participants are perceived and trained, the controls introduced at strategic points, and the resources assigned to implement policies and controls.

Although more scholars are now writing about the expanding scope of prosecutorial discretion in Germany, for a significant period the prevailing scholarship maintained that institutional and legal mechanisms effectively circumscribed discretion (Weigend 1978). For at least two decades, even in the face of rising crime rates and fiscal challenges, scholars continued to insist that prosecutors faced little pressure to dispose of cases quickly. As resource limitations became more pronounced, advocates of the German system argued that the principle of mandatory prosecution still constrained prosecution of serious crimes. By implication, prosecutors now only exercised discretion with respect to low level crimes. In the late 1970s, both Sessar (1979: 161) and Thomas Weigend (1978: 45–46) claimed that the government dealt with the impact of rising caseloads by increasing the numbers of prosecutorial staff.

The position of some theorists has begun to shift towards making more restrained claims on behalf of the principle of legality. For example, in 2004, Weigend argued that: '[t]oday prosecution is in effect mandatory only with respect to most felonies' (2004: 215). As Nigel Jamieson has written (1996: 122), stereotypical pictures of the civil law tradition, objectivity and the prosecutor's limited discretion constrained comparative scholars from accurately describing the state of German penal practice:

> The danger is that walking the tightrope of such cultural conventions institutes a ritual. A cozy but unthinking familiarity can be created out of such verbal stereotypes that subvert the substantive impact of the original communication. And so we learn to recite creeds of faith that are mere verbal shells – like rote-taught multiplication tables or Latin declensions. Meaning nothing to us, such creeds could just as easily be communist or Christian. [...] His source-oriented concern holds him so far back from his target that he is at risk of 'going native', which in the case of comparative law means that the whole point of the cross-cultural communication has been lost.

Today, there has been a dramatic turnaround in the orientation of German scholarship. To begin with, scholars cannot ignore the fact that both courts and law-makers have now legitimised the practice of plea bargaining. Now, many scholars have swung to the opposite bench and sharply criticised the rise of charge bargaining practices as a threat to the right to a fair trial and the system's truth-finding function (Kobor 2008: 123). Some scholars, focused primarily on the rise of plea bargaining, have overlooked the extent to which the principles of legality and objectivity are embedded in organisational practice (Rauxloh 2011: 326–29).

In reality, German prosecutors have always exercised discretion. In directing the course of investigation, deciding what charges to file and in determining how much initiative to take in a case, prosecutors are guided by their judgment, training and levels of organisational control that shape how they interpret and apply the penal code. To pierce the veil of cultural conventions in the German system, one need only compare the differences in case dismissal rates between different German *Länder* to find that wide variations in practice have existed for decades. The statistics demonstrate a remarkable divergence in practice. For example, the percentage of cases that prosecutors dismiss ranges from a high of 71.2 per cent in the city-state of Hamburg to a low of 52.2 per cent in Bavaria (Statistisches Bundesamt 2011: 10). A report, issued by a German government agency, states that differences in police training and prosecutors' 'judgment' throughout the country account for these variations in prosecution rates (ibid: 11).

The face of justice is not constituted by the law standing alone, as the geography of local practice plays a determinant role. Indeed, in 1979, Sessar pointed out that, as far back as 1970, case dismissal rates throughout Germany varied dramatically from region to region. In reviewing nationwide prosecution statistics from 1970, he noted: 'The first indications of discrepancies between law and practice come from the yearly statistics of the various prosecution offices. Among the 93 offices the ratio of charges to dismissals varied by up to 30% in 1970. The smaller the office (hence, the smaller the district), the higher the number of charges per case' (1979: 262). Surprisingly, although scholars have claimed that resource constraints and rising caseloads have fuelled the rise in plea bargaining in the past decade, there was a 2 per cent increase in dismissal rates between 2000 and 2009 (Statistisches Bundesamt 2011: 11).

Problems in translation

So far, I have demonstrated how scholars' fixation on legal texts, rather than practice, portrayed the German criminal justice system as one in which code provisions effectively constrained prosecutorial discretion. This textual centrism obscured the reality of a model in which discretion to some extent certainly always existed and in which discretionary decision-making practices blossomed in the shadow of the law. Although scholars' allegiance to the text of the code certainly perverted comparative legal research focused on the German criminal justice system, mistakes in translation also hampered efforts to pierce text-centric claims.

In particular, the ability of outsiders to challenge the low-discretion thesis was hampered by the translation of the German words for major (*Verbrechen*) and minor (*Vergehen*) crimes. Scholars, who substituted the word 'felony' for 'major crimes', rather than closely examining the list of so-called major crimes, mistakenly argued that the law hamstrung prosecutors' discretion in all cases involving serious crimes. Indeed, according to that translation of the term *Verbrechen*, it appeared that German law prohibited prosecutors from exercising discretion with respect to all felony cases. The proliferation of this claim buttressed assertions by scholars who argued that German prosecutors had little discretion to dismiss or defer cases. No less an expert than Michael Bohlander, a former German judge, translated *Verbrechen* as 'felonies' in his treatise entitled *Principles of German Criminal Law* (2009: 4, 27).

Scholars also erred when defining the term 'felony'. For example, Gabriel Hallevy, in his book entitled *A Modern Treatise on the Principle of Legality in Criminal Law*, defined the word 'felony' as a sentence with a minimum incarceration period of one year (2010: 20). In fact, in most US jurisdictions, a judge may sentence a felon to a term of probation. Hallevy extrapolates further and states that the borderline between *Verbrechen* and *Vergehen* in German criminal law is that the maximum penalty for *Vergehen* is one year's imprisonment (ibid). It is easy to see how a comparative law scholar reading this description would conclude that *Verbrechen* was the German equivalent to a felony.

These loose and incorrect translations led to analytical errors when scholars addressed the scope of German prosecutors' discretionary decision-making. If one takes the time to probe the meaning of the word *Vergehen*, one discovers that, according to the German Criminal Code, a crime qualifies as a *Vergehen* (low-level crime) as long as the *minimum sentence* for the crime prescribed by statute falls below one year of imprisonment. In contrast, in the United States, the sentencing range for many felonies begins with probation, rather than with a minimum sentence of one year of incarceration. As a result, many crimes classified as felonies in the United States *do not qualify* as a major crime in the German system. One can quickly understand the significance of this difference when one examines the gross number of crimes committed on an annual basis in Germany.

According to my computations, the percentage of actual crimes that qualify as *Vergehen* (low-level crimes) exceeds 85 per cent. Thus, even if you adopt without question the statement that German prosecutors exercise little discretion with respect to prosecution of major crimes, it is apparent that German prosecutors exercise discretion in close to 85 per cent of cases. Even before the formal introduction of plea bargaining, those numbers do not describe a system in which discretion is constrained. One can understand the ramifications of this mistranslation by examining a partial list of crimes that are typically classified as felonies in the United States but fall under the category of *Vergehen* in Germany: obstruction of an election, bribery of members of parliament, providing support to a terrorist organisation, sexual abuse of children under 14 years old as rape. From this partial list, we can see that the proposition that prosecutorial discretion is restricted to 'low-level' crimes, even if true, does not prove that prosecutorial discretion is limited in scope.

Practice as the gateway to language

To enter 'law's cosmos', we need to understand what it means to 'think like a lawyer' – in particular a lawyer who practises in a foreign legal culture. While comparative legal scholarship that addresses the German penal system has acknowledged that a gap between the penal code and criminal practice exists, we have failed explicitly to explore how local cultures of meaning shape how prosecutors interpret the law. We can no longer be content to employ a top-down approach to understand the interplay between culture and law. Researchers must observe the law in practice and continually interrogate human sources of knowledge, checking and rechecking the meaning of particular concepts in the larger cultural context.

Only by shifting and sorting through the knowledge of how law operates on the ground level and building a thick description of practice can translators and researchers build the foundation for a real understanding of a foreign legal system. Where gaps between law and practice exist, interviews alone may not reveal the 'truth'. As late as 2006, when I first began to interview German prosecutors in the field, senior level prosecutors admitted, although with great reluctance, that plea bargaining had crept its way into German legal practice in contravention of the German Code of Criminal Procedure. The exchange below indicates how two prosecutors struggled with this gap between the system's positivist legacy and the constraints of legal practice.

> Boyne: I have heard conflicting information about whether there's plea bargaining in Germany or not.[2]
> Senior Prosecutor 1: [Shakes his head – indicating no].
> Boyne: Let me put it a different way. How do you deal with the fact that, when your caseload gets very heavy and you don't have enough time to take all your cases to trial?
> Senior Prosecutor 2: Yes. Yes. The problem is that is the trial becomes more and more complicated sometimes a kind of bargaining happens. But that's [with the] the judge.

Early in the research process, I realised that the data disclosed that many senior level prosecutors appeared to be trapped into replaying tapes of the mythology of the German system. Although I continued to interview prosecutors, I sharpened the focus of my questions. I would sit down with prosecutors and individual case files and I would let them guide me through the decision-making process at various stages of a case. This decision-by-decision discussion of case files painted a fluid portrait of discretionary decision-making.

> Prosecutor: The city of *Frauenwaldau* gave the [case] file to me ... And now I have to decide what I want to [do about] the case. And now I have different possibilities. I can invite [the suspect] here and [interview] him

on my own what he has to say. But as you know, I have a lot of files, and if I do this, I will sit here the whole day, the whole night. So, in general, I send [the file] to the police and the police should [interview] him. Another possibility is that is that I write him [and tell him] that he can write me back … In some cases, we do that. For example, if they don't live [here], maybe they live to the south or maybe they live abroad … then it's very difficult … In this case the easiest way is to write him and then he can write back what he wants to say to the [allegation] but in normal cases like this, these people live [here] I will send this file to the police to [interview] these people … So first, [I] send the file to the police … and I tell the police to [interview these individuals] as suspect[s]. I can also [interview them] as witnesses. But I want to [interview them] as suspect[s] … Okay and I want to see the file back in about six weeks.[3]

The discussion of prosecutors' decisions in numerous cases naturally revealed the rubric of organisational factors that affect decision-making. Statements made at key decision points such as 'if I am unclear what decision to make, I will ask my colleagues' referred to a collegiate style of decision-making not found in office organisational charts. Curiously, in whatever prosecution office I studied, at mid-morning my interview subject would invite me to share coffee with a previously scheduled small group of prosecutors. The nature of the group differed from office to office – in some, the younger prosecutors met together, in others the members of the department might meet. There was no set pattern. In all of these meetings, I observed prosecutors sharing information about cases, judges and legal decisions. This informal consensus building created informal shared norms of local legal practice. Prosecutors would pose questions such as 'How would you handle a case in which…?' Other colleagues would reflect on similar cases they had handled. 'Should I propose this penalty?' Some of these same questions might very well be posed in a US prosecution office. There was a key notable difference, however. Missing in these discussions was any sense of individual agency. I heard very little bragging about cases that had been won or pride-laced discussions of how an individual prosecutor had achieved a particular verdict or sentence.

It is a bridge too far to claim that US prosecutors are possessed with a 'conviction mentality' and that all German prosecutors' concept of success is decoupled from their trial performance. However, in my interviews with and observations of German prosecutors, I discovered that they viewed their role in more collective, rather than individual, terms. A prosecutor's self-concept is largely disconnected from a notion of individual agency. It is this absence of a sense of individual agency, as well as a relatively flat hierarchical structure, that creates a container in which 'objective' decision-making can emerge. Informal structures within prosecution offices, such as the morning coffee meetings, encourage a more consensus driven style of decision-making. New prosecutors draw on their colleagues' unwritten knowledge of particular judges, norms and sense of fairness to inform their decision-making. This practice is not found in any code book. It is not taught in law schools. Yet it functions as institutional glue that both crafts a local legal culture and shapes decision-making. When I asked individual prosecutors how they learned to be a prosecutor, they pointed back to the training they received during their probationary periods in which their work was strictly supervised by a mentor. They also mentioned controls instituted by their supervisor, as well as the sense of direction imposed by the office leader.

When I first began interviewing German prosecutors, one of my original research questions, was: 'What case are you most proud of?' The purpose of the question was to get the interview subject to start talking about their decision-making process in a case in which they had played an instrumental role. At the time of penning the question, I had read about the inquisitorial structure of the system and, indeed, had spent a semester attending criminal law classes in a German law school. I 'knew' on an intellectual level that the role of the prosecutor in the German system was to find the truth by functioning as an objective decision-maker. Yet, my perspective of the prosecutor's role was also shaped by the five years that I had spent working as a prosecutor in the United States. My ability to understand the German system was coloured by my own experience working in a party-driven system in which the actions of the parties carry the case forward. In retrospect, that question only makes sense to a prosecutor operating in a party-based criminal justice system where trial success is viewed as an individual success and trials are viewed as a battle between two opposing sides. Pizzi has described the mindset of US prosecutors as an investment in achieving a victory in each individual case (1999).

Armed with a German-English dictionary, I had no problem phrasing the question using German words. Yet the words themselves lacked a referential frame within Germany's Continental system because, at least in theory, prosecutors function as non-partisan officials rather than as agents who actively shape system outcomes. My question was problematic from another perspective as well, as in Continental systems prosecutors perceive their role, in part, as judicial. Thus, the majority of German prosecutors did not view themselves as courtroom warriors, but rather as dispassionate civil servants who function, in their truth-finding role, as part of the judicial team. After several prosecutors told me that they did not understand the question, I finally realised that most prosecutors in the German system do not equate case outcomes with individual achievement.

While Germany's civil law tradition shapes in part how prosecutors view the law and their relationship to it, institutional norms in German prosecution offices reflect a 'different se[t] of basic understandings of how criminal cases should be tried and prosecuted' (Langer 2004: 4). Although comparative legal scholars have made much of the different structures of truth-finding in inquisitorial and adversarial systems, less attention has been given to what Máximo Langer has referred to as the '*structures of interpretation and meaning* through which the actors of a given criminal justice system understand both criminal procedure and their role within the system' (ibid: 10, original emphasis). More than just two different paths to the truth, they reflect two different methods of understanding. As Langer explains (ibid):

> Within these two procedural structures of interpretation and meaning or 'procedural languages', the same terms or signifiers often have different meanings. For instance, in the adversarial system, the word 'prosecutor' means a party in a dispute with an interest at stake in the outcome of the procedure; in the inquisitorial system, however, the word signifies an impartial magistrate of the state whose role is to investigate the truth.

Law and culture

While many comparatists have focused their attention on the competing normative visions of the inquisitorial and adversarial systems, my research shows that organisational factors, rather than the system's normative aims or the text of the code, shape the contours of prosecutorial decision-making. Prosecutorial behaviour is primarily shaped by organisational incentives and the nature of routine practice, rather than the law. Within the German prosecution service, profound differences exist in prosecutors' self-understanding. Despite the fact that prosecutors on paper function as 'second judges', their active investigative role in some types of case such as drug cases undercuts their ability to function objectively. Investigation of drug cases requires prosecutors to become proactively involved in targeting certain suspects with wiretaps and the use of informants. These activities give drug crime prosecutors a stronger vested stake in case outcomes than prosecutors in general.

I became aware of these differences in vested interests when a young prosecutor in a general crimes department related to me what happened to her when she was assigned to handle a drug case in court one day in addition to her normal case load. The prosecutor told me that she received a call from a colleague in the drug crimes department chastising her for unknowingly deviating from the drug department's sentencing guidelines, despite the fact that she had concurred with the presiding judge's suggestion.[4] Another prosecutor candidly shared with me that she had been transferred out of the drug crimes department because her supervisor told her that she had the wrong perspective (*Perspektive*) for the drug department. Thus, the nature of the caseload that a particular department handles may shape prosecutors' work practices. Because drug crime prosecutors work closely with the police from the beginning of a case, a tight camaraderie develops that undercuts a prosecutor's willingness to act as a check on police behaviour.

Conclusion

The comparatist must situate the language of a particular nation-state's legal texts within the text's surrounding legal culture – in particular, the culture of legal practice. Absent this contextual mapping, the text stands alone unfastened to the context which helps to define it. This problem is inherently more difficult when text-to-text translation must also negotiate the transfer of language and meaning between two legal systems built on different legal epistemological edifices – such as that which exists between civil and common law systems.[5] In that case, scholars must ensure that the 'text' that they are seeking to understand is not one that exists merely in prescriptive rules, but also one that reflects actual legal practice. This is particularly true in systems where evolutionary changes in legal practice have created a large gap between how the law works on the ground and how the law was designed to function. As Jamieson (1996: 127) has written:

> This task requires from the translator a power to transcend his own deep knowledge of the source material. In terms of targeting the serious reader, the comparative lawyer thus becomes more of a metaphysician than a mechanic, and never a mere morphologist.

Notes

* I would like to thank Cynthia Alkon and Kwai Ng for their helpful comments on an earlier draft as well as the participants in Washington University's Junior Scholar Workshop. In addition, I would be lost without the reference assistance of reference librarian Richard Humphrey. I am also indebted to Alex Berger's research assistance.
1 Without a doubt, this is a simplified view of comparative law as a more comprehensive comparison would also include socialist law, religious law and dual systems.
2 German Prosecutor Interview 10 June 2004. Interview subjects are anonymous but represented in my records by numerical identifiers.
3 German Prosecutor Interview 18 November 2005. *Frauenwaldau* is a pseudonym.
4 German Prosecutor Interview 8 December 2005.
5 Here I borrow Larry Laudan's definition of 'legal epistemology': 'Legal epistemology, properly conceived, involves both a) the *descriptive* project of determining which existing rules promote and which thwart truth seeking and b) the *normative* one of proposing changes in existing rules to eliminate or modify those rules that turn out to be serious obstacles to finding the truth' (2006: 3, original emphasis).

Bibliography

Bohlander, M. (2009) *Principles of German Criminal Law*, Oxford: Hart.
Boyne, S.M. (2010) 'Uncertainty and the Search for Truth at Trial: Defining Prosecutorial "Objectivity" in German Sexual Assault Cases', *Washington and Lee Law Review*, 67: 1287–359.
Chroma, M. (2004) *Legal Translation and the Dictionary*, Tübingen: M. Niemeyer.
Damaška, M. (1997) 'Truth in Adjudication', *Hastings Law Journal*, 49: 289–308.
Davis, K.C. (1976) *Discretionary Justice in Europe and America*, Urbana: University of Illinois Press.
Endicott, T. (2010) 'Law and Language', in E.N. Zalta (ed.) *The Stanford Encyclopedia of Philosophy* http://plato.stanford.edu/archives/fall2010/entries/law-language/ (accessed 1 October 2013).

Glanert, S. (2008) 'Speaking Language to Law: The Case of Europe', *Legal Studies*, 28: 161–71.

Goldstein A.S. (1974) 'Reflections on Two Models: Inquisitorial Themes in American Criminal Procedure', *Stanford Law Review*, 26: 1009–25.

—— and Marcus, M. (1977) 'The Myth of Judicial Supervision in Three "Inquisitorial" Systems: France, Italy, and Germany', *Yale Law Journal*, 87: 240–83.

Groot, G.-R. de (2006) 'Legal Translation,' in J.M. Smits (ed.) *Elgar Encyclopedia of Comparative Law*, Cheltenham: E. Elgar.

Hallevy, G. (2010) *A Modern Treatise on the Principle of Legality in Criminal Law*, Berlin: Springer Verlag.

Herrmann, J. (1976) 'The German Prosecutor', in K.C. Davis (ed.) *Discretionary Justice in Europe and America*, Champaign: University of Illinois Press.

—— (1992) 'Bargaining Justice – A Bargain for German Criminal Justice?', *University of Pittsburgh Law Review*, 53: 755–76.

Hodgson J. (2002) 'Hierarchy, Bureaucracy, and Ideology in French Criminal Justice: Some Empirical Observations', *Journal of Law and Society*, 29: 227–57.

Itzcovich, G. (2012) 'Book Review' [A.L. Kjær and S. Adamo (eds) *Linguistic Diversity and European Democracy*, London: Ashgate, 2011], *European Law Journal*, 18: 478–84.

Jamieson, N. (1996) 'Source and Target-Oriented Comparative Law', *American Journal of Comparative Law*, 44: 121–29.

Jolowicz, J.A. (2000) *On Civil Procedure*, Cambridge: Cambridge University Press.

Kagan, R.A. (2003) *Adversarial Legalism: The American Way of Law*, Cambridge, MA: Harvard University Press.

Kasirer, N. (2001) 'François Gény's *libre recherche scientifique* as a Guide for Legal Translation', *Louisiana Law Review*, 61: 331–52.

—— (2002) 'Bijuralism in Law's Empire and in Law's Cosmos', *Journal of Legal Education*, 52: 29–41.

Kobor, S. (2008) *Bargaining in the Criminal Justice Systems of the United States and Germany*, Frankfurt: P. Lang.

Langbein, J.H. (1974) 'Controlling Prosecutorial Discretion in Germany, *University of Chicago Law Review*, 41: 439–67.

—— (1985) 'The German Advantage in Civil Procedure', *University of Chicago Law Review*, 52: 823–64.

—— and Weinreb, L.L. (1978) 'Continental Criminal Procedure: "Myth" and Reality', *Yale Law Journal*, 87: 1549–69.

Langer, M. (2004) 'From Legal Transplants to Legal Translations: The Globalization of Plea Bargaining and the Americanization Thesis in Criminal Procedure', *Harvard International Law Journal*, 45: 1–64.

Laudan, L. (2006) *Truth, Error, and Criminal Law: An Essay in Legal Epistemology*, Cambridge: Cambridge University Press.

Peruginelli, G. (2007) 'Towards a Common Understanding of Law in a Multilanguage World: The Role of Cross-language Legal Information Retrieval Systems', *European Legal Forum*, 2: 64–71.

Pizzi, W.T. (1999) *Trials Without Truth: Why Our System of Criminal Trials Has Become an Expensive Failure and What We Need to Do to Rebuild It*, New York: New York University Press.

Poirier, M.R. (1995) 'On Whose Authority?: Linguists' Claim of Expertise to Interpret Statutes', *Washington University Law Quarterly*, 73: 1025–42.

Posner, R.A. (1988) *Law and Literature*, 1st edn, Cambridge, MA: Harvard University Press.

Rauxloh, R.E. (2011) 'Formalization of Plea Bargaining in Germany: Will the New Legislation Be Able to Square the Circle?', *Fordham International Law Journal*, 34: 296–331.

Roxin, C. (1997) 'Zur Rechtsstellung der Staatsanwaltschaft damals und heute', *Deutsche Richterzeitung*, 3: 109–21.

Šarčević, S. (1997) *New Approach to Legal Translation*, The Hague. Kluwer.

—— (2000) 'Legal Translation and Translation Theory: A Receiver-Oriented Approach' http://www.tradulex.com/Actes2000/sarcevic.pdf (accessed 1 October 2013).

—— (2012) 'Challenges to the Legal Translator', in P. Tiersma and L. Solan (eds) *The Oxford Handbook of Language and Law*, Oxford: Oxford University Press.

Schram, G. (1969) 'The Obligation to Prosecute in West Germany', *American Journal of Comparative Law*, 17: 627–32.

Sessar, K. (1979) 'Prosecutorial Discretion in Germany', in W.F. McDonald (ed.) *The Prosecutor*, Beverly Hills, CA: Sage.

Statistisches Bundesamt (2011) *Justiz auf einen Blick*, Wiesbaden https://www. destatis.de/DE/Publikationen/Thematisch/Rechtspflege/Querschnitt/ BroschuereJustizBlick0100001099004.pdf?__blob=publicationFile (accessed 1 October 2013).

Wagner, W. (1974) 'Der objektive Staatsanwalt – Idee und Wirklichkeit', *Juristenzeitung*, 29: 212–18.

Weigend, T. (1978) *Anklagepflicht und Ermessen: Die Stellung des Staatsanwalts zwischen Legalitäts- und Opportunitätsprinzip nach deutschem und amerikanischem Recht*, Baden-Baden: Nomos.

—— (2003) 'Is the Criminal Process about Truth? A German Perspective', *Harvard Journal of Law and Public Policy*, 26: 157–73.

—— (2004) 'The Prosecution Service in the German Administration of Criminal Justice', in P.J.P. Tak (ed.) *Tasks and Powers of the Prosecution Services in the EU Member States*, vol I, Nijmegen: Wolf.

Wolf, M. (2008) 'Interference from the *Third Space*? The Construction of Cultural Identity Through Translation', in M. Muñoz-Calvo, C. Buesa-Gómez and M.Á. Ruiz-Moneva (eds) *New Trends in Translation and Cultural Identity*, Newcastle upon Tyne: Cambridge Scholars.

Yule, G. (2010) *The Study of Language*, 4th edn, Cambridge: Cambridge University Press.

Chapter 9

The powerless translator: an argument based on legal culturemes

*Raluca Bercea**

On law and legal translators

By virtue of their endeavour, translators are powerful figures: they may choose merely to reflect, illustrate, render, explain, debate, recreate or propose a second-ary version of a given text. They sometimes obey the imperative of being faithful to the original text, hiding their presence in the translated version thereof, while, on the contrary, on other occasions, boldly assume the task of being the alterna-tive author of the source text, supplementing its meaning through the recreation process encompassed by translation. In both hypotheses, translators are bound to make creative choices in order to offer the reader a fully intelligible textual product, the minimum requirement therefore being to 'see to it that the target text has the same meaning potential as the original text' (Engberg 2002: 376).

Translation may consist, accordingly, of a loyal reflection of the original, of an accurate transfer of its meaning or, on the contrary, of a process of cultural mediation. At their best, translations (and translators) will have an emancipatory effect on source texts, by revealing not only their explicit but also their implicit dimension to a reader coming from a different cultural background. It has been argued, therefore, that any good translation reaches 'a point where it purports to do justice to the text through a process of incessant negotiation with it' (Glanert and Legrand 2013: 19). At their worst, translations will violate original texts in the name of the ideology embraced by the translator (Cassin 2006: 167).

Lawrence Venuti theorises in this respect 'the violence that resides in the very purpose and activity of translation' that he understands as 'the forcible replace-ment of the linguistic and cultural differences of the foreign text with a text that is intelligible to the translating-language reader' and to which he attributes 'enor-mous power in the construction of identities for foreign cultures, and hence [...] [a potential part to play] in ethnic discrimination, geopolitical confrontations, colonialism, terrorism, war' (2008: 14). At the extreme, translators might be considered the genuine masters of both source and target texts, while translations, understood as speech acts, will be precisely what translators want them to be.

Legal translators, however, benefit only from limited powers, mainly because of the convention that the original text (most frequently a legal rule) and its translated version should fulfil the same function in corresponding legal contexts. Put differently, the purpose of legal translation is 'the creation of a target-language text that is interpreted in the same way by readers familiar with the target-language legal system as the source-language text is interpreted by readers familiar with the source-language legal system' (Engberg 2002: 375–76). Fictions such as perfect equivalence of the various official versions of the same legal text, as well as techniques such as co-drafting, illustrate the inherent linguistic difficulties of such a bold goal.

As has been observed, it is the status of the legal rule itself – and only that – which confers on legal translation its specificity (Glanert 2011: 153). Moreover, law in general, as a field, conditions translation on account of its profoundly particular features. Relevantly, law is remarkably closed, if not 'sealed' (Vick 2004: 189), in more than one sense of the word: developing original schemes of intelligibility, ignoring all reality that has not been captured by its own concepts, opaque to any discourse other than its own, rejecting interdisciplinarity, promoting a hermetic point of view of the world, sustaining a most original epistemology.

Legal hermeticism is usually explained by law's normative and institutional character. As law is meant to regulate society in general, but also a certain society, with specific, irreducible features, law belongs to a tradition; but tradition is considered to be static, stable and inexorable (Bercea 2013a: 2). Equally, law should remain relatively uncomplicated, since interdisciplinary complications generate uncertainty, while uncertainty is detrimental to predictability and ultimately to the rule of law (Samuel 2009: 437). Indeed, coherent with the authority paradigm within which they operate, lawyers may well criticise a legal text both from the point of view of its contents or form and with respect to the social effects that it is supposed to generate, but they cannot deny its character of being *law* (ibid). Furthermore, if it is true that each discipline acquires its epistemological strength out of its members' consensus, the law has developed a remarkably coherent professional corpus, theorised as *'l'entité doctrinale'*, which exercises its control on legal meaning itself for the purpose of avoiding distortions and excluding contradictions (Jestaz and Jamin 1997: 167).

However, the opacity that the legal field has developed is also the result of at least two more factors (Bercea 2013a: 2). The first might be referred to as the law's self-sufficiency or self-claimed supremacy. Indeed, law's pre-eminence in comparison with any other field of knowledge represents the lawyers' most intimate statement of faith. In the continental European *nomothetical* tradition, law is (and represents the study of) legal text (*la loi*), which itself is traditionally sacred (Legrand 1995: 311, 2011a: 3). Therefore, out of its 'transcendentality' (Legrand 2012: 116), law has to remain pure. Rather contradictorily, the second factor resides in law's striving 'to preserve [its scientific] capital' (Legrand 2011b: 598). In other words, in order to be perceived as a respectable cognitive approach, legal science itself has had to promote the attributes of the pure positive sciences, recreating law according to an aesthetised pattern, focusing on systemicity, generality and predictable regularities.

Traditionally, what matters for lawyers is that binding law within one jurisdiction should be described without distortion. Coherent with the general positivist scientific trend of the 20th century, such an approach will naturally and conveniently emphasise the strictly conceptual, systematic, logical, neutrally articulated and objectively assessable dimensions of law. The hermetic character of the legal field can be said to represent an attempt to express the desire of the discipline for scientific respectability, which has gradually become an epistemological mark thereof. Needless to mention, law's purity and utmost coherence have been gained at a price that is now said to threaten the discipline 'with philosophical and epistemological bankruptcy' (Samuel 2009: 432), while law's institutionalisation and professionalisation have turned legal knowledge into a '[d]isciplinary ghett[o]' (Fish 1991: 100).

The normative and institutional character of the legal field determines as a prerequisite not only the closure of the field itself, as already mentioned, but also legal translators' obligatory alienation in respect of all their previous extra-legal knowledge. Against this background, one could speak of knowledge fundamentalism in the sense that law recreates its object through its own discourse, whose translation will prove to be even more self-restraining. I intend to analyse the impact that the specific character of the legal field has on translation. First, I will argue that law's hermeticism has forced lawyers to develop schemes of intelligibility that are restrictive as far as their approach to language is concerned. Secondly, I will take the view that despite the translator's necessary effacement once confronted with normativity, legal translation remains an act of communication in a context in which language is, perhaps more than other discourses, culturally embedded. This will allow me to conclude that the real difficulty faced by the legal translator is not of a legal (be it normative or institutional) nature but of a cultural nature, which I will express against the background of the concept of the 'legal cultureme'.

How lawyers approach language

The way in which lawyers use language may clearly be described according to common concepts developed in general linguistics. Perhaps the most relevant for linguistic analysis of legal discourse are the concepts of reference, truth and meaning as understood in semantics, those of implied content and context as defined in pragmatics or that of interpretation as imposed by the various trends in hermeneutics. What might strike the linguist when analysing legal discourse from this perspective is that the legal field has developed patterns of reasoning and schemes of proceeding that often run against what would be considered the basic findings of today's approaches to the various linguistic phenomena. Indeed, from a linguistic standpoint, lawyers' practice seems to express their inability to establish a nuanced relation to language, while in fact it translates law's attempts to keep the field transcendental, therefore closed.

Acting in their traditional capacity as '*la bouche de la loi*' (Montesquieu 1748:

XI, 6), nomothetical judges all over Europe – be they national or European judges – will try to interpret legal rules taking as irrefragable assumptions both their completeness and their unequivocal, unproblematic and direct link to the real world. Nevertheless, far from being undisputable, 'the idea of the autonomous normativity of legal texts and words contained in such texts is connected to a specific view of language' (Engberg 2002: 380). Sequences such as 'it is for the Court to find the right meaning of the article' are typical of current judicial reasoning, contradicting the requirement of a responsible involvement in construing meaning that connects translation to legal (judicial) interpretation: 'in legal interpretation as well as in legal translation, the dynamic [...] approach forces the interpreter or the translator to take the responsibility he actually has by depriving him of the pseudo-objective instrument by which context-independent meaning functions' (ibid: 387–88). Our already theorised 'irresistible referential instinct' (Pavel 1970: 96) has become second nature in law and pushes judges falsely to link legal words to a presumable univocal reality conditioning and subsequently validating their true meaning (Bercea 2009: 43) according to a simplistic pattern denounced in pragmatics by John Austin: 'It was for too long the assumption of philosophers that the business of a "statement" can only be to "describe" some state of affairs, or to "state some fact", which it must do either truly or falsely' (1975: 1).

Frequently, however, judges may be forced to ascertain a feeble degree of stability of meaning (if any) and the absence of truth in legal normative productions; after all, a deeper incursion into the history of philosophy will show that truth (and, *a fortiori*, legal truth) can 'fairly be approached as a cultural artefact' (Legrand 2012: 126). Thus, judges will find out not only that law is not exhausted by a rule, but also that legal rules are neither self-sufficient nor self-explanatory and that words do not mean much outside of their wider contexts.

A typical interpretive dilemma was faced by human rights judges in Strasbourg in the case of *Schalk and Kopf v Austria*, when assessing whether Article 12 of the European Convention on Human Rights (the Convention), pursuant to which '[m]en and women of marriageable age have the right to marry and to found a family, according to the national laws governing the exercise of this right', also refers to homosexual marriages.[1] The judges' approach followed a well established path, beginning with the sacramental formula 'looked at in isolation, the wording of Article 12 [means]' (para 55). Such a choice *a priori* voids interpretation to failure. Indeed, the Court readily found that it cannot establish the literal meaning of the text. Grammar alone is unable to cabin the possible semantic extension of the key sequence 'men and women' to one signification only. In effect, these words can potentially mean 'a man with a woman' or 'a man with a man' or 'a woman with a woman'. Similarly, the familiar legal fiction of the 'states' will' that is expected to have assigned meaning to each problematic sequence proves to be unhelpful in this occurrence, any form of cooperative exchange of information being impossible in the particular interpretive context represented by judicial enforcement of law. As Andrei Marmor would have put it in pragmatic terms, pointing to the gap that separates in certain respects the way in which the context and the implication rules function in legal discourse as compared to the basic guidelines that allow us to understand what a speaker says, asserts and implies in a neuter conversational context, '[j]udges [...] are not parties to the legislative conversation, so to speak' (2008: 434).

Carrying their typical interpretive attempt further, the judges decide that 'regard must be had to the historical context in which the Convention was adopted' (para 55), corrected by means of an evolutionary understanding of the text, which is to be interpreted in present-day conditions. This would allow us to assume that judges implicitly take into account the process of semiosis that prevents signs from being associated with a unique and stable meaning and provides them with a virtually infinite capacity to signify, as each interpreter could enrich each sign with a new significance. However, the lesson is unfamiliar to the Court, always in pursuit of a fixed immutable meaning, and therefore trying to establish that meaning through reference to other legal texts, hopefully less problematic from an interpretive point of view: 'Turning to the comparison between Article 12 of the Convention and Article 9 of the Charter of Fundamental Rights of the European Union ("the Charter"), the Court has already noted that the latter has deliberately dropped the reference to men and women' (para 60).

Here, the Court makes a reference to the commentary to the Charter, which 'confirms that Article 9 is meant to be broader in scope than the corresponding articles in other human rights instruments', adding that 'the reference to domestic law reflects the diversity of national regulations, which range from allowing same-sex marriage to explicitly forbidding it'. Finally, the Court cites the words of the commentary: 'it may be argued that there is no obstacle to recognize same-sex relationships in the context of marriage' (para 60). The meaning of the legal words seems, therefore, to have changed over time, so that law may no longer be said to be exhausted by a single supposedly complete rule. This conclusion does not stop the judges from mechanically applying their current intelligibility schemes and multiplying the textual perspective, as if, indeed, law might be exhausted by more rules. When this second legal text appears insufficient in its turn (for what could be the universal, atemporal and all-encompassing significance of 'marriage' after all?), the Court regards the practice of a number of contracting states that have extended marriage to same-sex partners, establishing, however, that 'this reflected their own vision of marriage in their societies and did not flow from an interpretation of the fundamental rights as laid down by the contracting states in the Convention in 1950' (para 53).

The quite worrying apprehension that life might not be exhausted by law occurs given that, when it comes to same-sex marriage, the Court explicitly withdraws by finding that 'the issue [...] concerns a sensitive area of social, political and religious controversy' (para 46), so that each national judge should establish the meaning of 'marriage' according to national approaches. This judicial solution may be (and has been) praised as one that reveals judges' sensitivity to the cultural diversity of the states parties to the European Convention on Human Rights (Bercea 2013b: 7).

If one expects, however, European human rights judges to act as the constitutional judges that they once were, and especially if one keeps in mind that the solution translates into fact the failure of a particular process of interpretation, one would require the European judges themselves to inject meanings into conventional words, rather than hide behind an allegedly unique, objective or authentic meaning that they will never properly grasp.

After all, 'legal terms can be viewed primarily as symbolic lexicons' that keep developing in order to cope with ever changing social needs (Poon Wai Yee 2005: 307), the judges' task being to interpret them, thus assigning them a situated meaning with respect to place and time. In that case, the judges would, of course, also have to be eager to assume the accessory task of producing arguments in favour of their interpretation that would be autonomous in respect of the legal text, although remaining faithful to it. This option happens to connect judicial interpretation to the latest assumptions in translation studies that postulate an eventually independent target text 'capable of functioning on its own in the new situation without necessary recourse to the source text' (Engberg 2002: 382) and closes the circle by returning once again to the matter of truth: 'To accept that translation is situated firmly within linguistic contingency is to begin to take responsibility for one's own perspectival apprehensions. [...] Linguistic contingency is one's opportunity' (Glanert and Legrand 2013: 8).

Cultural translation: memes, traductemes and culturemes

How to translate meaningfully, then, not only normative legal productions as such, that have so far been the unique concern of legal translators, but also the specifically legal use of language through institutionalised judicial interpretive practice that might vary from source to target culture? For, despite the feigned legal translator's effacement once confronted with normativity, legal translation remains an act of communication in a context in which, first, legal language is, perhaps more than in other discourses, culturally embedded (Glanert 2011: 144), secondly, the same (legal) communication act occurring in an identical (legal) context but within a different culture finds itself culturally marked and, thirdly, given the unique pragmatics of legal texts, elements that are typically settled in a regular conversational context remain open in the legal context (Marmor 2008: 423); yet, they must be resolved by the translator.

This series of difficulties will add to the fact that, as in any other translation operation, meaning does not exist in itself, being undisputedly the result of the translator's interpretive construction and of the reader's understanding: 'Translation is not an untroubled communication of a foreign text, but an interpretation that is always limited by its address to specific audiences' (Venuti 2008: 14). As in the general hypothesis, the translator's freedom is always conditioned by pertinence, which is to be assessed both in relationship with the legal source text itself and with the cultural context thereof, being understood that, given the normative component of legal texts, the legal effects of a concept are frequently the decisive element in assessing the degree of acceptability associated with a certain translation. All translators, including legal ones, will therefore have to deal with the issue of cultural distance, as they behave as mediators with a double cultural identity and, moreover, as non-neuter mediators whose presence is by definition inscribed in the target text: 'If translation is to be construed as a discursive, social, cultural practice and as a norm-governed, decision-oriented, strategic activity [...] it follows that the translation process produces not only semantic meaning, but also aesthetic, ideological and political meaning' (Lane-Mercier 1997: 44). This accessory meaning is indicative of the 'values, beliefs, images and attitudes circulating within [...] [the translator's] cultural context', of the translator's 'interpretation of the source text', of the translator's 'aesthetic, ideological and political agendas', and of the 'interpretative possibilities made available to the target-text readers through the translators' strategies and decisions' (ibid).

By overstepping the autarchy of structural research in linguistics and opening language studies to the extra-linguistic element, nowadays traductology has already stated that the cultural translator will have to reconstitute the extra-linguistic parameters of a speech situation, searching for the meaning of a complete enunciation (Lungu Badea 2004: 9). In such a context, clearly a legal (cultural) translator will primarily have to facilitate access to the legal culture reflected by the source text, explicating a dimension that law as such purportedly obscures. Legal translators will largely have to assume the task of fine-tuning the explicitness and implicitness of the source text in the text they recreate, being obvious that it is not so much the linguistic but the extra-linguistic implicitness of the source text that remains problematic. As has already been remarked, 'in legal translation linguistic units cannot be exchanged in isolation from legal cultural concepts' (Poon Wai Yee 2005: 307).

The cultural element is undoubtedly difficult to structure and therefore to organise by the rules of a foreign language. This is the main reason why a legal cultural translation will always represent an interpretation (mere equivalence at the abstract level of the language system will not necessarily ensure textual equivalence and it would hardly be expected for the legal translator to succeed where all translators have failed). After all, translation in general concerns less the language and more a specific manifestation thereof, and the purpose of a successful translation would be not only to ensure linguistic transfer but also meaningfully to achieve it within the framework of cultural transfer (Lungu Badea 2004: 79–106). Indeed, '[w]e can "hear" culture only by "listening to" language in a certain way' (Silverstein 2004: 621). To what extent, however, can a cultural legal translation be a successful enterprise?

An interdisciplinary approach would require reference to the general theory of information and its compression algorithms. One of the most remarkable applications of this theory concerns genes, our most familiar means of biological reproduction. Against this general background, Richard Dawkins has formulated the hypothesis that culture is our second system of replication consisting of units that he has called 'memes': a meme is a 'unit of information residing in a brain' (1982: 9). According to Dawkins, the size or range of memes may vary and their types as well (eg an idea, a habit, a lecture). They may imprint themselves on the brains of the receiving individuals so that a copy (not necessarily exact) of the original meme is graven in the receiving brain. Juan Delius has defined memes as 'material configurations in neutral memory that code behavioural cultural traits' (1989: 46).

Attempts have therefore been made to formalise 'cultural selection' according to the patterns of and in relationship with purely biological selection. Not only have memes been said to enable reproduction of cultural units from one individual to another and from one generation to another, but it has also been argued that culture as a system (or systems) of memes and their behaviour can affect the gene pool, while genes can affect culture (Vermeer 1997: 162). Synthetically put, cultures have been considered pools of interdependent memes. One step further has consisted in declaring memes an important element in explaining cultural specificity with direct bearing on translating and translation theory: there is no longer 'the' text, either as a fixed unit or as a member of one well established intertextuality (rendered by the notion of 'texteme'); memes may circulate in and out of texts and groups of texts according to the actual condition of the 'user' (or 'replicator'); text reception and production in translating is considered to be determined by memes which, in their turn, seem to be only partly controllable by their 'host' (the translator). All in all, translating means 'transcultural meme replication with translations as transcultural meme vehicles' (ibid: 163).

Independently of information theories and their potential impact on traductology, following the structuralist logics of other fields of linguistics, the modern theory of translation has identified and described the minimum units that the translator operates with ('traductemes'). Remarkably, traductologists have delimited themselves from a rigorous structuralist approach by conceiving traductemes as not referring to a strictly linguistic context but as also aiming to render the atmosphere that surrounds and conditions linguistic production. Quite similarly, the enlarged definition of memes refers not only to material brain configurations but also to their non-material contents. Traductemes are thus construed as an elastic, variable concept, irreducibly inscribed in an individual process and therefore resistant to standardisation (Lungu Badea 2004: 40).

In some hypotheses, the minimum translation units thus defined happen to limit the translator's options and strategies or, in extreme cases, make translation impossible. Such impossibility is of a different nature than the general postulate of inherent intraductibility formulated by pessimists such as Ferdinand de Saussure, Roman Jakobson, Benjamin Lee Whorf and Edward Sapir or Eugene Nida as consisting of the general failure of a sign to occupy the same place in the economy of a foreign language as in the one it translates (Hagège 1985: 47). The limiting units mentioned above are, most frequently, linguistic signs (words, collocations, phrases) profoundly marked from a cultural point of view and thus identified as 'culturemes'.

In this perspective, a cultureme would be considered the minimum linguistic unit endowed with and carrying cultural information. Additionally, a genuine cultureme will at the same time constitute and reflect the cultural identity of a given entity. The concept has been used so far by Els Oksaar (1988) within theories reflecting on interculturality, cultural transfer and cultural differences, but also by Hans Vermeer (1997) or Andrew Chesterman (2000) for the purpose of assessing the possibility of translating cultural difference.

The essential feature of a cultureme would be monoculturality, hard core culturemes being irreducible to similar units belonging to other cultures. Monoculturality distinguishes culturemes from the 'cultural concepts' used in anthropology (Silverstein 2004: 621). If, indeed, one could speak of a cultureme in the broad sense whenever one deals with a unit relevant for the cultural identity of a given community that corresponds to a certain degree with a similar unit within a different culture, in the strict sense of the word the cultureme seizes the idea that the cultural unit under discussion is characterised by an element conferring uniqueness on it, this particular element being the one that distinguishes it out of its identitarian importance for the members of the cultural community to which it belongs.

Contrary to the requirements of the translation paradigm centred on equivalence, only a variable degree of correspondence (if any) can be established by the translator when dealing with culturemes. In addition, culturemes can be described as having a relative character, depending on both the translator's and the receiver's knowledge, expectations and general background, and as being autonomous from translation proper; frequently, culturemes will remain unnoticed by the translator who may mistake them for mere traductemes, despite the fact that within the source culture their existence and identitarian importance are undisputable (Lungu Badea 2004: 69).

Against this background, a legal cultureme would be the minimum unit relevant for the very identity of a legal culture, or the smallest legally relevant carrier of a given legal structure. Therefore, legal culturemes will explain why different legal cultures are of irreducible nature by expressing parts of their identity. In such a key should be read arguments such as the following: 'The litigant in the English legal system [...] can certainly assert that [he] ha[s] in such or such a situation an action against some public or private body and [he] can probably assert that [he] ha[s] a "legitimate interest" or "expectation". What [he] cannot claim is a right to the actual substance, or object, of the action itself – [he] cannot claim a right, as a citizen, to succeed' (Samuel 1987: 286). Or again: 'the common law does not know of the differentiation between real and personal rights (*jus in rem* and *jus in personam*) so central to the civil law tradition. Thus, for example, the person who loses money in the bank account of another may recover by bringing an action *in personam* on the basis of a *jus in rem* against the debt in the bank!' (Legrand 1996: 67).

The same function could fulfil the well established distinction between public and private law within the continental European legal tradition that has been more than once approximated by the distinction between law and equity within the common law. Inevitably, borderline situations may arise: equivalence between the subjective right in continental Europe and the cause of action in the common law might illustrate the cultureme's important property of behaving like a functional correspondent, but not as an equivalent. Similarly, the French '*cause*' has been equated to the English 'consideration', despite the fact that each legal culture involved in the equation will claim the uniqueness and irreducible character of its own legal institution.

Since one cannot give up and decide that law cannot be translated, in each case mentioned above the translator's approach has been centred on functional correspondence, despite the fact that what is involved is precisely the impossibility of establishing a clear correspondence between cultural legal units that the translation process accidentally and contingently brings together. Focus on how these problematic units of legal translation function rather than on what they are, what they mean or what they imply about the culture that has embedded them suggests that culturemes are dealt with by translators as translation's 'black boxes'. Unable indeed to grasp the content of the box (because, despite its belonging to the same legal code that should speak with one language, the legal cultureme is profoundly culturally coloured), the translator has to rely on the box as a structure, that is, to rely on the exterior of the box itself and particularly on the part played by this box as a minimum structure within the larger structure represented in the occurrence by a given legal system.

Differently put, in the attempt to understand the meaning, the translator will first try to determine the function of the conspicuous element accessible to her knowledge. Thus, for not being able to assess the meaning of the box labelled 'consideration', the translator will rely on the fact that the box labelled 'cause' seems to fulfil the same function within the target legal culture. The choice of equivalence based on functionality translates here, in fact, a relevant parameter characterising the translation process itself, namely the existence of a cultural distance that needs to be rendered from one language to another.

As for the cultural ignorance that opacity towards the contents of the 'black box' may reveal, it is remarkable that the inability to seize the meaning of the cultureme is not so much and not only the translator's inability, but particularly and also the inability of lawyers in their capacity of readers in the target language. If law belongs to an elite, if it is esoteric, if, again, it speaks with one voice to the elected, that is to all the members of the doctrinal entity selected by law in its attempt to remain the sealed system described here, it must be emphasised that all this applies to law conceived in its transcendentality, to law untouched by anything else that would conveniently be placed outside law. This might explain, therefore, why a French lawyer and an English one, perfectly trained in contract law, will cautiously regard their mutual allegedly corresponding concepts occurring in their respective contract theories as black boxes with obscure contents. After all, legal culture is not law, according to the purity maxims developed by the legal field to protect its opacity.

Translating legal culturemes: difficulties

When functioning within translation, the cultureme becomes a traducteme the very identification of which supposes, first, the understanding by translators of units of meaning and thought rather than their proficiency in respect of common functional linguistic units. Secondly, the meaning of a cultureme (and especially a legal one) will represent the translators' construction and not their objective reflection and the univocal appropriate result thereof. Andrew Chesterman has defined an empirical model to be used by translators when operating within a framework implying cultural transfer (2000: 6). In this hypothesis, the translator is in fact expected to adopt a twofold strategy. First, she needs to acknowledge the units of information and the culturemes in the source text and to select and express them enunciatively. Secondly, the translator must elaborate a corresponding structure, at once adequate and recognisable, in the target language.

Applied to legal texts, the maxims of good cultural translation state that '[a] translator should follow the target text's grammatical form if the same legal effects intended by the original text can be achieved', and that 'if a legal issue is involved, it is best for the translated text to follow the form or style of the original text' (Poon Wai Yee 2005: 309). Here again the legal translator's identity seems to be that of a secondary and accessory author of the source text, whose unique task is to make the text available for the target reader for whom the original only exists in its translated embodiment.

From the perspective of legal cultural translation, however, one is forced to notice that legal translators face unavoidable difficulties when confronted with genuine legal culturemes because of at least two series of concurring factors. On the one hand, translators are supposed to approximate the cultural significance of the units that they use. But genuine culturemes are never equivalent, and their alleged correspondence calls for highly specific and refined cultural knowledge. On the other hand, and simultaneously, translators are supposed to identify meaningful linguistic units functioning similarly in corresponding legal situations, an imperative that implies linguists' utmost legal competence. One can indeed speak in this respect of the legal translator's perilinguistic competence (Ladmiral 1994: 61).

In the same line of arguments that would reveal the double linkage that a legal translator has to face, it has been argued that equivalence is determined 'on the one hand by the historical-cultural conditions under which texts are produced and received in the target language, and on the other by a range of sometimes contradictory and scarcely reconcilable linguistic-textual and extra-linguistic factors and conditions' (Poon Wai Yee 2005: 312). In fact, even according to the structural analysis applied to language, the cognitive function thereof seems to depend less on the grammatical system and more on our experience placed in a complementary relationship with meta-linguistic operations.

In the particular hypothesis of a legal translation, one would not speak of a definite impossibility to translate, but rather of the extreme difficulty of transferring or recreating the ambience of the source legal culture. In some cases, culturemes' relativity makes their very identification by the translator problematic, and such accidents will turn the cultureme from the 'black box' into the 'black hole' of a translation. Venuti argues that 'differences [in translation] can never be entirely removed, but they necessarily undergo a reduction and exclusion of possibilities – and an exorbitant gain of other possibilities specific to the translating language' (2008: 14).

Frequently, legal culturemes will partially disappear through translation (the English 'contract' paronymically and mimetically translated by the French '*contrat*' and introduced in the atmosphere of French contractual relations), while others will hopefully be recreated ('consideration' unproblematically translated by '*cause*', 'remedy' translated by '*remède*' or 'estoppel' by '*préclusion*'). The concern arising from such treatment is not so much the translator's personal creative involvement in law, a field that is traditionally sealed by the sacred nature of the legal text enacted by a legislator (and not by a translator).

In fact, as proven before, the idea that either a translation is creative or it does not exist at all already functions as an *acquis* in today's translation studies. The current risks of any translation of a legal cultureme are rather unauthenticity, inappropriateness, aleatoricism, meaning loss or artificial meaning gain, ethnocentrism or xenocentrism, and so on. Indeed, coherently with the universal logics of translation, sometimes the legal cultureme functions as an element of tension constraining the translator to naturalise the source text within a pure ethnocentric translation. After all: '[w]hatever difference the translation conveys is now imprinted by the receiving culture, assimilated to its positions of intelligibility, its canons and taboos, its codes and ideologies', so that translation has 'to bring back a cultural other as the recognizable, the familiar, even the same' (ibid: 14). On the contrary, in other hypotheses, a hard-core legal cultureme will challenge translators' omniscience and omnipotence, rendering them powerless.

When the cultural distance that it measures is considerable, the source word revealing that distance has to be kept as such in the target language accompanied by a gloss or a note explicitly associating the translators' voice with the intertext and representing the translators' shame (Lungu Badea 2004: 129). This would be a sign both of the translators' failure and of the deep untranslatability of the concept.

Suppose the parameters of an ideal communication circuit: the legal source text is not obscure, the author knows what he wants to say and the reader reasonably understands most of the text's meaning. Yet a legal cultureme is there, unproblematically decryptable within the source culture and requiring to be rendered by the translator in the target language for the purpose of being offered to readers belonging to the target culture. The cultureme only properly signifies within a specific cultural atmosphere, whose implied virtualities will ideally also be transferred by translation. Moreover, legal concepts are themselves virtual and transversal, allowing themselves to be interpreted according to social needs.

However, will the virtualities of the source concept (including those arising from its embeddedness in the source culture) be the same as the virtualities of its target 'functional equivalent'?

Several other questions should be raised in the context of cultural legal translation: is the possibility of the translation itself conditioned by the existence of equivalence or at least by a certain degree of correspondence between the legal cultures meeting within the translation process? What is the significance to be assigned to the coexistence of parallel legal translations? Should such coexistence mean that from inside the language no equivalence is possible, therefore it is for the legislator to intervene and arbitrarily institute it? Who validates legal cultural equivalence? Which legal culture constitutes the privileged point of reference and according to what rule? Should translators opt for an ethnocentric translation whenever dealing with the need to convey a legal cultureme in the attempt to naturalise the source text, or rather should they choose to be faithful to the latter's content and cultural ambience which would hopefully per se activate full significance? Is the historical common cultural European background sufficient to grant a reasonable degree of sameness, therefore the possibility of legal translation within Europe? Are the various autonomous concepts flourishing in European law to be understood as transgressing national legal culturemes and thus rendering domestic legal translation superfluous? One will also have to evaluate the translating strategies of compensating or adjusting the meaning and to assess their usefulness in the legal context in which translators find themselves deprived of their habitual power. Of utmost importance, since translation in general often tends to become autonomous in relationship to the source text, one should be prepared to take into consideration a genuine aesthetics of legal translation.

Not to translate has become nowadays an impossible choice in law. Negotiation has therefore been said to represent a reasonable palliative to the apparent impossibility of legal translation. Modern translators must be successful within and despite difference, formal correspondence being replaced by a sort of either dynamic or functional equivalence. But then there are differences and differences, and the utmost difference will perhaps lead to failure of negotiation. If, in a certain sense, a legal text should be conceived as a palimpsest of the legal culture within which it functions, hard core culturemes mark the true limit of the legal translator's power.

Notes

* The author's participation at the International Conference 'Comparative Law — Engaging Translation', organised by the Kent Centre for European and Comparative Law, Kent Law School, Canterbury, UK on 21–22 June 2012, was financed by the POSDRU/89/1.5/S/63663 programme. The research for this chapter was also financed by the POSDRU/89/1.5/S/63663 programme.
1 *Schalk and Kopf v Austria* (Application no 30141/04) (2010) ECHR 218.

Bibliography

Austin, J.L. (1975) *How to Do Things With Words*, J.O. Urmson and M. Sbisa (eds), 2nd edn, Cambridge, MA: Harvard University Press.

Bercea, R. (2009) 'Toute comparaison des droits est une fiction', in P. Legrand (ed.) *Comparer les droits, résolument*, Paris: Presses Universitaires de France.

—— (2013a) 'How to Use Philosophy When Being a (Comparative) Lawyer', *Procedia – Social and Behavioral Sciences*, 71: 160–67.

—— (2013b) 'The European Court of Human Rights: The Beginning of a Systematic Comparative Law Approach?', in P.-L. Runcan, G. Raţă and C. Goian (eds) *Applied Social Sciences: Administration and Management*, Newcastle-upon-Tyne: Cambridge Scholars.

Cassin, B. (2006) 'Violence de la traduction: traduire l'intraduisible', in *Vingt-deuxièmes Assises de la traduction littéraire (Arles 2005): Traduire la violence*, Arles: Actes Sud.

Chesterman, A. (2000) *Memes of Translation: The Spread of Ideas in Translation Theory*, Amsterdam: J. Benjamins.

Dawkins, R. (1982) *The Extended Phenotype: The Gene as the Unit of Selection*, Oxford: Oxford University Press.

Delius, J.D. (1989) 'Of Mind, Memes and Brain Bugs: A Natural History of Culture', in W.A. Koch (ed.) *The Nature of Culture*, Bochum: Brockmeyer.

Engberg, J. (2002) 'Legal Meaning Assumptions – What are the Consequences for Legal Interpretation and Legal Translation?', *International Journal for the Semiotics of Law*, 15: 375–88.

Fish, S. (1991) 'Being Interdisciplinary Is So Very Hard to Do', *Issues in Integrative Studies*, 9: 99–112.

Gémar, J.-C. (2002) 'L'interprétation du texte juridique ou le dilemme du traducteur', in R. Sacco (ed.) *L'Interprétation des textes juridiques rédigés dans plus d'une langue*, Turin: L'Harmattan.

Glanert, S. (2011) *De la traductibilité du droit*, Paris: Dalloz.

—— and Legrand P. (2013) 'Foreign Law in Translation: If Truth Be Told …', in M. Freeman and F. Smith (eds) *Current Legal Issues: Law and Language*, Oxford: Oxford University Press.

Hagège, C. (1985) *L'Homme de paroles*, Paris: Fayard.

Jestaz, P. and Jamin, C. (1997) 'L'entité doctrinale française', *Dalloz*, 'Chroniques': 167–75.

Ladmiral, J.-R. (1994) *Traduire: théorèmes pour la traduction*, Paris: Gallimard.

Lane-Mercier, G. (1997) 'Translating the Untranslatable: The Translator's Aesthetic, Ideological and Political Responsibility', *Target: International Journal of Translation Studies*, 9: 43–68.

Legrand, P. (1995) '*Antiqui juris civilis fabulas*', *University of Toronto Law Journal*, 45: 311–62.

—— (1996) 'European Legal Systems Are Not Converging', *International and Comparative Law Quarterly*, 45: 52–81.

—— (2011a) *Le Droit comparé*, 1st edn, Paris: Presses Universitaires de France.

—— (2011b) 'Siting Foreign Law: How Derrida Can Help', *Duke Journal of Comparative and International Law*, 21: 595–629.

—— (2012) 'Foreign Law: Understanding Understanding', *Journal of Comparative Law*, 6: 67–177.

Lungu Badea, G. (2004) *Teoria culturemelor, teoria traducerii*, Timisoara: West University Publishing House.

Marmor, A. (2008) 'The Pragmatics of Legal Language', *Ratio Juris*, 21: 423–52.

Montesquieu, C. (1748) *De l'esprit des lois*, in *Œuvres complètes*, R. Caillois (ed.), vol II, Paris: Gallimard, 1951.

Oksaar, E. (1988) *Kulturemtheorie: Ein Beitrag zur Sprachverwendungsforschung*, Göttingen: Vandenhoeck & Ruprecht.

Pavel, T. (1970) *L'Univers de la fiction*, Paris: Éditions du Seuil.

Poon Wai Yee, E. (2005) 'The Cultural Transfer in Legal Translation', *International Journal for the Semiotics of Law*, 18: 307–23.

Samuel, G. (1987) '"Le droit subjectif" and English Law', *Cambridge Law Journal*, 46: 264–86.

—— (2009) 'Interdisciplinarity and the Authority Paradigm: Should Law Be Taken Seriously by Scientists and Social Scientists?', *Journal of Law and Society*, 36: 431–59.

Silverstein, M. (2004) '"Cultural" Concepts and the Language-Culture Nexus', *Current Anthropology*, 45: 621–51.

Venuti, L. (2008) *The Translator's Invisibility: A History of Translation*, 2nd edn, London: Routledge.

Vermeer, H.J. (1997) 'Translation and the "Meme"', *Target: International Journal of Translation Studies*, 9: 155–66.

Vick, D. (2004) 'Interdisciplinarity and the Discipline of Law', *Journal of Law and Society*, 31: 163–93.

Part III

Translation beyond translation

Chapter 10

Translating religious principles into German law: boundaries and contradictions

Pascale Fournier and Régine Tremblay

Introduction: religious principles as a 'social' order?

Over recent decades, two important debates have echoed each other in Western European countries. The first argument, which is quite ancient, touches upon the place of religious principles in a legal system and their distinction from (state) law. The second discussion, of more recent origin, pertains to the 'integration' of minorities through recognition of their distinct religious normative orders. Despite fundamental differences, both discourses share many interesting meeting points and raise important issues. Some of these matters, which only become more complex when one tries to translate religious normative principles into state law, will be the watermarks in this chapter.

First, one must keep in mind that religious principles are stateless: they are not tied to a state per se and they do not have a fixed form (or state). This raises the question of how one can translate religious normative principles within a specific state and in a comprehensive fashion. Secondly, it is difficult to evaluate to what extent state law is secular and to study the various forms of state law over time. How, then, can a state translate religious principles within its boundaries and in line with its laws? Some authors have defended recognition of all non-Western customs in the name of 'progressive integration of what is after all [...] a single world' (Kollewijn 1951: 325). Others have argued in favour of 'allowing [Muslims] to have the social space within which *Shari'a*-mindedness can flourish, thereby allowing pious Muslims to live a faith-based life' (Turner and Arslan 2011: 156). Many have idealised religious principles as harmonious. In this chapter, we problematise such an idealised picture of religious principles and explore elements that should be taken into account before religious principles can be translated into positive law. Based on fieldwork, we present religious family law as contested from the inside and open to decisions, strategies and manipulations that incessantly alter its content and meaning.

The product of our fieldwork arises from the particular context of Germany, a country that shares many traits with other continental European polities as far as recognition of religious laws is concerned. Germany has been the focus of debates regarding the search for 'pluralistic modes of incorporation' (Koenig 2005: 228) of communities along the lines of their religious socio-legal orders. These discussions specifically addressed whether Muslims might organise their community along religious lines through an entity called a 'public law corporation', as Christians and Jews are allowed to do in Germany (Rohe 2004: 87). With very few exceptions, Germany does not recognise religious law in a domestic context but a debate is raging about translating religious norms into positive law. This chapter outlines the challenges to eventual recognition. It argues that while these hurdles are considerable, they are downplayed or underestimated by many legal scholars. In order to support our claim, we present the findings of fieldwork undertaken among Jewish and Muslim communities in Germany and introduce data from formal interviews with eight Jewish and Muslim women conducted in 2011. The fieldwork focuses on Jewish and Islamic religious laws and their relation to state law in Germany.

First we present the basic rules of Islamic and Jewish law and the German state law that regulates them. Next we contend that the boundaries for shaping and applying religious norms are blurry. Indeed, principles are constantly redefined by parties and adjudicators, while adjudicatory outcomes and procedures for religious marriage and divorce are often uneven and depend on the choices and decisions of particular parties, adjudicators and stakeholders. We argue that these conflicting outcomes might be explained by boundless discretion and informality in the religious adjudication process, but that this structure is not foreign to so-called secular family law. Thus, if the project of recognising religious principles is to be maintained in the context of family law, it must take stock of the conceptual and practical conflicts that inhere to the sphere of family law and indeed to law more generally. These arguments are intended as a contribution to the burgeoning literature on the interaction between secular state law and 'unofficial' religious norms (Moon 2008; Nichols 2012).

The German legal landscape: religion and the state

When Jews and Muslims marry in Western countries, their ceremony often includes both a religious and a civil element. Under both traditions, husbands and wives have distinct rights and responsibilities within marriage. Access to religious divorce is drawn sharply along gender lines (Estin 2008: 464). Under Islamic family law, marriage establishes a system of reciprocity in which each party is assigned a set of contractual rights and duties towards the other (Abu-Odeh 2004). A marriage contract can only be concluded through the principles of offer (*ijab*) and acceptance (*qabul*) by the two principals or their proxies (Nasir 2009: 45). Upon marriage, the husband acquires the right to his wife's obedience (ibid: 98) and the right to restrict her movements outside the matrimonial home (ibid: 80). For her part, the wife acquires the right to her *mahr*[1] (Esposito and DeLong-Bas 2001: 23; Fournier 2010: *passim*) and the right to maintenance (Esposito and DeLong-Bas 2001: 25). Like Muslim marriage, Jewish marriage is finalised according to contractual principles. The parties execute a marriage contract (a *ketubah*, plural *ketubot*), often written in Aramaic (Reiss and Broyde 2005: 202), which lists the duties of each spouse.

Unlike the Muslim marriage contract, which is negotiated between the parties and is therefore unique to them and their relationship, the *ketubah* is fairly standard. As put by Elliot Dorff and Arthur Rosett: 'the parties may determine by contract only those elements of the relationship which the law permits them to decide' (1988: 453). Based on the Torah's articulation of a husband's duties towards his wife, this contract includes requirements for adequate food, clothing, shelter and regular intercourse, as well as a sum to maintain the wife in the event of death or divorce (traditionally, the sum necessary for the woman to support herself for one year) (Epstein 1927: 163).

Islamic legal institutions such as *talaq* divorce, *khul* divorce and *faskh* divorce determine the degree to which each party may or may not initiate divorce and the different costs associated with each transaction. According to classical Islamic family law, women have the agency to use the *khul* or *faskh* divorce, but may not use the *talaq* divorce. The *khul* divorce is initiated judicially by the woman, although with the understanding that such a route will dissolve the husband's duty to pay the deferred *mahr* (El Alami and Hinchcliffe 1996: 27–28; Abdal-Rehim 1996: 105). The *faskh* divorce is a fault-based divorce initiated by the wife before the Islamic tribunal, and it is by nature limited to specific grounds (Abdal-Rehim 1996: 105). In the case of termination of marriage by *faskh* divorce, unlike in the case of *khul* divorce, the wife is entitled to *mahr* (El Alami and Hinchcliffe 1996: 29). Finally, the *talaq* divorce (repudiation) is a unilateral act which dissolves the marriage contract through a declaration by the husband only. The law recognises the power of the husband to divorce his wife by saying '*talaq*' (meaning 'divorce') three times without the need for him to ask for enforcement of his declaration by the court (ibid: 22). However, this unlimited 'freedom' of the husband to divorce at will in the private sphere involves the (costly) obligation to pay *mahr* in full as soon as the third *talaq* has been pronounced (Esposito and DeLong-Bas 2001: 23).

Unlike Muslim women, who may initiate divorce through *khul* or *faskh*, Jewish women are not in a position to obtain a religious divorce from their husbands. In order to be '*halachically*' correct (Jacobs and De Vries 2007: 251), a Jewish marriage may only end in the death of a spouse or the voluntary grant of a divorce (*get*) by the husband (Haut 1983: 18) and its simultaneous acceptance by the wife (Yefet 2009: 443–44). The husband thus has the exclusive power to deliver a *get* (Bible Deuteronomy 24: 1), which comes in the form of a surprisingly brief document written mostly in the Aramaic language. If a Jewish woman is entitled to a *get* and has not received one owing to her husband's refusal, she is referred to as an *agunah* (plural *agunot*) (Bible Ruth 1: 13); literally, a 'chained' or 'anchored' woman. Several limitations are placed on a divorced Jewish woman who wishes to enter into religious remarriage without a *get*. First, if she marries a man by civil ceremony, the relationship is considered adulterous under Jewish law. Therefore, the woman is never permitted to enter into religious marriage with that man

(Cohn 2004: 66). Secondly, children born to a woman who has not received a *get* are labelled *mamzer* (plural *mamzerin*). Such children are sometimes 'effectively excluded from organized Judaism' (Nichols 2007: 155), as they are illegitimate and may never marry anyone but another *mamzer*. Although a wife can in theory refuse a *get* issued by her husband, in practice the consequences for the man are neither as serious nor as far-reaching as they are for an *agunah*: '[a] man who remarries without a Jewish divorce has not committed adultery, but has only violated a rabbinic decree mandating monogamy; he is nonetheless considered married to his second wife, and his children are legitimate' (ibid).

The German legal system only very scantily recognises Islamic and Jewish divorce law. Until 1999, a citizenship applicant had to provide evidence of at least one German ancestor in order to receive German citizenship, making it almost impossible for foreigners to become citizens (Article 116 of the Grundgesetz, the German Basic Law). Germany's citizenship policy has thus been described as 'one of the most restrictive in the EU' (Green 2005: 922). In short, even though foreign law is made applicable to all non-German citizens, of which there are many in the Muslim immigrant communities, *talaq* and *get* divorces are only recognised if all relevant gestures were conducted outside of German territory. Moreover, German domestic family law, which applies to German citizens, does not allow for pronouncement of *talaq* divorces or delivery of *get* divorces. German courts have been consistent in their treatment of *talaq* divorce: this form of religious divorce will be recognised only if it has been carried out entirely in a jurisdiction which allows such a divorce (Siehr 2005: 352).

In general, German courts will not perform *get* divorces themselves nor will they pressure the husband to grant the divorce, but will refer the parties to the appropriate jurisdiction: the rabbinical authorities.[2] Refusal to grant a *get* is problematic for the wife, since she can legally obtain a divorce before a German court, but without a religious divorce she will remain an *agunah*. German courts have confirmed that freedom of religion exonerates Jewish men from all coercion as to giving a *get*, whether coercion results from domestic court decisions or recognition of foreign judgments.[3]

For a German citizen, German divorce laws and procedures are the same whether or not one follows the laws of a religious tradition. Like most Western countries, Germany has a no-fault divorce system (Robbers 2006: 286; Foster and Sule 2010: 520–21).[4] Provisions related to divorce are found in sections 1564–48 of the Bürgerliches Gesetzbuch (BGB), the German Civil Code. The first of these provisions specifically states that 'a marriage may be dissolved by divorce only by judicial decision on the petition of one or both spouses' (section 1564 of the BGB). A religious authority does not have jurisdiction to grant a divorce under German law (Siehr 2005: 352). In Germany, only a court can pronounce a divorce.

Formal recognition of religious norms in German law is not yet accomplished. One exception, however, is the possibility for Jewish and Muslim individuals to have recourse to religious arbitration. Unlike in other polities such as parts of

Canada (Fournier 2010: 120), religious arbitration is not precluded in Germany, whether in family law or in other private matters (Rohe 2009: 97–98). The possibility of seeking religious arbitration is attracting heavy questioning and criticism in Germany (Popp 2011).

From plural belongings and boundaries to the shaping of religious principles

By interviewing eight Muslim and Jewish women in Germany, we aimed to investigate the socio-legal reality and understanding of religious family norms. The interviews took place mainly in Berlin in summer 2011. The original plan was to interview women in Berlin only, without translators. This meant that the women we would interview had to be able to speak English, a trait that in itself would limit the number and type of women participating. As it proved difficult to find English-speaking women in Berlin willing to talk about their divorces, in the end some of the interviews were conducted through translators, while one participant was from outside Berlin. The interviews took place in the midst of intensive networking and fieldwork in sectors of the German Muslim and Jewish communities. Although we advertised for volunteers through a website (http://talaqgetgermany.wordpress. com), emails to academic groups and public posters, the majority of interviewees came to us by word of mouth and contacts within the Berlin Jewish and Muslim communities, a method approved by the Office of Research Ethics and Integrity of the University of Ottawa in response to our application.

Our participants come from a variety of backgrounds. Two of them had converted to their current religions: one to Judaism, the other to Islam (Participants #5 and #6). Despite our concern for a varied sample, some groups remain underrepresented. For example, none of the Jewish women interviewed is Orthodox, and none of the Muslim women would describe herself as very conservative or fundamentalist. None of them was extremely poor, although several were by no means well off. Many of the women spoke English as a third or fourth language. Almost all were educated at the undergraduate level and were working. All of these traits must be taken into account when trying to draw any conclusion about what the women's accounts say about divorce and use of religious principles in Germany. The women interviewed are not representative of their entire communities, although some similarities in experience among the participants point to consistent themes. All were asked the same basic questions. Depending on the answers, these were then followed by more specific queries.

We use a 'story-telling' approach to depict how legal agents navigate the religious and socio-economic endowments that community life produces. If it is difficult to draw policy conclusions from mere stories (Fajer 1994: 1845), we have nevertheless tried to combine our stories with empirical data and socio-legal literature, to draw some general conclusions from our fieldwork. Qualitative interview analysis brings new, marginalised accounts of religious customs as experienced by religious women and thus builds on existing scholarship from its margins. More specifically, this section explores the context of religious law, its internal boundaries and its interactions with the civil law, focusing on how parties and adjudicators redesign those boundaries through legal behaviours.

Under classical Islamic law, the Islamic court (*qadi*) usually does not arbitrate *talaq* divorces – for instance, a woman in Malaysia can ask the court to declare a *talaq* divorce (Pelezt 2002: 169) – but rather adjudicates *khul* divorces[5] and *faskh* divorces. In the latter instance, 'a wife who is unhappy in her marriage and who wishes to obtain a dissolution must petition the court but only in so far as she can demonstrate to the court (*qadi*) that the limited grounds under which divorce can be granted have been met' (Elĭ Alami and Hinchcliffe 1996: 29; see also Abu-Odeh 2004: 1106). In Germany, no organised system of *qadis* exists, so religious leaders known as imams, a word literally translatable as 'prayer leader', 'fulfill more responsibilities that could be attributed to the Islamic religious sphere' (Kamp 2008: 143). German imams celebrate Islamic marriages and adjudicate divorces (ibid: 144). In this way, they 'become central figures of the community' (Kastoryano 2004: 1237).

Unlike the heterogeneous venues and audiences of Islamic religious divorce, the act of Jewish religious divorce is systematically overseen by one party: a *beth din* (plural *battei din*). This tribunal of three Jewish judges (*dayanim*) functions according to formalities born of centuries of religious tradition. The *beth din* oversees the process but does not execute the divorce. 'No one – not the government, not the courts, not even a rabbi – is authorized to divorce a couple except for the husband' (Yefet 2009: 442–43). Therefore, the power of the *beth din* lies in its persuasive authority rather than its ability to mandate results. As a result of the Second World War (Bodemann 1990: 40), German Jewish communities have relied on American, British and Israeli rabbis, given their institutional disorganisation and demographic instability (Eddy 2006). The influence of foreign rabbis and *battei din*, a recurrent occurrence in our participants' testimonies, participates in shaping the boundaries of religious principles in Germany.

The contemporary German Muslim context also seems to leave some space for a decline in importance of the religious sphere among immigrant communities. Recent surveys reported by the German weekly *Der Spiegel* in August 2012 show a rising will among Muslim Germans of Turkish origin to 'integrate into German society' and secular institutions, along with a paradoxically increasing religiousness (Hawley 2012). This uneven influence of the religious sphere was another recurring theme in our fieldwork. The ability of religious individuals to pick and choose normative belongings contributes in important ways to fashioning religious law in action. Many participants mentioned that religious rules and rulings could be ignored by one party, who would then turn to the civil sphere to uphold his or her interests:

Participant #1:
Interviewer: During or before your marriage, did you ever discuss the *talaq* type of divorce with your husband [...]?

Participant: No, never, because we were both not that religious. I mean, we were both just very young, and I think for us the legal [civil] marriage was a lot more binding than the other thing, that was just a show for the family [...].
[...]
Interviewer: What did your ex-husband think of the religious divorce?
Participant: I think he didn't care at that point because he was more involved with English and German people, when he broke away from me he broke away from the Muslim society and he just lived as he pleased.

Sometimes, the Jewish or Islamic authorities will themselves contribute to lessening the influence of their religious normative order by aligning with the civil sphere and 'surrendering' to its grasp. This will be the case, for instance, when a woman convinces the adjudicator to recognise a civil divorce, even though the latter cannot in itself lead to a religious divorce by strict application of Jewish or Islamic legal rules:

Participant #2:
Interviewer: Once you have the secular divorce you're also divorced in God's eyes.
Participant: Yes, normally in our religion you have to have a divorce [...] but because I was never overly religious and because in my case, this is a special case. My case was my mom died when I was very little, so the family sort of broke apart a bit. [...] So in my case it was all a lot more liberal.

Participant #4:
Interviewer: So did your rabbi recognise your civil divorce from Germany?
Participant: Yes, of course. He was living here, of course.

It would thus appear that civil law sometimes trumps religious law. However, it should be noted that there is no uniformity in this civil/religious interaction. In some other situations, the adjudicators will stubbornly refuse to consider what the civil law decrees, and will instead stick to their own internal legal rules and criteria to grant religious divorce and to celebrate religious marriages (Participants #1 and 2).

Reciprocally, religious law sometimes trumps civil law. For Jewish participants, one theme was that if their families or their spouses were from Israel, then the German civil marriage was of especially little consequence: in Israel, virtually all marriages are religious (Lerner 2009: 447). One woman said that her spouse, whose family was from Israel, did not tell his parents they had celebrated a German civil marriage. His mother was upset until the man clarified that it had only been a civil ceremony. The couple had a religious ceremony soon afterwards, and the parents considered that their absence from the civil ceremony was of no consequence:

Participant #3:
The religious marriage was for my parents-in-law very important, because they didn't know [what] a civil contract [is], they didn't know that; they're from Israel. [...]
And then in the afternoon [...] we went for dinner [with the husband's parents]. [...] [M]y husband stood up and [told his parents we were married]. And [...] my mother-in-law was up and down the ceiling: 'How could you marry without me!' It was a mess [...]. Then my husband said it was not a Jewish ceremony, it was a civil. [...] So, then she says: 'That's ok, I don't care! Ok, fine fine'. [...]. We made the Jewish [ceremony] and then everything was ok.

It would thus seem, from the perception of the participants, that religious and civil norms are constantly reconfiguring their respective spheres of influence in unpredictable ways. Some religious individuals will attempt to bend the religious adjudication in their favour by making it align with the civil sphere. Whether that strategy is successful or not, both parties will often (but not always) have the opportunity to ignore religious law and turn to the civil sphere, thus rewriting religion's boundaries every time.

In addition to considerable paradoxical interplay between the civil and religious spheres, our fieldwork suggests that the voices of the law are plural and internal to the religious normative order. That is to say, the legal power of official figures such as imams or rabbis is overshadowed and influenced by other stakeholders in religious communities, such as friends, families and members of the community. Such reactions spur the parties to adopt several tactics to secure the approval or support of some stakeholders, effectively 'bargaining in the shadow of the law' (Mnookin and Kornhauser 1979: 950). However, there is no way to predict what the stakeholders' influence will be:

Participant #2:
I was lucky. There are many families that put a lot of pressure on women so that they cannot get divorced, simply because they are very religious. But in my case, my family is rather relaxed and more liberal and this is why I consider myself lucky that I could just make my own decision and follow it through.

We see that the concrete implications of religious law are dependent on the actions of third parties, so that the law is constantly mediated by intricate family loyalties, community networks, friendships, and what Michel Foucault called 'the little tactics of the habitat' (Foucault 1977: 149). This perpetual redesigning of the boundaries of religious customs serves as a reminder of legal pluralism's insight that 'law arises from, belongs to, and responds to everyone' (Macdonald 2002: 8). Normative orders do not simply exist, with clear contours and outer limits, but are constantly created by legal subjects themselves, as they 'participate in the multiple normative communities by which they recognize and create their own legal subjectivity' (Kleinhans and Macdonald 1997: 38). It is this 'everyday law' that we have tried to unearth in the context of religious norms, discovering that many on-the-ground difficulties to idealising and conceiving religious principles as a fixed legal entity.[6] Translation of religious norms under conditions of German positive law thus becomes a complex enterprise.

From adjudicatory contradictions and boundaries to the application of religious principles

This section shifts the analysis to the mechanisms of religious law, focusing on the roles of Islamic and Jewish adjudicators, namely on the application of religious principles. Julie Macfarlane, one of the few scholars conducting empirical research on Muslim practices in the West, has found that imams in North America often assume roles that go beyond those assigned by classical Islamic law to *qadis*. Macfarlane has noted that the adjudicatory role of imams is inconsistent, generating wildly diverging outcomes (2012). We have sought to examine whether decisions and adjudication by German imams present any consistency. Our findings mirror those of Macfarlane: religious adjudication and bargaining in Germany leads to wildly diverging results.

Often, the adjudicators and the parties will disregard the substantive and procedural rules of Islamic law. This leads to strikingly varied results, such as uneven requirements for marriage celebration. For instance, a marriage will sometimes be performed in the absence of the imam, as in the case of Participant #8, even though other women, such as Participant #2, asserted that the presence of the imam is an essential condition for a valid Muslim marriage:

> Participant #8:
> We did the marriage at home, and you don't need an imam [...] to do this. You can go to an imam or to a mosque, but you can do it at home. And there was my father, and his father – the family. And brothers and sisters. So we had witnesses, and everything. [...] His father made the *nikah* [Muslim marriage contract].

The same selective observance of procedural and substantive rules can be noticed among certain Jewish *battei din* and rabbis. Specifically, the *get* ceremonial requirements were sometimes bent by rabbis, who would create their own *get* procedures, humiliating and insulting women (Participant #4). However, other religious adjudicators bend the procedural rules in favour of women. It would thus seem that the vagaries of religious law can go both ways. Some imams allow women to pronounce the *talaq* divorce, which under Islamic law can only be done by the man (Hussain 2011: 120–22):

Participant #1:
Participant: Well I did the divorce with an imam. My husband wasn't there
[…]. [The imam] just said something and I had to say it three times and then
I was divorced.
Interviewer: Do you remember what you had to say three times?
Participant: […] [I]t was uh 'I divorce with Allah's permission, I divorce
you, I divorce you, I divorce you' and that was it. […] It took 30 seconds
or something.
Interviewer: So they let you initiate the religious divorce without his consent?
Participant: Yes, because by that time we'd lived separately and everybody
knew he was violent, everybody knew that he was having loads of extra-
marital affairs, you know, loads of them, and so he was considered unworthy
of being a Muslim […].

The substantive rules of divorce are also bent and applied irregularly, as the case
of grounds for divorce illustrates. Under Islamic law, grounds to issue an Islamic
faskh divorce decree include impotence on the part of the husband, insufficient
material support and companionship ('the loneliness of the marriage bed'), non-
fulfilment of the marriage contract, mental or physical abuse, or a husband's lack
of piety (Abdal-Rehim 1996: 105; Esposito and DeLong-Bas 2001: 32–34).
However, some imams apply these divorce grounds unevenly, being reticent to
grant divorce for insufficient material support and physical abuse, while favouring
divorce claims on grounds of homosexuality or impotence:

Participant #1:
[I]f he's gay, then you'll find any imam [to adjudicate the divorce], if he's
unable to father a child, again you'll find any imam. But if he beats you and
leaves you hungry and you know that kind of stuff, […] you have to sit there
and do all your dirty washing out in front of witnesses in order to [divorce]
[…].

We have found that some imams are reluctant to enforce post-divorce alimony
(Participant #2), even though the woman is entitled to three months of additional maintenance under Islamic law (Nasir 2009: 142). The *mahr* seems to be
an element that is enforced selectively, even though it is central to the Muslim
custom of marriage and divorce:

Participant #1:
We signed some sort of contract saying in case of divorce what he would
have to pay me, which of course never happened. […] It was never again an
issue. The minute it came to finances, there was no Muslim blood in him at
all […]. I know many who sign the religious contract, and then you might as
well use it as toilet paper because it has no meaning.

The same complex indeterminacy can be found in some doctrines of Jewish law. If a Jewish man refuses to grant the *get*, the wife is left with very little religious recourse. Hence, the opportunity for 'strategic behavior' (Estin 2008: 464) in civil divorce proceedings is remarkable, making the *get* an ideal tool for blackmail. Lisa Fishbayn writes that: '[t]he power men enjoy under Jewish law to withhold a *get* is of concern to civil law because this power becomes an effective bargaining endowment in the resolution of civil family law disputes' (2008: 85). The boundary between civil and religious principles is permeable. That being said, the Jewish *agunah* has been provided with some countervailing bargaining instruments. If Jewish women cannot grant a *get* of their own initiative, they may refuse their husbands' *get*, which will prevent the rabbinical authorities from dissolving the marriage contract. It is regarded as against the spirit of Jewish law for a wife to be able to dismiss her husband by granting him a *get* (Mielziner 1987: 117). Jewish women may refuse consent to the *get* for reasons related to the best interests of their children, to extract further concessions from the husband or for pecuniary incentives.[7] Jewish men who are citizens of Israel may respond to this bargaining by obtaining official permission from an Israeli rabbinical court to marry a second wife, effectively circumventing the wife's refusal. A line has to be drawn between refusing the *get* and negotiating over granting one. Some of our participants' experiences very well illustrated the indeterminacy of such religious rules.[8]

It would seem that religious law's inconsistencies stem not from its misapplication, but from its structure. Our fieldwork supports Susan Weiss's view that Jewish law 'is not a collection of harsh and uniform rules, but rather embraces various and contradictory voices [and the] outcome of a given case depends upon the rabbinical authority consulted, the "facts" he deems worthy of emphasis, and the voices he chooses to heed' (2004: 63). The same extends to Islamic law, so that religious principles do not seem to be a homogeneous body of oppressive rules but an open-ended toolbox used in various contradictory ways by different rabbis, imams and parties.

The growing mass of feminist scholarship reinterpreting the internal legal doctrines of Jewish law (Graetz 2005: 4; Sassoon 2011) and Islamic law (Barlas 2002: 3; Mernissi 1985: 52) is interesting in this regard, as it underlines that religious norms are, in fact, malleable and can be invoked to support many conflicting conclusions. Undoubtedly, inconsistencies in the application of religious norms often stem from arbitrary applications of the law, a phenomenon exacerbated by the informality surrounding religious family law in Germany. Perhaps these phenomena can be seen as products of the very nature of religious law, which, just like any state law, can be indeterminate and fashioned by the bargaining parties themselves. Recognising these legal rules and practices would thus lead to many unpredictable distributive consequences, which must be acknowledged and studied empirically before a fruitful conversation on the nature of religious law and its translation into German law – or state law generally – can continue.

Conclusion: legal scholarship in times of diaspora and migration

This chapter has outlined several conceptual difficulties and challenges to seeing religious law as a 'social', harmonious sphere of identity that can be easily recognised, translated and valued by the state. We have explored the processes through which the internal and external boundaries of religious normative orders come to be defined and have revealed the incessant cross-cutting of civil and religious orders. It would seem that religious legal subjects are busy constantly redrawing the lines of competing normative orders, so that clear-cut recognition of the boundaries of one or the other is practically unworkable. Parties and adjudicators seem to be able to bend the religious rules to favour one party or the other.

Our conclusions can be extended to other legal orders, including state law (Rittich 2001: 929; Kennedy 2002: 116–17). The instability and openness to manipulation we have outlined may not be peculiar to religious law, but rather constitute attributes of all legal systems. Relying on socio-legal literature and fieldwork, we have suggested that the malleability of religious law is neither due to arbitrary, 'bad' law-making nor to new norms that diverge from black-letter religious law. Instead, the contradictory outcomes of religious principles might be attributable to the indeterminacy of religious law, its internal gaps, conflicts and ambiguities that leave the door open to choice, agency, and 'strategic behavior' in legal interpretation (Kennedy 1998: 180).

It does not follow from our exposition that religious norms should never be recognised. Defending this would be hypocritical, given that many Western legal rules are rooted in Christianity. Nor does our analysis imply that civil, state law is 'better' than religious law or that it is more determinate or egalitarian. There is a need to distance ourselves from the over-valuation of secularity, and to question the false dichotomy between religious law and secular law.

Our study rather offers a humble awareness of the complexity of legal orders. In a context where international migration and the transnational flow of people are ever-increasing, it is imperative for law to take stock of the many conflicting implications of proposed policy decisions. A turn to private relational dynamics thus seems to be lacking in legal scholarship on minority legal systems. To be sure, brilliant legal accounts of the complex hybridity of legal identities and belongings are currently emerging (Van Praagh 1996: 214). Fascinating fieldwork has also been produced on the topic of legal subjects' navigation of informal, religious legal orders (Campbell 2010; Macfarlane 2012). However, a broader turn towards the empirical study of these socio-legal complexities will become even more necessary as time progresses. Moreover, the difficulty of translating stateless normative principles into state law should be explored. Armed with this curiosity, legal scholars can perhaps begin the study of religious legal orders afresh.

Notes

1 *Mahr*, meaning 'reward' or 'nuptial gift', is the expression used in Islamic family law to describe the 'payment that the wife is entitled to receive from the husband in consideration of the marriage' (Esposito and DeLong-Bas 2001: 23).

2 See Kammergericht (KG) Berlin (Berlin Court of Appeal), 1 January 1993 – FamRZ 1994, 839, 839–40.

3 See Oberlandesgericht [OLG] Oldenburg (Oldenburg Court of Appeal), 7 March 2006 – 12 UF 125/05 – FamRZ 2006, 950; Bundesgerichtshof (BGH) (German Federal Court of Justice), 28 May 2008 – XII ZR 61/06 – FamRZ 2008, 1409.

4 The only ground for divorce is a demonstrable *Zerrüttungsprinzip* – 'an inevitable breakdown of the marriage' (Foster and Sule 2010: 520–21). This doctrine is found in the German Civil Code, which defines a breakdown of marriage as occurring when 'the conjugal community of the spouses no longer exists and it cannot be expected that the spouses restore it' (section 1565 I of the BGB). In principle, the German Civil Code requires that spouses live apart for one year before a divorce is available. However, an earlier divorce may be granted if 'continuation of the marriage would be an unreasonable hardship for the petitioner for reasons that lie in the person of the other spouse' (section 1565 II of the BGB).

5 In cases of mutual consent, where the wife waives the deferred portion of *mahr*, divorce can be finalised outside the court system. However, in most cases the parties will disagree as to the amount and file their respective claims with the *qadi*. Moreover, in some countries such as Egypt, the wife can even obtain a *khul* divorce from the *qadi* without the husband's consent (Mashhour 2005: 583).

6 For an empirical study of norm-generating everyday interactions, see Austin Sarat (1990: 344–45).

7 Although little evidence exists with regard to the frequency with which this bargaining power is used by women, a study issued by the Chief Rabbinate of the state of Israel reports that within divorce proceedings commenced from 2005 to 2007, some 180 women were 'chained' to their husbands and a slightly higher number of men were 'chained' by their wives. In nearly 350 divorce cases that were active as of 2005, 19 per cent of the cases continue to be unresolved because of the man's refusal to grant a *get*, while 20 per cent of the cases showed that women failed to cooperate with the divorce proceedings (Fendel 2007).

8 For example, some participants' husbands went to Israel to argue (successfully) that the women were refusing a *get*, even though the husbands had never even attempted to give a *get* and were in fact refusing to do so:

> Participant # 4:
> Participant: I think until today he doesn't understand why I left him, because he was very hurt about this.
> [...]
> Interviewer: But had he tried to give you the *get*?
> Participant: No! Never, never. [...] He didn't have to get a *get*, he just had to get a permission to remarry. [...] He went to the rabbis in Haifa [Israel]. [...] He didn't say why he doesn't have a *get*, and they accepted it like this, so they permitted him to remarry [...]. He argued that I was refusing to accept the *get*.

Bibliography

Abdal-Rehim, A.-R. (1996) 'The Family and Gender Laws in Egypt During the Ottoman Period', in A. El Azhary Sonbol (ed.) *Women, the Family, and Divorce Laws in Islamic History*, Syracuse, NY: Syracuse University Press.

Abu-Odeh, L. (2004) 'Modernizing Muslim Family Law: The Case of Egypt', *Vanderbilt Journal of Transnational Law*, 37: 1043–146.

Barlas, A. (2002) *'Believing Women' in Islam: Unreading Patriarchal Interpretations of the Qur'an*, Austin: University of Texas Press.

Bodemann, Y.M. (1990) 'The State in the Construction of Ethnicity and Ideological Labor: The Case of German Jewry', *Critical Sociology*, 17: 35–46.

Campbell, A. (2010) 'Bountiful's Plural Marriages', *International Journal of Law in Context*, 6: 343–61.

Cohn, M. (2004) 'Women, Religious Law and Religious Courts in Israel – The Jewish Case', *Retfaerd (Scandinavian Journal of Social Sciences)*, 107: 57–76.

Dorff, E.N. and Rosett, A. (1988) *A Living Tree: The Roots and Growth of Jewish Law*, Albany: State University of New York Press.

Eddy, M. (2006) 'A New Start for Rabbis in Germany', *Philadelphia Inquirer*, 14 September: A12.

El Alami, D. and Hinchcliffe, D. (1996) *Islamic Marriage and Divorce Laws of the Arab World*, The Hague: Kluwer.

Epstein, L.M. (1927) *The Jewish Marriage Contract: A Study of the Status of the Woman in Jewish Law*, Clark, NJ: Lawbook Exchange, 2005.

Esposito, J.L. and DeLong-Bas, N.J. (2001) *Women in Muslim Family Law*, 2nd edn, Syracuse, NY: Syracuse University Press.

Estin, A.L. (2008) 'Unofficial Family Law', *Iowa Law Review*, 94: 449–80.

Fajer, M.A. (1994) 'Authority, Credibility, and Pre-Understanding: A Defense of Outsider Narratives in Legal Scholarship', *Georgetown Law Journal*, 82: 1845–67.

Fendel, H. (2007) 'Rabbinate Stats: 180 Women, 185 Men "Chained" by Spouses', *Israel National News*, 23 August http://www.israelnationalnews.com/News/News.aspx/123472 (accessed 1 October 2013).

Fishbayn, L. (2008) 'Gender, Multiculturalism and Dialogue: The Case of Jewish Divorce', *Canadian Journal of Law and Jurisprudence*, 21: 71–96.

Foster, N. and Sule, S. (2010) *German Legal System and Laws*, 4th edn, Oxford: Oxford University Press.

Foucault, M. (1977) 'The Eye of Power', in M. Foucault, *Power/Knowledge: Selected Interviews and Other Writings 1972–1977*, C. Gordon (ed. and trans.), New York: Pantheon Books, 1980.

Fournier, P. (2010) *Muslim Marriage in Western Courts: Lost in Transplantation*, Farnham: Ashgate.

Graetz, N. (2005) *Unlocking the Garden: A Feminist Jewish Look at the Bible, Midrash and God*, Piscataway, NJ: Gorgias Press.

Green, S. (2005) 'Between Ideology and Pragmatism: The Politics of Dual Nationality in Germany', *International Migration Review*, 39: 921–52.

Haut, I.H. (1983) *Divorce in Jewish Law and Life*, vol V, Brooklyn, NY: Sepher-Hermon Press.

Hawley, C. (2012) 'Young Turks Increasingly Favor Integration and Religion', *Spiegel*

Online, 17 August http://www.spiegel.de/international/germany/survey-turks-in-germany-willing-to-integrate-but-more-religious-a-850607.html (accessed 1 October 2013).

Hussain, J. (2011) *Islam: Its Law and Society*, 3rd edn, Sydney: Federation Press.

Jacobs, L. and De Vries, B. (2007) 'Halakhah', in M. Berenbaum and F. Skolnik (eds) *Encyclopaedia Judaica*, 2nd edn, vol VIII, Detroit, MI: Macmillan.

Kamp, M. (2008) 'Prayer Leader, Counselor, Teacher, Social Worker, and Public Relations Officer – On the Roles and Functions of Imams in Germany', in A. Al-Hamarneh and J. Thielmann (eds) *Islam and Muslims in Germany*, Leiden: Brill.

Kastoryano, R. (2004) 'Religion and Incorporation: Islam in France and Germany', *International Migration Review*, 38: 1234–55.

Kennedy, D. (1998) *A Critique of Adjudication*, Cambridge, MA: Harvard University Press.

—— (2002) 'The International Human Rights Movement: Part of the Problem?', *Harvard Human Rights Journal*, 15: 101–25.

Kleinhans, M.-M. and Macdonald, R.A. (1997) 'What is a *Critical* Legal Pluralism?', *Canadian Journal of Law and Society*, 12(2): 25–46.

Koenig, M. (2005) 'Incorporating Muslim Migrants in Western Nation States – A Comparison of the United Kingdom, France, and Germany', *Journal of International Migration and Integration*, 6: 219–34.

Kollewijn, R.D. (1951) 'Conflicts of Western and Non-Western Law', *International Law Quarterly*, 4: 307–25.

Lerner, H. (2009) 'Entrenching the Status-Quo: Religion and State in Israel's Constitutional Proposals', *Constellations*, 16: 445–61.

Macdonald, R.A. (2002) *Lessons of Everyday Law*, Montreal: McGill-Queen's University Press.

Macfarlane J. (2012) *Islamic Divorce in North America: A Shari'a Path in a Secular Society*, Oxford: Oxford University Press.

Mashhour, A. (2005) 'Islamic Law and Gender Equality – Could There be a Common Ground? A Study of Divorce and Polygamy in Sharia Law and Contemporary Legislation in Tunisia and Egypt', *Human Rights Quarterly*, 27: 562–96.

Mernissi, F. (1985) *Beyond the Veil: Male-Female Dynamics in Modern Muslim Society*, 2nd edn, Bloomington: Indiana University Press.

Mielziner, M. (1987) *The Jewish Law of Marriage and Divorce in Ancient and Modern Times and its Relation to the Law of the State*, Littleton, CO: F.B. Rothman.

Mnookin, R.H. and Kornhauser, L. (1979) 'Bargaining in the Shadow of the Law: The Case of Divorce', *Yale Law Journal*, 88: 950–97.

Moon, R. (ed.) (2008) *Law and Religious Pluralism in Canada*, Vancouver: UBC Press.

Nasir, J.J. (2009) *The Islamic Law of Personal Status*, 3rd edn, Leiden: Brill.

Nichols, J.A. (2007) 'Multi-Tiered Marriage: Ideas and Influences from New York and Louisiana to the International Community', *Vanderbilt Journal of Transnational Law*, 40: 135–96.

—— (ed.) (2012) *Marriage and Divorce in a Multicultural Context, Multi-Tiered Marriage and the Boundaries of Civil Law and Religion*, Cambridge: Cambridge University Press.

Peletz, M.G. (2002) *Islamic Modern: Religious Courts and Cultural Politics in Malaysia*, Princeton, NJ: Princeton University Press.

Popp, M. (2011) 'Parallel Justice: Islamic "Arbitrators" Shadow German law', *Spiegel Online*, 1 September http://www.spiegel.de/international/germany/parallel-justice-islamic-arbitrators-shadow-german-law-a-783361.html (accessed 1 October 2013).

Praagh, S. Van (1996) 'The Chutzpah of Chasidism', *Canadian Journal of Law and Society*, 11(2): 193–215.

Reiss, J. and Broyde, M.J. (2005) 'Prenuptial Agreements in Talmudic, Medieval, and Modern Jewish Thought', in M.J. Broyde and M. Ausubel (eds) *Marriage, Sex, and Family in Judaism*, Lanham, MD: Rowman & Littlefield.

Rittich, K. (2001) 'Who's Afraid of the *Critique of Adjudication*? Tracing the Discourse of Law in Development', *Cardozo Law Review*, 22: 929–45.

Robbers, G. (2006) *An Introduction to German Law*, 4th edn, Baden-Baden: Nomos.

Rohe, M. (2004) 'The Legal Treatment of Muslims in Germany', in R. Aluffi B.-P. and G. Zincone (eds) *The Legal Treatment of Islamic Minorities in Europe*, Leuven: Peeters.

—— (2009) 'Shari'a in a European Context', in R. Grillo and others (eds) *Legal Practice and Cultural Diversity*, Farnham: Ashgate.

Sarat, A. (1990) '"… The Law Is All Over": Power, Resistance and the Legal Consciousness of the Welfare Poor', *Yale Journal of Law and the Humanities*, 2: 343–79.

Sassoon, I. (2011) *The Status of Women in Jewish Tradition*, Cambridge: Cambridge University Press.

Siehr, K. (2005) 'Private International Law', in J. Zekoll and M. Reimann (eds) *Introduction to German Law*, 2nd edn, The Hague: Kluwer.

Turner, B.S. and Arslan, B.Z. (2011) '*Shari'a* and Legal Pluralism in the West', *European Journal of Social Theory*, 14: 139–59.

Weiss, S. (2004) 'Israeli Divorce Law: The Maldistribution of Power, its Abuses, and the "Status" of Jewish Women', in R. Elior (ed.) *Men and Women: Gender, Judaism and Democracy*, Jerusalem: Urim Publications.

Yefet, K.C. (2009) 'Unchaining the *Agunot*: Enlisting the Israeli Constitution in the Service of Women's Marital Freedom', *Yale Journal of Law and Feminism*, 20: 441–503.

Chapter 11

Of friendless and stained men: grafting medieval sanctions onto modern democratic law

Luca Follis

In 1954, 17 jurisdictions in the United States still had the sanction of civil death on their books. The disability which came to the United States under English common law, and which gained its own independent existence after the outlawing of attainder in the constitution, seems to have been beset by translation and transferability problems from the very start. The meaning, origins and material effects of the sanction were argued and debated in American state courts throughout the 19th and 20th centuries. In Britain, civil death came as a consequence of attainder or entry into a religious order and seems to have reached its highpoint in the 15th and 16th centuries (Lander 1961). Yet transported across the Atlantic and grafted on to the statutes of the new democratic states it became a wholly different legal instrument intimately connected to the penal imaginary and the legitimation of state punishment (Smith 2009).

A number of jurisdictions still retain the language of civil death within their criminal and civil law, even if the blanket ban on legal personality that they maintained is now heavily qualified. At the same time, however, the enduring legacy of civil death is that it provided the vocabulary and legitimacy for the rearticulation of modern day legal principles of 'less-eligibility'. Thus, despite the fact that the 19th century formulation of civil death may have been a casualty of the judicial activism of the late 1960s and 1970s and the dismantling of the so-called federal 'hands-off' doctrine, most states maintain rather strict and comprehensive statutory disabilities for convicted felons that touch on everything from access to social welfare programmes, voting rights, employment eligibility, adoption proceedings and educational loans. Taken as a whole, these statutory enactments cover a broader range of those privileges enjoyed by citizens than common law or 19th century civil death could envisage and curtail a convict's capacity for social determination to a dramatic degree (Follis 2013).

This chapter considers the transmission, transfer or (if we bend the meaning of the term slightly) translation of civil death across the Atlantic and the various paradoxes and indeterminacies that its interpretation seeded in American criminal law. To this end, I will first briefly describe how early modern and medieval common law understood the disability and the institutional context that framed its application. I will then move to a discussion of the cultural and legal foundations of legal death in New York, the first state to frame the disability as a statute. Drawing on Robert Cover's (1983, 1986, 1986a) theory of legal interpretation, I will analyse how the gap between the common-law understanding of civil death and its austere statutory construction was negotiated in the case law of New York, Alabama and Oklahoma. I will focus on Cover's suggestion that legal meaning emerges in a back and forth between normative interpretations on the one hand (the work of judges proper) and the field and forms of action that flow from the decision on the other. For Cover, the intelligibility of interpretations relies on this 'dialogical' process largely because judicial decisions take effect in a field saturated with violence and violence requires explanation and justification.

In what follows I argue that Cover's model of interpretation helps us grapple with the myriad of equivocations and contradictions inherent in the case law of civil death. The blanket deprivations contained in the sanction, divorced as they were from the institutional and cultural field of action within which they gained meaning, significantly problematised the task of recovering, or discovering, the scope and meaning of civil death – as well as the sort of violence that it might inadvertently authorise. As we will see, however, most judges sought to pare down its most debilitating effects, creatively engaging the 'fogs and fictions' of medieval jurisprudence to challenge the epistemic foundations upon which state statutes were based. They did so by recovering the exceptions and qualifications that might make the contradictions inherent in legal death sustainable and intelligible under democratic law.

Attainder and its ghost

One way to understand civil death is to treat it as an umbrella category for a broad array of disabilities that bracket or annihilate a criminal's legal personality. In this sense, as a legal expression of the principle of criminal 'less eligibility' (Rusche and Kirchheimer 1939: 152–57), it has proven a dogged mainstay of political and social organisation. A form of civil death (*atimia*) was known to ancient and classical Greece and Roman law provided for at least three separate varieties of criminal dispossession (*capitis deminutio, sacratio* and *infamia*). Early modern and medieval Europe also deployed legal death in the form of outlawry and infamy (von Bar 1916; Bennett 1930; Damaška 1968; Manville 1980; Agamben 1995).

Civil death in England typically flowed from the condition of outlawry or from attainder. Before the Norman Conquest, the outlaw occupied a liminal place at the intersection of the not yet mutually exclusive spheres of private and public justice (Goebel 1976). As author of a flagrant offence the outlaw was deemed the 'friendless man' and considered as dangerous as a wild animal (that is, he could be killed with impunity): '[A]n outlawed felon was said to have *caput lupinum* [wolf's head], and might be knocked on the head like a wolf, by any one that should meet him; because, having renounced all law, he was to be dealt with as in a state of nature' (Blackstone 1769: 319–20).

The right to kill the outlaw persisted until early in the reign of Edward III when it was restricted to a sheriff in possession of a lawful warrant (Palgrave 1832: 210–12). During this time the nature of outlawry also shifted and took a more procedural turn. Outlawry became either a mode of compelling the appearance of an absconder (and hence a mechanism for dealing with his estate/inheritance should he fail to appear) or a species of attainder (Coke 1628: Book 2 ch 2 at 197).

Attainder was the primary vehicle for the imposition of civil death; it applied to all those convicted of a capital crime or treason and had three consequences: forfeiture of property and office, corruption of blood and civil death. Corruption of blood, perhaps the most potent penalty associated with attainder, declared the condemned's blood stained and blocked the capacity of heirs to inherit through him. If the convict was of noble or gentle birth before the attainder, his direct lineage was made base and ignoble. The bloodstain poisoned the family vine, rupturing relationships of homage and villeinage, and thrusting its victims from the hierarchy of mutual obligations and pledges that animated feudal life (Smith 1870).

However, given that the penalty for treason and felony was death, attainder and civil death appear to have largely been mechanisms for managing the earthly affairs of the dead or the soon to be dead. In those cases where the criminal was not put to death (including when someone claimed benefit of clergy, entered a religious order and became legally dead) civil death usually meant a de facto sentence of banishment (in which case the convicted man left his crimes behind) or internal exile.

Additionally, attainder was often used as a political weapon by monarchs against insurrectionists or enemies and might result in death, pardon or a reversal of the attainder (Bellamy 1979, 1984). Thus the matter was quite complex at common law and to emerge biologically alive and legally dead usually signalled an act of clemency or pardon. It might be read as the enduring mark of disgrace for having survived the ordeal of justice. Finally, it appears that the term civil death itself seems to have served primarily descriptive purposes – that is, as an evocative term for depicting the condition of one attainted, outlawed or entering a religious order – and does not appear to have been a penalty proper.

The emergence of civil death

The appearance of civil death in the legal codes of the newly independent American states can be traced to New York State and three 18th century acts of the New York legislature. On 21 February 1788 the legislature declared that all felonies would be punishable by death and that the estate (real and personal) of the felon would thereafter be forfeited to the state. Eight years later, on 26 March 1796, the legislature changed direction by substituting life imprisonment as punishment for felonies in all cases except treason, murder and stealing from a church. The Act further mandated that: 'no conviction of attainder of any person for any offense, except treason, should thereafter work a forfeiture of goods, chattels, lands, tenements, or hereditaments, or any right therein' (*Platner v Sherwood* 1822: 122).[1] In his address to the legislature in 1798, Governor Jay noted that the body had failed to clarify how the introduction of the prison as the main punishment for felony (as opposed to death) changed the status of convicts. He suggested the legislature ought: 'either expressly to declare, or impliedly to decide, whether in any and what respects the convictions in those cases extinguish or affect civil rights and relations' (New York State 1825: 55). The governor's prompting was followed on 29 March 1799 by the following statute:

> [T]hat in all cases where any person, hereafter, may be duly convicted and attainted of any felony, hereafter to be committed, or of aiding, &c., and shall be adjudged to imprisonment for life in the state prison, such person shall be deemed and taken to be civilly dead to all intents and purposes.
>
> (*Platner v Sherwood* 1822: 121)

The language chosen by the legislature to frame the disability was hardly accidental. It drew upon the spirit and logic of attainder, a penalty that held a unique place in the state's history. Between the Declaration of Independence and the Treaty of Peace in 1783, the colonial, provincial or state legislature produced approximately 60 statutory enactments concerning attainder. Between 1783 and 1813, the state legislature published an additional 48 pieces of legislation to normalise the effects of its long confiscation policy. The 1788 Act was one of the final statutory enactments of attainder by the legislature before its repeal of all state laws inconsistent with the Treaty of Peace with Great Britain. Two days after the Act, the Office of Commissioner of Forfeitures, a powerful committee constituted in 1776 for 'inquiring into, detecting and defeating all conspiracies which may be formed in this state against the liberties of America' was abolished (Reppy 1948: 16–17, 1949: 248–49).

New York's prolific enactment of attainder statutes was in keeping with the manner in which attainder had been deployed by English monarchs throughout the middle ages: it represented a political weapon and efficient mechanism of economic and land dispossession levelled against enemies or insurrectionists. All attainder acts previous to the 1788 law referred to crimes committed during the War of Independence since the New York constitution, passed in 1777, expressly prohibited attainder for crimes not committed during war. Thus, while the 1788 Act referenced the same normative universe as attainder, and to a large extent evoked its elements in slightly altered form, it was a relatively new variant (that is, it only worked for forfeiture and did not involve the loss of civil rights or the formal status of being attainted). The Act offered clear legal continuity between revolutionary/martial violence and the birth of modern criminal law, vesting the authority for both in the state's prerogative to make war on its enemies.

When, in 1796, the legislature reformed the penal code to make all felonies (except three) punishable by life imprisonment, it again drew upon the language of attainder to clarify that forfeiture, as set out in the state constitution and the

US constitution, was abolished. However, as Jay noted, the statute's wording implied that there might be acts of attainder that did not work for forfeiture or corruption of blood but would still have some effect. The 1799 Act seems designed to clarify precisely what this new disability would entail. In this sense it represented a hybrid of colonial, revolutionary and republican law. The statute remained couched in the language, symbols and metaphors of common law and has subsequently been interpreted by some courts as a mere declaration of the continued validity of common law civil death.

However, it certainly was not the straightforward and unproblematic act of transmission that the above genealogy would seem to indicate. First, life imprisonment was a penalty unknown at common law and, as we have seen, civil death was never a stand-alone punishment (it was descriptive of the civil state of those attainted, banished or declared infamous). Secondly, the inclusion of the wording 'for all intents and purposes' seemingly extended the effects of civil death beyond the disabilities that attended the common law status since in the latter there was an intricate web of exceptions (eg one could be sued or prosecuted and thus defend oneself) and additional sanctions (that is, corruption of blood and forfeiture), which potentially qualified complete legal annihilation. Thirdly, it was not merely the institutional form of punishment that had changed but also the cultural and social context within which punishment was embedded (eg Americans took an expansive view of equality, liberty and property). This was a shift that, as I argue in the next section, would figure prominently in the question of how civil death should be interpreted.

Incidents of law

Robert Cover (1983, 1986a) claimed that judicial interpretation is never a 'free' (in the sense of strictly hermeneutic) enterprise; it is always addressed to a field of institutional action and provides the mandate for agents arranged within this field to act upon, respond to or implement a particular decision. There is a direct link between acts of interpretation and the actions that flow from them, making legal decision-making a structurally embedded practice. How agents will act forms one of the parameters for interpretation and helps shape its context. Judges take active cognisance of how their opinions will probably be put into practice, primarily because of the enormous stakes involved in what they do: 'legal interpretation is either played out on the field of pain and death or it is something less (or more) than law' (Cover 1986a: 1607). Interpretations provide justifications for violence that has occurred or will occur, as well as occasioning the imposition of violence on others.[2]

'On one level judges may appear to be and may in fact be, offering their understanding of the normative world to their intended audience. But on another level they are engaging a violent mechanism through which a substantial part of their audience loses its capacity to think autonomously' (ibid: 1615). Cover's understanding of violence is broader than the imposition (or the threat) of physical force and admits the epistemic violence of legal interpretations alongside the many routine instances of dispossession and pain that flow from judicial decisions (Beckett 2011).

When judges interpret law, they confront two interrelated problems. The first concerns the strict hermeneutical 'meaning' and reading of the legal text. The second is related to the question of implementation (that is, how to ensure that social agents will act in line with and under the sign of their interpretations) (Sarat and Kearns 1995: 235). The former is tied to the social organisation of roles, in that judges are conscious of the wider judicial community and the fact that any work of interpretation must be recognisable by one's colleagues as a reasonable or legitimate justification for violence. However, while this normative community is one part of the audience to which interpretations are addressed, the main audience consists of those that will carry out the judge's orders.

Decrees become deeds through a system of social organisation and taken-for-granted cooperation. For example, in the act of criminal sentencing a judicial order sets in motion a machinery of violence which: (i) incapacitates the offender; (ii) imposes and carries out a sentence of imprisonment; and (iii) protects the judges and other elements of the criminal justice system from reprisals (Cover 1986a: 1618–19). That machinery of violence is made of gaolers, police officers, court officers and prison guards, all of whom routinely overcome their cultural and moral inhibitions against doing violence to step up to a judge's orders.

This division of labour allows for a relative stability in the operation of legal violence in as much as judges can authorise it, safe in the knowledge that in fact they will not have to physically carry it out (thus overcoming their own cultural and moral inhibitions) while the agents of violence can shift the moral responsibility for the acts they commit to the judges that authorised them. However, this means that judges carry the grand share of moral responsibility for the act and it also puts emphasis on the necessity of controlling those that will carry it out (Sarat and Kearns 1995: 237). As Austin Sarat and Thomas Kearns (ibid: 239) note:

> Legal interpretation, in this account, is deeply and profoundly shaped by an awareness of the contingent character of implementation; meaning is altered and transformed in order to ensure that action follows utterance. An excellent reading of a legal text is one that garners not just the praise of critics, but also triggers necessary responses in those charged with carrying out the acts of violence it authorizes.

The problem with such a situation is that it brings into relief the tension between producing the most coherent, satisfactory legal reading on the one hand and producing a reading that will be efficient and pragmatic enough to generate the most responsive act on the other hand. In choosing between these competing modes of framing the legitimacy of a violent act, law displays and reinforces its *jurispathic* tendencies.[3] That is to say, there is a sense in which generating the kind of strong justifications required to transform a decree into violence is itself an act of violence that prioritises the 'objectivity' of its own narrative: 'legal interpretation seeks to show not only that its decisions are technically sustainable, but that they are worthy of being lived in and through the pain that is done in their name' (ibid: 246).

The link between interpretation and action necessarily involves the transformation of thought by action: if the conditions of action appear front and centre (when weighing the available matrix of narratives that could justify an act) narratives that tend to correspond to conditions necessary for the social organisation of violence will be prioritised. But what happens to meaning if judges are unsure what actions or what violence will flow from their interpretation? As we will see, the problem of interpreting the doctrine of civil death posed precisely this question.

The legislature's 1799 Act ruptured the interpretive scaffolding that could render the violence implied in civil death meaningful and intelligible. Beyond New York, in the numerous states that transcribed its 1799 statute into their penal codes, civil death found firm legislative footing because of its intuitive sense – at once bolstered by the austere depersonalisation of 19th century penal regimes and the ambiguous relationship between English common law and American state law. However, uncoupled from the common law catalogue of deprivations, punishments and mitigated statuses – as well as the complex social relationships and institutional interdependencies that supported it, judges found themselves trying to divine precisely what sort of violence their interpretations would or could authorise. How deep into the social body did the convict's now severed social relationships, contractual obligations and debts penetrate and what sort of justice would be possible for those still tethered to the legally dead? Besides the question of physical force, a zero-sum ban on legal personality potentially deregulated a broad catalogue of symbolic and structural violence that might be levelled against the convict. Thus, rather than an authorisation of or justification for force, the violence of civil death involved a removal of the convict and his agency from law's purview.

Avery v Everett, decided in 1888, illustrates well the tension between interpretation and action, meaning and violence.[4] The case concerned the inheritance of John H. Southwick, who had left his estate to his wife for life and upon her marriage or death, willed the inheritance flow to his son Charles. She died shortly after her husband and Charles should ordinarily have inherited the family estate. However, in the interim, Charles had been convicted of second-degree murder, sentenced to state prison and was under the disability of civil death. Augustus, Southwick's nephew and next in line, filed a motion to eject Charles's claim to the estate and asked the court to recognise his interest in the property. On the face of it, *Avery* should have been a straightforward case: Charles had no claim. However, despite a century's worth of arbitration, the meaning of civil death remained unclear.

For example, *Graham v Adams* (1801) and *O'Brien v Hagan* (1853) agreed that civil death terminated any court action to which a convict was party.[5] Similarly, the court in *In re Deming* (1810) found that, despite a pardon, the sale of Deming's estate and the interest his heirs had accrued from it – as well as the remarriage of his wife – were unalterable consequences of his civil death.[6] Yet, by 1860, Judge Balcom was writing in *Freeman v Frank* that a defendant's civil death did not render him immune from a rape suit.[7]

Bowles v Haberman (1884), argued only four years before *Avery*, gives a sense of just how much remained equivocal.[8] Bowles, the plaintiff in that case, had received a favourable judgment against Haberman and the latter's appeal was pending at the time Bowles was convicted of felony. When Haberman moved to have Bowles's rights suspended because of his civil death and the appeal hearing stayed during his imprisonment, the court denied the motion, arguing that regardless of his legal death, Bowles retained the right to defend himself from suits against him. At the same time, however, Judge Earl's opinion intimated that significant undecided questions potentially qualified the efficacy of this right of legal self-defence and that, although theoretically a right existed, substantively it might not be actionable: '[i]t may be that he cannot move the argument of the appeal, that his rights are so far suspended that he cannot take any steps in the action or upon the appeal' (*Bowles v Haberman* 1884: 250).

Avery is distinctive because it sets aside much of the above case law and focuses exclusively on the point of transmission or translation between the common law and the New York statute. To this end, the court's opinion plumbs Chitty, Blackstone and Coke to recover the meaning and interpretation of legal death, resituating the breadcrumb of legal continuity primarily in English rather than domestic sources. As we have seen, the 1799 construction of civil death stated that a sentence of imprisonment for life rendered a convict civilly dead 'for all intents and purposes'; when the statute was re-enacted in 1813, the legislature omitted the above phrase. The court in *Avery* (Andrews J) focused on what difference, if any, this shift in statutory construction had on the material effects of legal death.

Was the 1799 construction merely declaratory of the common law status or did it somehow go beyond the disabilities available in England? Alternatively, how did the omission of this phrase shift the terms of the sanction? Did the absence of 'for all intents and purposes' indicate that for some intents or purposes convicts might be considered legally alive? In the absence of any legislative description or notes of what rights were suspended, the 1799 and 1813 enactments represented a sort of cipher to divine the contours of legal death and the type of violence it could authorise. The court relied heavily on two opinions, *Troup v Wood* (1820) and *Platner v Sherwood* (1822), which specifically considered the shift in meaning occasioned by the phrase 'for all intents and purposes'. Both cases concerned property owned by Henry Platner, a convicted forger sentenced to life imprisonment three months after the legislature's 1799 Act.

In *Troup v Wood* (1820), Platner's representative filed a bill to set aside the sale of Platner's land at auction to settle a judgment debt (against him) in favour of Abraham Bachman.[9] Chancellor Kent invalidated the sale of land on a number of grounds, including that the debt had been paid in 1798 and that the procurement and seizure of the land for sale (as well as its sale) were fraudulent. In passing Kent also noted that, regardless of the fraud, the sale would be invalid because the *scire facias* used by the defendant to restore the judgment debt against Platner was addressed to him and, given his civil death at the time, should have been addressed to his representatives. Kent's interpretation was that the legislature's Act of March 1799 was merely declaratory of the continuance of common law civil death:

> The party was incapacitated, forever, from discharging any of the civil relations equally as if transported, or banished for life, or become a monk professed [...]. And we perceive, that the Legislature [...] seemed to be aware that the other common law consequences of the conviction would still follow, for they declared by express provision, that no such conviction should work forfeiture of property, real or personal.
>
> (*Troup v Wood* 1820: 248)

Platner v Sherwood was brought by Platner himself (pardoned by Governor Lewis in 1806) to set aside sales of other land made while he was imprisoned under the same judgment and execution as the previous case. Sherwood (following the ruling in *Troup* in which he was a co-defendant) responded with a demurrer to the bill, arguing that Platner's civil death legally divested him of his estate and thus rendered Platner incapable of compelling him to answer the bill. Kent ruled that Platner's crime occurred prior to the legislature's 1799 enactment and thus fell outside the disability's scope, although he also took the opportunity to revise his earlier opinion.

Relying on Lord Coke's *Institutes* and the few English common law cases that dealt with the inheritance of the assets of civilly dead convicts, Kent distinguished between the strictest variants of civil death at common law (abjuration and banishment) and those that flowed from attainder or profession. In discussing the latter instance (that is, the effects of joining a religious order), he noted that the religious entrant became dead in law, an executor administered his estate in the same fashion as if he were factually dead and his land was inherited by his heirs (*Platner v Sherwood* 1822: 129). However, even in this relatively straightforward case, civil death provided glimmers of an afterlife: the new recruit's wife did not inherit until his natural death and he could still sue through a proxy.

Throughout, the opinion emphasised the myriad of exceptions and qualifications that limited the extent to which one legally dead might be considered the same as one dead in fact. However, according to Kent, while this was the case in England and before the revolution, the 1799 statute created a new rule and was meant to extend the effects of civil death well beyond what was understood at common law. This was the interpretive anchor for the court's opinion in *Avery*. Andrews J argued, somewhat disingenuously given Kent's point above, that the

1813 legislative revision (which omitted the troublesome phrase) represented a signal from the legislature that it intended the disability to revert to its common law origins. He then deployed the common law strategically and creatively to recover the 'meaning' of civil death and to place the forms of violence it indirectly authorised within an institutional (and hence predictable) form still answerable to law (*Avery v Everett* 1888: 332).

The fact that *Platner* and *Troup* figure so prominently in Andrews's opinion, despite the fact that he clearly disagreed with the Chancellor's interpretation, is important. In the background of the opinion is the fraud perpetrated against Platner, itself an evocative example of the kind of criminal opportunism a complete ban on legal personality might engender and protect. It involved land in five different counties worth US$136,000.00 that was seized (with the collusion of the sheriff) and sold to the defendant for less than US$800.00 to pay a debt of US$773.00 that had already been paid in 1798. By the time *Troup* was decided in 1820, Kent estimated the value of the land to have accrued to some US$409,000.00.

It is clear that Platner's situation represented an important touchstone for the court when it declared: 'the inference seems almost irresistible that the doctrine that civil death, consequent upon a life sentence, divests the criminal of his estate, has no foundation in our law' (*Avery v Everett* 1888: 333). Despite this, the court went on: 'the disabilities flowing from the situation of *civiliter mortuus* have a wide scope, without including this incident' (ibid). In articulating here the full range of disabilities and negative rights a convict retained, the Andrews court defined the parameters of legitimate and legal violence under civil death and imposed limited footholds for a convict's legal self-protection:

> The statute [...] assumes that a life sentence of the husband, ipso facto, dissolves his marriage. The convict cannot sue, although he may be sued, and his property is answerable to his creditors. But he may defend an action brought against him. He cannot enter into executor contracts and call in aid the courts to enforce them, but he may transfer his property by will or deed. His political rights are taken from him, his wife and children owe him no fealty or obedience.
>
> (*Avery v Everett* 1888: 332)

Yet the revisionist line contained in the majority opinion was recognised and critiqued in the lone dissent. According to Earl J, both the 1799 statute and its 1813 amendment were attempts by the legislature to simplify the law by removing common law confusion and uncertainty and to bring it into 'harmony with our social organization and governmental system' (*Avery v Everett* 1888: 335). To that end, it had stipulated that the life convict no longer 'possessed any rights growing out of organised society or depending upon or given by law. As to all such rights, he was, in law, dead and buried' (*Avery v Everett* 1888: 334).

The 1813 revision retained the implications of the 1799 statute in more concise and plain language, rather than signalling a return to the 'archaisms, uncertainties and confusion' of common law (*Avery v Everett* 1888: 336). After all, he reasoned, why, under any wise system of laws, should a convict retain his title to property when he cannot protect it by action, recover it through proceedings or draw upon it for enjoyment? Why shouldn't the property simply descend to his heirs or next of kin? The majority had emptied the statute of its core meaning and called forth an atavistic spectre, a creature of law neither fully dead nor wholly alive.

The gap between Earl J's dissent and the majority opinion lays bare the epistemic stakes involved. According to Earl J's reading, a blanket ban on legal personality is not only preferable from a normative and hermeneutic standpoint but it is also an efficient and technically sustainable blueprint for institutional action (or inaction). Earl J's critique charges the majority with an act of interpretive violence (that is, setting aside a clear rule from the legislature and a number of cases) in an attempt to render predictable the lawful violence that might flow from civil death and to limit the capacity for lawless violence that the disability could engender. We will see a similar dynamic at work in the interpretation of civil death in Alabama in the next section.

The rights of the dead

Holmes v King (1927), decided before the Supreme Court of Alabama, similarly sought to recover the practical meaning of 'civil death' and its impact on a convict's property.[10] The Alabama statute provided that a convict sentenced to life imprisonment was civilly dead but, unlike in New York, also stipulated that such convict may 'at any time within six months after his sentence, make and publish his last will and testament'. At issue was what happened to a convict's property if he failed to produce a will during this period.

Judge Bouldin, writing the court's opinion, compared the wide variance in the material effects of civil death in New York (reviewing *Troup*, *Platner* and *Avery*), California, Kansas and Missouri. While the California statute declared that a civilly dead convict was to be treated as 'dead in fact' in terms of property, a later unrelated statute permitted a convict to 'make or acknowledge a sale or conveyance of property' (*In re Nerac* 1868; *Coffee v Haynes* 1899).[11] In Missouri and Kansas, on the other hand, a convict under the disability was treated as truly deceased and the state provided for the administration and distribution of his estate as in the case of a natural death (*Williams v Shackleford* 1889 and *Gray v Stewart* 1904).[12]

Given the wide variability in the state cases the court, following the lead in *Avery*, returned to the common law to divine which variant of civil death underpinned the Alabama statute. It distinguished between the literal common law understanding of civil death (that is, in cases of religion, banishment or abjuration) and the more limited sense of attainder for treason or felony. While in the former case civil death meant that an individual's estate passed on to his heirs as if he was dead in fact, in the latter case civil death also brought corruption of blood (which forbade transmission to heirs and forfeited estates to the crown). However, before the corruption could take effect and the estates could be forfeited, a separate proceeding (known as 'office found') was required to establish the attainder and to make the king's right to the land a matter for the solemn record. In the interim, the title remained in the convict's name, although his civil death still gave him no standing to pursue a legal action or to enforce a contract.

Commenting on the breadth of the disability and specifically citing the influence of the 'leading case' of *Avery v Everett*, Bouldin J argued that the legislature had not intended civil death to have the same effect as before 'office found' – that is, that the convict retain the title but be unable effectively to take any legally valid action upon it. Such an interpretation was inconsistent with the core assumptions of property and contract law:

> The strange anomaly of a contract without mutuality, the subjection to suit without power to bring one, so strip property of its incidents as to virtually cast it adrift [...]. We are impressed such a situation was never in the contemplation of our lawmakers.
>
> (*Holmes v King* 1927: 415)

However, despite its nod to *Avery*, the sort of violence contemplated above seems altogether different from that which appears in the New York case. In the former, the Andrews court was clearly concerned with hemming in the potential actions of others (both state agents and fellow citizens) and clearly articulating the degree of disadvantage and exclusion of the criminal other. Bouldin J's opinion, on the other hand, is hardly revisionist. The violence it contemplates and which figures prominently in his reading of civil death refers to the unintended consequences that such a doctrine could imply for the institution of property and the internal coherence of law: '[I]t seems anomalous to think of a person making a will after he is dead. But the idea of "civil death" is a creature of law, and may have such incidents as law declares. Such was the case at common law' (ibid).

If *Avery* leveraged the common law to switch the epistemic foundations of civil death away from the legislature's blanket ban, *Holmes* is concerned with the broader epistemic rupture that choosing the wrong variant of civil death might unleash into the arbitration of contracts and property.[13] Accordingly, the court decreed that civil death in Alabama had the same effect as entering religious orders or banishment at common law: the convict's estate was to be administered like that of a dead man (it passed on to his heirs) but his will remained ambulatory for six months after sentencing. Besides recovery of the right to dispose of property, *Holmes* effectively reified civil death in Alabama as a complete death-in-law.

Bouldin J's interpretation in *Holmes* was upheld in *Vann v Rogers* (1932), where civil death carried the same effect as death with respect to the tolling of statutes of limitation and in *Wright v Price* (1933), where a father was found to have no voice in an adoption proceeding because of his civil death.[14] Thus, until 1941, when *Breed v Atlanta, B. & C. Railroad Co.* was decided, Alabama upheld a complete ban on legal personality except during the narrow six-month property window.[15] The court, however, took a different interpretive route in *Breed*, a case in which the potential for unregulated violence implied in civil death statutes was made painfully explicit. Was a civilly dead convict entitled to protection under an Alabama statute designed to prevent homicide?

The plaintiff, administrator of the deceased Joe Breed, brought a wrongful death suit against Atlanta B. & C. Railroad Co. As Breed was crossing a section of rail track he had been hit by the company's train and died as a result of his injuries. The plaintiff claimed that his death had been caused by the 'wanton, willful or intentional conduct' of the railroad's agents. The case was reminiscent of an earlier suit for damages by a life convict against a railroad company (*Quick v Western Railway of Alabama* 1922).[16] In that case, John Quick sought damages from Western Railroad for running him over while he crossed the track. The same court denied the claim on the grounds that a civilly dead convict was under disability to sue. *Breed*, in contrast, represented a dramatic about-face; the court embarked on a lengthy consideration of civil and natural rights. While the former could be abrogated by law (and were in the case of civil death), natural rights, such as the right to life, were inalienable: 'If he has the natural right to life, by what process of reasoning should the law to prevent homicides not shield him by wrongful act as any other human being?' (*Breed v Atlanta, B. & C. Railroad Co.* 1941: 647).

If the previous case law had emphasised the primacy of internal coherence over and against the law's withdrawal from managing the problem of violence in legal death, *Breed* brought this question powerfully to the fore. If civil death even muted convict claims to *ex post facto* justice, then the disability might as well provide a blanket invitation to extra-legal violence. Not surprisingly, however, the opinion in *Breed* was followed by a forceful dissent by Chief Justice Gardner.

According to Gardner CJ's reading, the homicide prevention statute in question specified that a personal representative gained a right of action only if an intestate could have maintained an action for the same act if it had failed to produce death. In this regard, the same court had ruled in *Quick* – a case which presented exactly this scenario – that a life convict was under disability to sue and could not maintain such an action; this rule, as we have seen, had been reaffirmed rather forcefully in *Holmes* a few years later.

Secondly, as Gardner CJ intimated, the statute was enacted in 1872. Since then, Alabama had been leasing most of its state prisoners to private contractors (primarily in the mining, lumber and railroad industries) and in addition to the high death tolls involved (in some years deaths in these camps approached 40 per cent) the convict lease routinely generated enduring physical disabilities.[17] What standing did the claims of these biologically alive but physically maimed convicts have? Gardner CJ, much like Earl J in *Avery*, charged his colleagues with a brand of epistemic violence (that is, injecting enduring inconsistency and contradiction at the core of civil death) in favour of paring down the disability's immanent violence:

> The opinion speaks of the natural right to life [...] [b]ut a life convict also has the natural right not to be injured, not to be made to suffer the loss of eyesight or his limbs or be made an invalid the remainder of his days [...]. And yet, under our 'civil death' statute confessedly he could recover nothing [...]. It is illogical to say that an injured life convict, maimed and suffering, can have no recovery so long as there remains a flicker of life but that the moment the flame goes out and life is extinct, there suddenly arises a cause of action in the administrator to recover damages for the very wrong, a redress of which was denied the convict while yet in life. No such result was intended.
>
> (*Breed v Atlanta, B. & C. Railroad Co.* 1941: 653)

Law, interpretation and death

Most civil death statutes followed New York's formulation: a blanket ban on civil rights without any clear elaboration of what this specifically did or did not entail. Read literally, as Gardner CJ and Earl J maintained they should be, these statutes efficiently atomised a convict's legal personality and would have potentially far-reaching effects as social relationships became more complex and as criminal justice reforms transformed the nature of imprisonment (eg the introduction of parole systems). In interpreting the statutes, the courts were generally faced with a choice between two paths of violence: fidelity to the legislatorial wording and hence withdrawing the capacity of law to arbitrate and manage the violence done to the convict *or* rupturing the hegemony of the legislature's ban by introducing alternative readings of the statute's epistemic foundations.

Not all alternative readings relied upon the common law as a normative touchstone, however. In Oklahoma, the Supreme Court built its interpretation of civil death on the basic incompatibility between American democracy and medieval jurisprudence. In *Byers v Sun Savings Bank* (1914), a convict had executed a note and mortgage while incarcerated as a way to pay his attorney fees.[18] When his creditors sought to foreclose, the convict replied that his civil death made him incapable of contracting and hence the mortgage and note were invalid. In writing the court's opinion Judge Harrison noted that, although the language of most state civil death statutes would seem to 'divest a citizen of all rights whatsoever and render him absolutely *civiliter mortuus*', the legal principles underpinning legal death brought the 'fogs and fictions' of feudal jurisprudence into modern statutes without recognising 'the effect of its literal significance or the extent of its infringement upon the spirit of our system of government' (*Byers v Sun Savings Bank* 1914: 732).

The court's opinion engaged in a lengthy discussion of the difference between civil, natural and political rights and emphasised that civil death statutes were out of step with the 'spirit of our fundamental laws' (ibid: 732). It then pointed out that state statutes still made it possible for a felon to be sued for divorce or prosecuted for a crime committed after conviction. Moreover, in no state was the fundamental principle of *habeas corpus* suspended by civil death, indicating that certain central natural rights (eg life and self-preservation) fell outside the statute's scope. But, clearly, even to enforce these rather limited rights, the court reasoned, the convict must have to be able to contract with an attorney and thus to acquire and dispose of his personal property to pay the attorney fees. Besides recovering a convict's right to contract, Harrison J's opinion also potentially opened the door to further rights.

Grooms et al v Thomas (1923) went even further: a convict serving a life sentence for murder inherited real estate from his sister and conveyed the title to third parties.[19] The conveyance was challenged by the sister's other heirs, who argued Grooms was incapable of inheriting the property and the title should go to them (the deceased's next of kin). Following the Court's approach in *Byers*, Judge Stephenson argued that what the plaintiffs sought amounted to forfeiture or corruption of blood; both penalties were expressly prohibited by the state and federal constitutions and had been recently abolished in England (33 and 34 Vict c 23). In a forceful rewriting of the state's civil death provisions, the court decided that a convict may 'convey the title to real property and inherit title to property as freely and fully as if he had not been convicted and imprisoned' (*Grooms et al v Thomas* 1923: 89).

The above Oklahoma cases present yet another understanding of the violence embedded and prefigured in judicial interpretations of civil death. In Henderson and Stephenson JJ's opinions, the very notion and practice of civil death is in open contradiction with the core principles of American democracy. The violence of law's withdrawal is broadly conceived, experienced by both convict and citizen and of a political significance that transcends the particulars of the two cases. Indeed, it is precisely because the harm generated by the doctrine is so widely distributed that the Oklahoma courts are in a position to effectively critique and subvert the common law foundations of the disability.

It may seem remarkable that more courts did not take a similar *jurispathic* direction and that most chose to find exceptions and qualifications to a ban on legal personality in medieval jurisprudence, rather than building their critiques on the clear normative and practical incongruence between legal death and democratic law. This is part and parcel of the doctrine's indeterminacy and instability. Civil death was clearly incompatible with American conceptions of property, liberty and equality. At the same time, however, the concept fit seamlessly within the imaginary of harsh justice and punishment maintained by most state penal regimes and the social organisation of violence that thrived therein.

No judge ever sentenced a convict to legal death; it appears like a ghost, of its own volition and as a symbolic counterpart to the authorised violence pregnant in a judge's criminal sentence. It is precisely this aspect of the doctrine (as a kind of quasi-autonomous machinery of violence and dispossession) that posed so many problems for its judicial legitimation. If action shapes interpretation, legitimate interpretations will be those that balance a clear rationale for action with established principles and criteria.

Civil death presented the courts with potentially unrestricted violence, perpetrated by actors whose actions could not be legitimated from within its interpretive framework (since they were not authorised as such) and whose effects reached well beyond the convict's legal demise. Thus, the jurisprudence of civil death also brings us to a broader point regarding law's relationship with and appreciation of violence. Despite a regular engagement with the machinery of death and force, law has difficulty recognising and reckoning with the kind of non-corporeal violence that flows not from a judicial decision but from its routine operation.

Notes

1 *Platner v Sherwood*, 6 Johns. Ch. 118 (1822).
2 For the purposes of this discussion I will bracket the question of whether this relationship is a quintessential attribute of criminal law or, as Cover maintained, it is true of law in general (in support of the latter view see, eg Benjamin 1921; Derrida 1990).
3 Robert Cover used the term 'jurispathic' to convey something similar to epistemic violence. That is the tendency of state law to represent itself as unitary and the sole source of right, in the process killing off other normative orders (Cover 1983: 40; Beckett 2011: 4).
4 *Avery v Everett*, 110 NY 317 (1888).
5 *Graham v Adams*, 2 Johns. 408 (1801); *O'Brien v Hagan*, 1 Duer, SCR, 664 (1853).
6 *In re Deming*, 10 Johns. 232 (1813).
7 *Freeman v Frank*, 10 Abb. Pr. 370 (1860).
8 *Bowles v Haberman*, 95 NY 246 (1884).
9 *Troup v Wood*, 4 Johns. Ch. 249 (1820).
10 *Holmes v King*, 216 Ala. 412 (1927).
11 *In re Nerac*, 35 Cal. 392 (1868); *Coffee v Haynes*, 124 Cal. 561 (1899).
12 *Williams v Shackleford*, 97 Mo. 322 (1889); *Gray v Stewart*, 70 Kan. 429 (1904).
13 For example, if the legislature had emphasised the more limited version (attainder), it would have generated an untenable situation where, in the absence of a will, the estate would have remained untouchable for the remainder of a convict's natural life.
14 *Vann v Rogers*, 225 Ala. 186 (1932); *Wright v Price*, 226 Ala. 468 (1933).
15 *Breed v Atlanta, B. & C. Railroad Co.*, 241 Ala. 640 (1941).
16 *Quick v Western Railway of Alabama*, 207 Ala. 376 (1922).
17 Alabama's railroads were deeply involved in the state's convict lease system. The first leasing contract calling for 100 Black convicts to work on the Georgia and Alabama Railroad for one year for the sum of US$2500.00 was awarded in 1868. Until the state abolished the convict lease in 1928 (carrying the dubious distinction of being the last Southern state to do so), most of its able-bodied convicts were leased to private corporations mining coal, felling lumber and laying railroad track in penal encampments across the state. Conditions were grim, inhuman and

mortality rates were staggering (Oshinsky 1996: 76–81; Lichtenstein 1996; Ayers 1984).

18 *Byers v Sun Savings Bank*, 41 Okla. 728 (1914).

19 *Grooms et al v Thomas et al*, 93 Okla. 87 (1923).

Bibliography

Agamben, G. (1995) *Homo Sacer: Sovereign Power and Bare Life*, trans. D. Heller-Roazen, Stanford, CA: Stanford University Press, 1998.

Ayers, E.L. (1984) *Vengeance and Justice: Crime and Punishment in the 19th-Century American South*, Oxford: Oxford University Press.

Beckett, J.A. (2011) 'The Violence of Wording: Robert Cover on Legal Interpretation', *No Foundations*, 8: 3–39.

Bellamy, J.G. (1979) *The Tudor Law of Treason*, London: Routledge.

—— (1984) *Criminal Law and Society in Late Medieval and Tudor England*, Gloucester: A. Sutton.

Bar, C.L. von (1916) *A History of Continental Criminal Law*, trans. T.S. Bell and others, Boston, MA: Little, Brown & Co.

Benjamin, W. (1921) 'Critique of Violence', trans. E. Jephcott, in *Walter Benjamin: Selected Writings*, M. Bullock and M. Jennings (ed.), vol I: 1913–1926, Cambridge, MA: Harvard University Press, 1996.

Bennett, H. (1930) '*Sacer Esto*', *Transactions and Proceedings of the American Philological Association*, 61: 5–18.

Blackstone, W. (1769) *Commentaries on the Laws of England*, vol IV, London: Strahan & Woodfall, 1795.

Coke, E. (1628) *The First Part of the Institutes of the Laws of England*, London: E. & R. Brooke, 1794.

Cover, R.M. (1983) '*Nomos* and Narrative', *Harvard Law Review*, 97: 4–68.

—— (1986) 'The Bonds of Constitutional Interpretation: Of the Word, the Deed and the Role', *Georgia Law Review*, 20: 815–33.

—— (1986a) 'Violence and the Word', *Yale Law Journal*, 95: 1601–29.

Damaška, M.R. (1968) 'Adverse Legal Consequences of Conviction and Their Removal: A Comparative Study', *Journal of Criminal Law*, 59: 347–60.

Derrida, J. (1990) 'Force of Law: The "Mystical Foundation of Authority"', trans. M. Quaintance, *Cardozo Law Review*, 11: 919–1045.

Follis, L. (2013) 'Resisting the Camp: Civil Death and the Practice of Sovereignty in New York State', *Law, Culture and the Humanities*, 9: 91–113.

Goebel, J. (1976) *Felony and Misdemeanor: A Study in the History of Criminal Law*, Philadelphia: University of Pennsylvania Press.

Lander, J.R. (1961) 'Attainder and Forfeiture, 1453 to 1509', *The Historical Journal* 4: 119–51.

Lichtenstein, A. (1996) *Twice the Work of Free Labor: The Political Economy of Convict Labor in the New South*, New York: Verso.

Manville, B. (1980) 'Solon's Law of Stasis and Atimia in Archaic Athens', *Transactions of the American Philological Association*, 110: 213–21.

New York State (1825) *The Speeches of the Different Governors of the Legislature of the State of New York*, Albany, NY: J.B. Van Steenbergh.

Oshinsky, D.M. (1996) *Worse than Slavery: Parchman Farm and the Ordeal of Jim Crow Justice*, New York: Simon & Schuster.

Palgrave, F. (1832) *The Rise and Progress of the English Commonwealth*, vol I, London: J. Murray.

Reppy, A. (1948) 'The Spectre of Attainder in New York (Part I)', *St John's Law Review*, 23: 1–67.

—— (1949) 'The Spectre of Attainder in New York (Part II)', *St John's Law Review*, 23: 243–90.

Rusche G. and Kirchheimer, O. (1939) *Punishment and Social Structure*, New Brunswick, NJ: Transaction, 2003.

Sarat, A. and Kearns, T.R. (1995) 'Making Peace with Violence: Robert Cover on Law and Legal Theory', in A. Sarat (ed.) *Law's Violence, and the Possibility of Justice*, Ann Arbor: University of Michigan Press.

Smith, C. (2009) *The Prison and the American Imagination*, New Haven, CT: Yale University Press.

Smith, P.V. (1870) 'On the Law of Forfeiture for Treason and Felony', *Bristol Selected Pamphlets*, University of Bristol Library http://www.jstor.org/stable/60248868 (accessed 1 October 2013).

Chapter 12

Abuse of tax law as a language of morality in modern times: a comparative analysis of France, Canada and Ireland

Bénédicte Sage-Fuller and Ferdinand Prinz zur Lippe*

Introduction: 'As certain as death and taxes'?

In his influential book, *The Wealth of Nations*, Adam Smith stated that a good tax system is one which meets the four criteria of equity, fairness, simplicity and certainty (1776: 452). He added (ibid) that it would be preferable that a tax system should have a great deal of inequity, rather than a little uncertainty:

> The certainty of what each individual ought to pay is, in taxation, a matter of so great importance, that a very considerable degree of inequality, it appears, I believe, from the experience of all nations, is not so great an evil as a very small degree of uncertainty.

It is admitted that in a state where the rule of law prevails, where a minimum standard of care and services is provided by public authorities to citizens, taxes are legitimate for the organisation of public life. It is also understood that the very same rule of law requires putting clear limits on state power and authority to levy taxes. That is why taxes are based on statutes enacted by Parliament, so that citizens can predict with certainty how much tax they will have to pay, and when.

Modern tax systems have become so complex that taxpayers use the services of tax experts, who make it their business to minimise their clients' tax liability. Tax avoidance is a game of statutory interpretation, which seeks the most favourable meaning out of the thousands of provisions in a tax code. It is estimated to cost millions or even billions of dollars in lost public revenue to society (OECD 2011: 6; Fleury 2010: 1). The 2013 G20 Summit emphasised the necessity to combat 'tax avoidance, harmful practices and aggressive tax planning'. Its final declaration stated as follows: 'In a context of severe fiscal consolidation and social hardship, in many countries ensuring that all taxpayers pay their fair share of taxes is more than ever a priority' (Russia G20 2013: 12).

In common law jurisdictions, Lord Tomlin's judgment in the UK's *Duke of Westminster*[1] tax case was for a long time the rationale for tax planning: 'Every man is entitled if he can to order his affairs so as that the tax attaching under the appropriate Acts is less than it otherwise would be' (*IRC v Duke of Westminster* 1936: 19).

Lord Tomlin convinced the majority of the court that a literal interpretation of tax statutes was required, and that any attempt to overcome a literal application in order to discover the 'substance of the matter' of a transaction 'seem[ed] to involve substituting "the incertain [sic] and crooked cord of discretion" for "the golden and straight metwand of the law"' (ibid).

Since then, many jurisdictions have moved away from this approach, either by modifying the rules of statutory interpretation in taxation, or by enacting legislation called 'General Anti-Avoidance Regulations' (GAAR), or both. GAAR is based on the idea that taxpayers 'abuse' the tax system by turning it to their advantage. They violate the spirit of a tax provision, even if they formally apply it correctly. The issue of statutory interpretation is obviously core to tax avoidance. However, rather than visiting that aspect of the problem, this chapter explores the meaning of the word 'abuse' of tax legislation at a jurisprudential level in the context of three jurisdictions, France, Canada and Ireland, and in two languages, French and English. Because the word 'abuse' connotes a moral judgment that the taxpayer did something wrong, even though she stayed squarely within the formal limits of the law, this analysis defends a reading of French, Canadian and Irish GAAR and related judicial decisions in the light of the theory of language of morality advanced by Scottish philosopher Alasdair MacIntyre.

MacIntyre's central thesis, developed mainly in the three editions of *After Virtue* (2007) and in *Whose Justice? Which Rationality?* (1988), is that the modern world has lost 'comprehension, both theoretical and practical, of morality' and that the language of morality nowadays is in a state of 'grave disorder' (MacIntyre 2007: 2–3; Knight 1998: 105). Nominalism and the Enlightenment rejected the Aristotelian account of human morality as oriented towards a goal, a *telos*. Therefore, determining whether human actions are good or evil is no longer done with reference to this moral goal of human life. Moral rules still exist but they are 'deprived of their teleological context' (MacIntyre 2007: 55). Thus, there is a gap between moral language and moral meaning (Lutz 2012: 70), moral language having ceased to express the values of the human *telos*. Indeed, MacIntyre argues that language has become a manipulative tool used by its utterer to convince or coerce another to side with her preferred view of the world (MacIntyre 2007: 77).

The modern language of morality thus creates 'moral fictions' and provides moral authority to those who speak it on the basis of such fictional morality. The manager, to take the example of a well known character in modern society, relies on systematic effectiveness to claim that she controls 'certain aspects of social reality'. In the name of effectiveness, she uses moral language to bend human behaviour into 'compliant patterns' (ibid: 73–74). The manager's authority is based on the belief that she knows and understands certain value-free social facts, and that she is an expert at making human behaviour conform to them. The problem, according to MacIntyre, is that it is a mistake to believe that social facts can be value-free. Their apprehension depends on interpretation, which is itself based on 'culturally developed standards', in this instance those of the manager herself (Lutz 2012: 66). The manager's effectiveness, being based on the moral fiction that she knows objective social facts, effectively manipulates others into moulding their behaviour according to her own cultural standards. What is represented as value-free facts in order to justify the managerial authority being deployed is more accurately based on a hidden value-laden interpretation of social facts.

In the same vein, this chapter argues that tax avoidance legislation (GAAR), in as much as it relies on the word 'abuse' with specific reference to tax legislation, also operates a manipulation under the guise of moral language, this time through the legal system.

Abuse and anti-avoidance legislation

Canada was the first country to introduce GAAR legislation in 1988. The then Minister of Finance, Michael Wilson, declared that while tax planning had become more sophisticated and audacious, Canadian taxpayers were unhappy to see some of their fellow citizens avoiding their taxes by exploiting tax rules (House of Commons Debates, Canada 1987: 7363). Section 245(4) of the Income Tax Act directs that a tax avoidance transaction is abusive if:

> (4) [...] if it may reasonably be considered that the transaction [...]
> (*b*) would result directly or indirectly in an abuse having regard to those provisions, other than this section, read as a whole.

Only one year later, the Irish legislature adopted a GAAR provision in section 86 of the Finance Act 1989, now section 811 of the Taxes Consolidation Act 1997, which similarly states that a transaction is not an abusive tax avoidance transaction if:

> (3)(ii) the transaction was undertaken or arranged for the purpose of obtaining the benefit of any relief, allowance or other abatement provided by any provision of the Acts and that the transaction would not result directly or indirectly in a misuse of the provision or an abuse of the provision having regard to the purposes for which it was provided.

After both Canada and Ireland had taken the view that tax planning can have an abusive character and adopted the concept of abuse of tax legislation, a third jurisdiction, France, more recently modified its tax law to introduce this concept, under the name *abus de droit fiscal*, in Article L64 of the Livre des procédures fiscales (Book of Fiscal Procedures, or LPF). Accordingly, transactions will be considered abusive if:

(1) […] either […] they are fictitious or […] they sought a literal application of texts or decisions, contrary to the original objectives of their authors, and […] they had for sole motivation to avoid or reduce the tax burden that the taxpayer would have had to bear, without those transactions.

Abuse as language of morality

To find a tax scheme abusive pursuant to GAAR provisions, a court of law cannot rely on a straightforward application of the law, since *ex hypothesi* the structure being considered falls precisely within the formal and literal application of the law. Instead, the court has to establish that the scheme violates the true purpose of the statute. French, Canadian and Irish courts have therefore had to decide cases where it was claimed that a certain tax scheme was abusive; in other words where claims of wrongfulness rather than of illegality were being made. It is argued here that, in these cases, judges have had to move within a grey area, where it was unclear that a taxpayer had behaved in a legally reprehensible way but where it was alleged that she had acted against moral standards. By holding that such a scheme is, or is not, abusive, judges in effect decide that it is morally wrong or morally right. A language is used, which suggests an underlying morality (Villey 1974: 3). Indeed, the words 'abuse' and *abus* express a moral judgment of wrongfulness.

The *Oxford Dictionaries* website defines abuse as 'the use of something to bad effect or to bad purpose'.[2] Meanwhile, the *Nouveau Petit Robert de la langue française 2014*, a well known French dictionary, defines *abus* as *usage mauvais, excessif ou injuste* ('bad, excessive or unjust use'). In both languages, the words 'bad', *mauvais, excessif* and *injuste* clearly indicate a negative moral judgment. In a taxation context, GAAR legislation based on the words 'abuse' or *abus* thus indicates that a taxpayer has done something bad, excessive or unjust, even though she stayed within the limits of the law. It is therefore argued that GAAR legislation uses a language of morality. Tax administrations claim that tax planning in its aggressive form 'undermine[s] the integrity and the fairness of the tax system' (Jérôme-Forget 2009: iii), whereas tax advisers reply that all they are doing is to apply the law literally, *à la* Duke of Westminster.

MacIntyre's analysis of how the language of morality deals with moral disagreement in modern society casts light on this matter. In Chapter 2 of *After Virtue*, he argues that moral disagreements are expressed 'in their interminable character' (2007: 6). He adds: 'I do not mean by this just that debates go on and on – although they do – but also that they apparently can find no terminus' (ibid). MacIntyre continues by saying that rival arguments are conceptually incommensurable. Not only does each claim feature its own logic, but the opposites are based on rival premises that cannot be weighed against each other as they each use a distinct set of 'normative or evaluative concepts' (ibid: 8). He refers to the example of healthcare. Proponents of liberty will argue that we should let medical doctors exercise their art privately alongside their public practices in order to allow them to earn more wealth freely. For their part, partisans of equality hold that all citizens should be treated equally by medical doctors and that private practices should not exist as they would confer an advantage to wealthier citizens and have negative repercussions on access to public healthcare for the others. Both sets of arguments are presented logically, yet they rest on two different premises, and for that reason they are conceptually irreconcilable (ibid).

The same explanation holds for tax planning. Proponents of the freedom to organise one's tax affairs optimally say that tax planning based on the literal application of tax legislation is a by-product of a legal system seeking to ensure legal certainty and predictability. Advocates of equality counter that tax planning results in loss of public revenue and unfairness and must be curtailed to maintain equality between taxpayers. MacIntyre shows that we find ourselves entangled in assertions and counter-assertions rather than being engaged in a discussion on the merits of rival normative concepts (ibid: 8).

MacIntyre continues his analysis by asserting that all arguments, despite being based on conflicting normative or evaluative concepts, are nonetheless presented as being impersonal rational claims (ibid). They are not offered as the utterance of personal choice, but rather as the expression of impersonal criteria. He uses the example of someone saying 'You must do this because it is your duty', rather than 'Do this because I say so' (ibid: 9). Calling on the notion of 'duty', without actually defining the rationale for this duty, means that the authority of the order appears to rest on an objective standard independent of the relationship between speaker and hearer. However, according to MacIntyre, this strategy really consists in a masquerade since the undefined duty is actually a personal preference of the speaker being presented under the cover of rational argument (ibid: 9–10).

Here again, it is helpful to apply MacIntyre's philosophical ideas to tax planning. A Canadian 1987 Tax Reform Supplementary Information justified the adoption of GAAR by stating that '[e]quity requires that firm measures be taken to block sophisticated strategies designed to yield tax advantages that were not intended by Parliament' (Sherman 1990: 995). The Canadian Government thus called on the principle of equity to justify GAAR legislative measures which, by its own admission, would introduce considerable legal uncertainty in the administration of the tax system. The principle of equity is not rationally defined, other than by political statements. However, it is readily admitted that GAAR would negatively but necessarily impact on the legal certainty afforded to taxpayers (Department of Finance, Canada 1987: 1, 55, 129).

On a practical level, a particular tax provision becomes binding law on the basis of a certain philosophical or political justification. In effect, the legislator tells the taxpayer: 'Do this because it is good'. But the goodness of the measure is contingent upon the very philosophical or political belief that motivated it in the first place, so what actually happens is more accurately that the legislator states: 'Do this because I say so'. When the philosophical and political beliefs of the legislator change with a new Parliament, the tax measure generally stays. Its rationale is no longer there, but its binding character remains. This is the nature of law in a democratic regime based on representation.

It is accepted that violation of the law brings negative consequences for the violator. Many may no longer remember the rationale for a specific measure, but the text is clear and the circumstances under which it would be breached are also ascertainable by citizens. However, determining what constitutes an abuse of the text requires knowledge of its rationale and because it may already be awkward to make sense of tax law at the time of enactment, it can become very difficult to ascertain it at the subsequent moment of application by courts of law. Yet, there are judgments to the effect that tax legislation is being abused.

To return to MacIntyre, he emphasises (2007: 10) how over time the words and expressions originally used by their authors will have changed in character and meaning: 'In the transition from the variety of contexts in which they were originally at home to our own contemporary culture, 'virtue' and 'justice' and 'piety' and 'duty' and even 'ought' have become other than they once were'.

Thus, the concepts of 'equity' and 'fairness', as they appear in the context of GAAR have a very different meaning from what Smith originally intended when he was describing the canons of a good tax system in *The Wealth of Nations*. With GAAR being based on the concept of 'abuse of legislation', equity is advanced to justify a great deal of legal uncertainty as a necessary evil at a time when tax systems have become extremely complex. In other words, not only have the French, Canadian and Irish legislators diminished the practical importance of legal certainty for a tax system, but they have done so in the name of equity and fairness. This is obviously completely at odds with what Smith said about good tax systems in 1776.

Thus, while the same words are being used two centuries apart on account of their same moralising power, their meaning and moral content differ. By the same token, there is great difficulty in ascertaining what the rationale of a specific tax measure actually is and what then constitutes its abuse. Of course, national tax administrations provide guidance to taxpayers on abuse;[3] indeed, they may even have specific GAAR committees to reduce uncertainty.[4] However, the point being emphasised here is that both the law and judges use a language of morality to characterise this abuse, without rationally explaining it. The next section will illustrate this claim with examples derived from French, Canadian and Irish tax planning and involving GAAR judgments.

France: seeking a tax advantage is abusive

The principle of abuse of tax legislation was introduced into French law in 2008, following the *Janfin* decision of the highest administrative court, the Conseil d'État (Council of State).[5] Prior to 2008, the general principle of *abus de droit* had been applicable to certain categories of taxes only.[6] New Article L64 of the LPF gives power to the French tax administration to refuse to take into account acts that constitute an *abus de droit* as being either fictitious or as having been undertaken on the basis of a literal application of legislative texts in a way running contrary to the intention of the legislator and exclusively with a view to reducing or avoiding tax. Experts observe that whereas optimally managing one's tax affairs is necessary for taxpayers and tax advisers, strategies should not go beyond certain boundaries. Such is the limit attaching to the exercise of any kind of freedom: it ought not to be abused (Cozian and Deboissy 2013: 793). Incidentally, tax advisers can be sued for failing to provide the best advice to their clients.

Article L64 of the LPF on *abus de droit fiscal* (abuse of tax law) concerns two types of behaviour: simulation and *fraude à la loi* (evasion or avoidance of the law) (Tetley 1994: 312–13).[7] There is a distinction between *fraude, abus de droit* and *fraude à la loi* (Cozian and Deboissy 2013: 794–95). It is important to exclude from this discussion the term *fraude*, which is the deliberate violation of tax legislation (close to the meaning of the English word 'fraud') and which therefore concerns tax evasion and not tax avoidance.

Abus de droit therefore includes *fraude à la loi* but not *fraude*. It covers situations of extremely advanced tax planning, sometimes qualified as 'aggressive', where the literal meaning of legislation is being relied upon in order to minimise or reduce tax liability. *Fraude à la loi* does not imply any kind of simulation or lie. It constitutes an *abus de droit* under Article L64 of the LPF when two cumulative conditions are met (ibid: 801). First, the taxpayer must have sought a literal application of legislative texts or decisions, which contradicts their author's intention. This determination requires discovering the purpose of the legal text and its economic rationale with regard to the objective reality that it sought to capture in the first place. Secondly, the motivations of the taxpayer must have been exclusively to reduce or minimise tax liability. If her actions can be explained by reference to another reason (whether commercial, familial, financial or economic), there will not be *fraude à la loi*. Accordingly, the doctrine of *abus de droit* under Article L64 of the LPF will then fail to apply (Fouquet 2009: 288).

Two examples illustrate the difficulty faced by courts of law when requested to adjudicate on allegations of *abus de droit* in tax law. In the 2009 decision of *Ministre de l'Economie et des Finances v Axa SA*, the Conseil d'État was asked to decide whether a repurchase option between Banque d'Orsay and Axa SA constituted an abuse of Article 158B of the Code Général des Impôts (General Tax Code, or CGI) on *crédits d'impôts* (tax credits).[8] Banque d'Orsay had purchased obligations from Axa SA. It had then quickly allocated dividends and benefited from the tax credit that Article 158B attaches to such distribution. It had later resold the obligations to Axa SA at the initial sale price minus the sum amounting to the distributed dividends and the tax credit. The tax effect of this repurchase option was that the tax credit, by being included in the repurchasing price, was made available to the sellers, although they had not accumulated sufficient profits to claim it directly from the French tax administration in the first place. The question for the *Conseil d'État* was whether this operation purported to rely on the literal application of the legislative provision on tax credits (Article 158B of the

CGI) and whether it amounted to a *fraude à la loi* (Article L64 of the LPF) and therefore to an *abus de droit*.

Two conditions must be met for a *fraude à la loi* to be recognised: first, that the transaction be artificial and without substance (that is to say, that it harbours purely fiscal motivations) and, secondly, that it be contrary to the objectives of the legislative provision (in this case Article 158B of the CGI). As regards the first requirement, the Conseil d'État held that repurchase options are not artificial because they entail the usual risk that the sellers would not buy back the obligations. In relation to the second demand, the Conseil d'État reviewed the legislative debates of 1965 and found that the intention of the legislator when it adopted the law on tax credits had been to encourage shareholding in companies, to develop the Paris financial market and to eliminate the double taxation of dividends. On this basis, the Conseil d'État found that the repurchasing operation of obligations between Banque d'Orsay and Axa SA was not contrary to the objectives of Article 158B of the CGI and therefore not abusive.

The decision in *Société Charcuterie du Pacifique* also concerned a tax credit claim, this time in the context of the building of a beach resort in French Polynesia.[9] A company called Te Tiare Beach Resort (TTBR) had lent 70 million CFP Francs (Francs Comptoirs Français du Pacifique, the currency used in French Polynesia) to Charcuterie du Pacifique (CDP). CDP then used the loan, together with 30 million CFP Francs of its own funds, to invest 100 million CFP Francs in capital in a company called Te Tiare Beach Resort II (TTBR II). Out of this capital investment, 30 per cent was of CDP's own funds and 70 per cent was a loan from TTBR. CDP obtained 50,000 shares in TTBR II in return for its investment in capital. TTBR was a shareholder in TTBR II, and the loan to CDP was repaid upon construction of the beach resort by handing over to TTBR the shares acquired in TTBR II.

The final piece of the puzzle is that Article 115-1-2 of the Code des Impôts Directs de la Polynésie Française (Code of Direct Taxation of French Polynesia, or CIDPF) allows for tax credits (*crédit d'impôt*) for the subscription of capital. TTBR was the developer and did not have the right to this tax credit, whereas CDP as investor could claim it. CDP therefore sought a tax credit from the tax administration with respect to the 100 million CFP Francs invested in TTBR II, and included half of the tax credit in the value of the shares in TTBR II handed back to TTBR in repayment of the loan. In effect, CDP and TTBR shared the value of the tax credit so obtained.

The Conseil d'État had to decide whether the tax credit claim was abusive. The same two conditions as obtained in *Ministre de l'Economie et des Finances v Axa SA* were analysed by the court, which considered the artificiality of the transactions and examined whether they were contrary to the objectives of the legislation. It was clear that the loan of 70 million CFP Francs from TTBR to CDP was purely artificial and had no motivation other than to help financing the acquisition of shares in TTBR II in order to gain a tax advantage. It was, however, equally clear to the Conseil d'État that the objectives of Article 115-1-2 of the CIDPF were precisely to encourage developments such as hotels and beach resorts in French Polynesia. In this case, CDP had invested funds in TTBR II, which in turn was going to build a beach resort with the 100 million CFP francs. The money was never actually transferred by TTBR to CDP, or even for that matter to TTBR II. The share transactions took place only on paper but the beach resort was actually built.

The Conseil d'État held that, despite the undisputed fact that the overall series of transactions was aimed to facilitate the construction of a hotel, the investment made by CDP was for 30 million CFP Francs, not 100 million. The loan of 70 million CFP Francs was never physically transferred from TTBR to CDP or from CDP to TTBR II, and CDP was never a creditor of TTBR with respect to that part of the capital funding. As a result, the tax credit that could be claimed by CDP only concerned the 30 per cent of the capital funding provided, that is, the 30 million CFP Francs actually transferred. The Conseil d'État held that the tax credit claim was therefore abusive.

These two examples show how difficult it is to assess abuse of tax legislation in practice. It would appear that the only difference as a matter of law between the two cases was that, according to the Conseil d'État's decision in the first dispute, Banque d'Orsay seemingly took a real risk that the sellers (Axa SA) might not repurchase the obligations bought, whereas in the second litigation, TTBR apparently did not take any real risk in lending some capital funding from Société Charcuterie du Pacifique to be invested in TTBR II. However, one could argue that Banque d'Orsay actually took less risk than TTBR in the sense that there was less risk of Axa SA not repurchasing the obligations than there was of TTBR losing its capital investment. Axa SA is an international financial institution and is therefore less likely to be in financial difficulty than a local developer of beach resorts on remote Pacific islands in French Polynesia. However, in the one case the transactions were held not to be abusive and incurred no negative moral judgment, whereas in the other they were found to be abusive with the ensuing connotation of moral wrongdoing.

The 'interminable character' of moral disagreement identified by MacIntyre is in evidence: while some readers will share the view taken by the Conseil d'État, others will argue the opposite. In any case, the decisions of the Conseil d'État, although final from a legal standpoint, cannot be taken to be authoritative as a matter of morality, despite having recourse to a language of morality. Under the guise of asserting 'do this because it is good', the Conseil d'État is actually saying 'do this because I say so'.

Canada: the violation of the 'spirit of the law' is abusive

Section 245 of the Income Tax Act, Canada's GAAR, was enacted in 1988. It aims at striking down avoidance transactions, which are transactions, or series of transactions (section 248(10) of the Income Tax Act),[10] giving a tax benefit to the taxpayer where they have not been arranged for any bona fide purpose other than to obtain the tax benefit (section 245(3)). The Act further requires that it can be reasonably considered that the transaction, or series of transactions, is a misuse of the tax provisions resulting in the tax benefit or an abuse of the provisions read as a whole (section 245(4)). The Supreme Court had the opportunity to apply this provision for the first time in *Canada Trustco Mortgage Co. v Canada* in 2005,[11] and then on three more occasions in *Mathew v Canada*,[12] *Lipson v Canada* in 2009[13] and finally in *Copthorne Holdings Ltd v Canada* in 2011.[14] The first and the last of these cases will be considered in some detail for the purpose of this chapter.

In *Canada Trustco Mortgage Co. v Canada* (*Trustco*), the issue was whether capital cost allowances (CCA) claimed by Trustco were sought abusively or not. Trustco was a mortgage lender and made profits from leased assets. It had purchased trailers, which it had then leased back to a seller. It subsequently reduced its income from the leases by claiming CCA on the trailers for the 1997 tax year. This strategy allowed for the deferment of the tax payments on profits to be diminished by the amount of the CCA. The Supreme Court of Canada held that a 'contextual and purposive approach' was necessary to identify the 'object, spirit or purpose' of the tax provision in question. Revenue Canada alleged that the 'costs' coming under the relevant CCA provisions could not encompass a scheme where there was no real economic risk involved for the taxpayer. The Supreme Court rejected this argument on the basis of an interpretation of the word 'cost' in the relevant provision in the context of the Income Tax Act, making specific reference to the purpose that the text was seeking to achieve. The Court found that it was irrelevant that the taxpayer had not incurred a real economic cost — the trailers in question had a 'cost' which came within the plain meaning of the CCA provision. According to the Court, there was no abuse of the CCA text, and Trustco was entitled to claim CCA with respect to the trailers.

By contrast, in the 2011 decision in *Copthorne Holdings Ltd v Canada* (*Copthorne*), the Supreme Court held that several transactions carried over a period of seven years, which had the effect of preserving the Paid-Up Capital (PUC) of an amalgamated company and which included the distribution of that PUC to the shareholder of the company as a return of capital rather than a distribution of dividends, represented an abuse of the relevant provisions. Sections 89(1), 87(3) and 84(3) of the Income Tax Act 1985 state explicitly that the PUC of an amalgamated company cannot exceed the sum of the amalgamating companies' PUCs; that for parent-subsidiary companies that are being amalgamated the PUC of the subsidiary is cancelled upon amalgamation; and that a company is deemed to have paid a dividend when redeeming shares, except when what is paid is its PUC.

What the taxpayer did, in this case, was to engage in a series of operations to transform a subsidiary and its parent company into two sister companies before proceeding to amalgamate them and redeeming shares to the level of the PUC of the amalgamated company. The PUC of the new company therefore consisted of the PUCs of the two sister companies. The redemption was deemed to have been a distribution of the PUC and was made tax-free in the hands of the shareholder. Had the transformation of the subsidiary into a sister company not taken place before the amalgamation and redemption of the shares, the tax-free distribution of PUC could only have concerned the amount corresponding to the PUC of the parent company, as the PUC of the subsidiary would then have been cancelled.

In order to label these operations as abusive, the Supreme Court of Canada made a number of interesting findings and statements with a view to discovering the 'object, spirit or purpose' (*Copthorne* 2011: 70) of the applicable tax provisions. Of course, nothing in the legislation explicitly prohibits a taxpayer from transforming a subsidiary into a sister company before proceeding to an amalgamation and redemption of shares, and the Supreme Court thus admitted that the PUC of the amalgamated company had been validly created. However, the Court found that these operations ran against the 'spirit' of the section of the Income Tax Act, which stated that the PUC of a subsidiary was cancelled upon amalgamation with its parent company. The Court determined that there was nothing surprising in not finding an explicit prohibition in the text of the legislation, since such omission was the very *raison d'être* of GAAR's section 245.

The Court held furtherthat: 'However, this does not mean that the text is irrelevant. In a GAAR assessment the text is considered to see if it sheds light on what the provision was intended to do' (*Copthorne* 2011: 88). In the case at hand, therefore, the Supreme Court proceeded to analyse the legislative provisions in order to determine the 'scheme' applicable to the distribution of PUC beyond what was explicitly written into the legislation. The Court found that the spirit of these provisions was that the distribution of PUC should be tax-free in the hands of the taxpayer in so far as this PUC was originally created with tax-paid money. That is why, according to the Court, the PUC of a subsidiary that does not feature such tax-paid money characterisation should not be distributed tax-free to a shareholder.

Here again, it can be seen that while the arguments of the Court are legally convincing in both cases, they are far from being rationally satisfying. In *Trustco*, the Court made the arbitrary decision that the word 'cost' should be interpreted literally and took the view that whether it had been actually incurred was irrelevant. By way of contrast, in *Corpthorne*, the Court made the arbitrary decision that a taxpayer could not claim a tax-free distribution of PUC since this capital had not actually been created. In both cases, the opposite decision could have been reached: *Trustco* could convincingly have been decided against the taxpayer and *Corpthorne* in her favour.

In effect, the Supreme Court of Canada is behaving just like the French courts in the decisions reviewed above. By stating that a transaction is abusive, the Supreme Court is making a moral judgment on the actions of the taxpayer, which cannot be said to be in breach of the law but are said to be violating its spirit. The Court is, however, lacking in rational arguments to justify its decisions. Instead, it uses what MacIntyre describes as the language of morality of modern times to assert its own 'culturally developed standards' as regards what constitutes an abuse of tax legislation. It is stating 'do this because it is good', but it is actually saying 'do this because I say so'.

Ireland: no clear principle to decide whether there is abuse or not

The Explanatory Memorandum to the Finance Act 1989, which introduced what is now section 811 of the Taxes Consolidation Act 1997, declared that the intention of the provision is as follows:

> The purpose of the section is to counteract certain circumstances which have little or no commercial reality but are carried out primarily to create an articifical tax deduction or to avoid or reduce a tax charge. Such a transaction is referred to in the section as a tax avoidance transaction.

The section has been used sparsely by the Revenue. Only one case, *Revenue Commissioners v O'Flynn Construction Co Ltd*, has been the focus of a judicial decision, in this instance by the Irish Supreme Court in December 2011 (*O'Flynn Construction*).[15] Three judges then concurred to dismiss the appeal brought by the taxpayer (O'Donnell, Fennelly and Finnegan JJ), while two judges dissented (McKechnie and Macken JJ). The main point of disagreement between O'Donnell J's majority judgment and McKechnie J's dissent is that the former held that the taxpayer had abused the applicable tax provision, whereas the latter considered that it had not. The two opinions must be considered in turn.

O'Flynn Construction involved a scheme whereby the benefit of export sales relief (ESR) was passed on by a manufacturing company to a construction company. Under the ESR scheme, profits created from qualifying exports are exempt from corporation tax. Dividends distributed from these profits are similarly tax-exempt in the hands of the shareholders. Mitchelstown Export Company Ltd had earned ESR of IR£1.2 million, but was not in a position to distribute dividends. An elaborate series of transactions was therefore devised, involving some 40 steps, in order to transfer the ESR to two other companies and to their shareholders. These two companies were not export companies but construction companies (O'Flynn Construction Ltd and others), which had distributable dividends against which the ESR was claimed, thereby allowing its distribution to benefit from the tax-exemption regimes. The issue was whether the series of 40 steps in order to arrive at this result was an abuse of the ESR. O'Donnell J was very aware of the difficulty in deciding whether there had been such abuse. He expressed this problem (*O'Flynn Construction* 2011: 76) as follows:

> On behalf of the taxpayer for example it might be said – and indeed was said – that the products here had been manufactured and exported, and employment generated, and that the State had agreed that profits derived from that activity would be exempt from tax and could generate tax free dividends, and

therefore that the State was at no loss and got what it bargained for – tax forgone on the amount of profits in return for employment sustaining and export creating manufacture. On the other hand, it could equally be said that the transaction or transactions at issue here – the introduction of funds [...], first by Dairygold and then by [O'Flynn Construction Ltd], and a multiple declaration of dividends – had nothing to do with achieving the export of goods or the maintenance of employment. The goods had been exported and any jobs created long before the series of transactions were put in place over the Christmas period of 1991.

O'Donnell J decided that there had been an abuse of the ESR provision. According to his analysis, the exports alone were not enough to generate tax reliefs in relation to corporation tax and income tax: the exporting company had also to produce a profit and declare a dividend. Therefore, he viewed the fact that the exporting company effectively passed on the ESR to other companies, which had made a profit and declared a dividend, as 'articificial and contrived' (ibid: 80) and as constituting an abuse of ESR. He held that: '[a] scheme which allows the shareholders in a non exporting company to benefit from Export Sales Relief on the profits of the non exporting company, is surely a misuse or abuse of the scheme having regard to the purpose for which the provision is provided' (ibid: 73).

Upon reading this judgment, a slight sense of uncertainty can be felt. The use of the word 'surely' in the sentence quoted above might be an indication that the judge was somewhat hesitant about his approach. Indeed, earlier in his judgment he made a cautious observation in response to examples that the Appeal Commissioners had given about so-called clear-cut cases of abuses of tax provisions: 'The absence of any clearly articulated and principled distinction between these cases, and the difficulty in suggesting any substantial content to the concepts of misuse and abuse, is telling' (ibid: 73). This statement contributes to the argument being advanced here. In cases where courts have to decide what constitutes an 'abuse' of a tax provision and in the absence of a rationale to make a moral judgment about it, the legal opinion often appears to be just another assertion, rather than a discussion on moral disagreement. Indeed, the dissenting judgment of McKechnie J that there was no abuse of the ESR is as plausible as O'Donnell J's assertion that there was. McKechnie J focused in particular on the issue of income tax-free distribution of dividends. After a lengthy assessment of the various legislative stages of the provision since its inception in 1956, he concluded (ibid: 96) that:

> What this assessment highlights, in stark terms, is that no attempt had been made over its thirty-five year life span, to regulate the tax status of such dividends: strikingly restrictions regarding matters such as the following were never put in places: (i) the temporal relationship as between profits earned, profits distributed and acquisition of shareholding, (ii) the legal personality

of the shareholder, the size of the shareholding and the duration of its retention, (iii) the legal proximity of shareholder to exporting company, (iv) the nature of the shareholder's business and its association with that of the exporting company, (v) the requirement for shareholder investment in the exporting company, or its size, use or when required, (vi) the due date by which such dividends would have to be distributed.

The relief was never restricted by the legislature in relation to these matters, despite having received considerable attention over more than three decades. Accordingly, McKechnie J felt that even if the taxpayer had devised a very complex scheme featuring 40 steps or so in order to allow the shareholders of a construction company to benefit from an export relief, it still did not abuse the purpose of the relief, which was to encourage the manufacturing industry in the broadest possible way.

It would be difficult to say which of these two judgments is the morally correct one. This case offers yet another example of what MacIntyre calls the 'interminable character' of modern moral disagreement: the two opinions are based on rival premises, have their own logic and are conceptually incommensurable. Even O'Donnell J, whose approach prevailed in the end, seemed slightly unsure that his view was the correct one. However, the language of morality was used to assert the court's preferred view and, yet again, as in France and in Canada, one very much feels that the court is saying 'do this because it is good', whereas it is actually proclaiming: 'do this because I say so'.

Conclusion

Whether in France, Canada or Ireland, GAAR legislation relies on the concept of 'abuse', or *abus*, of tax legislation in order to disqualify transactions or deeds made by taxpayers following literal applications of tax legislation. Making reference to GAAR legislation, courts consider that such transactions abuse the spirit of tax legislation in circumstances where they nonetheless adhere to its literal application. The law itself is not violated, only its 'spirit', which is assessed by reference to what judges consider abusive. In this regard, the guidance documents issued by tax administrations offer little legal certainty as they are not law.

MacIntyre's analysis of the modern language of morality argues that it hides the subjective choices of its utterers, and that it is used to manipulate others under the guise of moral authority. Accordingly, it can be said that the language of GAAR legislation is a language of morality of modern times in as much as it uses the artifice of moral language by labelling something as abusive, bad, *excessif* or *injuste*. As the various examples derived from the French Conseil d'État and the Canadian and Irish Supreme Courts show, there does not appear to be a clear principled approach to deciding GAAR cases. In every instance, a court of law decides one way, but could easily have decided differently. Ultimately, it seems that it is the personal, subjective and arbitrary decision made by a court that constitutes the underlying basis of the legal opinion. In every case, judges appear to be saying 'do this because it is good', whereas they are actually asserting 'do this because I say so'. Ironically, when GAAR legislation is applied, taxpayers are effectively being accused of manipulating the tax system. However, as MacIntyre convincingly shows, it is the utterer who is involved in manipulation, not the addressee of the statement. Careful analysis reveals that moral GAAR language appears to facilitate manipulation of the taxpayer by the tax system, rather than the other way round.

To be sure, there are significant similarities in the languages used by the three courts of law that have been discussed here. Thus, the moralising tone is the same in the three countries under examination: the legislators and the judges *feel* that the taxpayer has done something wrong, and they *feel* this in the same way whether they are French, Canadian or Irish, whether they express themselves in French or in English or whether they are operating in a common law or a civil law context. This finding indicates that the language of morality used in these three situations features an international element, which is the same in France, Canada and Ireland. Indeed, tax planning is an international phenomenon that is being exacerbated by globalisation. Yet it remains to be seen what is the morality behind the language used in GAAR legislation. Indeed, is there more to it than the illusion of morality? Can we plausibly claim that norms and values of international morality in tax planning are emerging at international level, which will eventually provide clear principles to decide GAAR cases? In this regard, it may be that abuse of tax law is developing into an international autonomous concept (Kjær 2011: 331).

In an article entitled 'Mythologies de l'international' ('Mythologies of the international'), Chantal Delsol writes that globalisation is engendering a world featuring its own internal logic, values, ends and behaviours (2006). This new world has its own culture and, for that matter, its own myths, which give coherence to the globalised entity. Delsol uses the word 'myth' in the classical sense to suggest a significant story; an interpretation of the universe. It is therefore possible that the language of anti-avoidance in taxation seeks to express such new myths of the globalised, internationalised world, in order to to combat aggressive tax avoidance. The moral authority of GAAR legislation would then be based on the myths that Delsol discusses in her text.

However, Delsol (ibid: 1083) warns about the dangers of these new myths, which may not be overtly expressed:

> International mythology follows religions, which it tries to replace. It acts as their substitute, bringing an interpretation of the world capable of making sense of existence [...]. But it shelters other weaknesses. It does not know that it believes. It believes that it knows. And this illusion of objectivity augurs many oppressions.

As highlighted by the 2013 G20 Summit, states currently experience very severe, if not catastrophic, fiscal deficits that can only be filled by tax revenues. In the context of this pressing necessity and given the fight against aggressive tax avoidance, the rule of law must continue to prevail over the dangers of manipulation and oppression that modern times can generate in the guise of the 'illusion of objectivity' of morality, whether on account of its language (MacIntyre) or its mythology (Delsol).

Notes

* This article was researched and written with the generous financial support of the College of Business and Law, University College Cork, Ireland. Our thanks go to Professors Diane Bruneau, Catherine Piché and Shane Kilcommins, Dr Dominic de Cogan, Dr Samuel Gregg and the anonymous reviewer for their constructive comments. Any remaining errors or omissions are ours alone.
1 *IRC v Duke of Westminster* [1936] AC 1 (HL).
2 *Oxford Dictionaries* http://www.oxforddictionaries.com/definition/english/ abuse?q=abuse (accessed 1 October 2013).
3 Concerning Canada, see Revenue Canada, Information Circular IC-88-2 (21 October 1988) and IC-88-2S1 (13 July 1990) http://www.cra-arc.gc.ca/menu/ ICSC_80-e.html (accessed 1 October 2013). As regards Ireland, see Revenue Commissioners, Notes For Guidance, Taxes Consolidation Act 1997, Finance Act 2013 Edition, Part 33: 11–17 http://www.revenue.ie/en/practitioner/ law/notes-for-guidance/tca/part33.pdf (accessed 1 October 2013).
4 Canada created the so-called 'GAAR Committee'. France, for its part, established the 'Comité de l'Abus de Droit Fiscal'.
5 CE (27 September 2006) No 260050, *Ministre v Sté Janfin*, JurisData No 2006-081020.
6 Former Article L64 of the Livre de Procédures Fiscales applied the doctrine of abuse of tax law to selected taxes relating to real estate sales (*droit d'enregistrement* and *taxe de publicité foncière*), income tax, corporation tax and turnover tax. Former Article L64A extended it to the Impôt de solidarité sur la fortune (a solidarity tax on wealth above a certain threshold) and to trade tax. See 'Livre des procédures fiscales', in *Code de procédure fiscale* (2007), 14th edn, Paris: Dalloz.
7 This translation is tentative and should not induce the reader to confuse 'tax evasion' with 'evasion or avoidance of the law'.
8 CE (7 September 2009) No 305586, *Ministre de l'Economie et des Finances v Axa SA*, JurisData No 2009-081542.
9 CE (12 March 2010) No 306368, *Société Charcuterie du Pacifique* RJF 6/10 No 620, concl. E. Geffray.
10 Canadian Income Tax Act 1985 s 248(10) defines, in its English version, a 'series of transactions' as follows: 'For the purpose of this Act, where there is a reference to a series of transactions or events, the series shall be deemed to include any related transactions or events completed in contemplation of the series'. The French version of the provision reads as follows: '*Pour l'application de la présente loi, la mention d'une série d'opérations ou d'événements vaut mention des opérations et événements liés terminés en vue de réaliser la série*'.
11 *Canada Trustco Mortgages Co v Canada* [2005] 2 SCR 601.
12 *Mathew v Canada* [2005] 2 SCR 643.
13 *Lipson v Canada* [2009] 1 SCR 3.
14 *Copthorne Holdings Ltd v Canada* [2011] SCR 63.
15 *Revenue Commissioners v O'Flynn Construction Ltd* [2011] IESC 47.

Bibliography

Aaronson, G. QC (2011) 'GAAR Study: A Study to Consider Whether a General Anti-Avoidance Rule Should be Introduced into the UK Tax System' (11 November) http://webarchive.nationalarchives.gov.uk/20130321041222/http://www.hm-treasury.gov.uk/d/gaar_final_report_111111.pdf (accessed 1 October 2013).

Cozian, M. and Deboissy, F. (2013) *Précis de fiscalité des entreprises*, 37th edn, Paris: Lexis Nexis.

Delsol, C. (2006) 'Mythologies de l'international', *Politique étrangère*, 4: 1075–83.

Department of Finance, Canada (1987) *Lower Rates, Fairer System*, White Paper, Fiscal Reform, 18 June.

Fleury, S. (2010) 'Abusive Tax Planning: The Problem and the Canadian Context', 18 February, Publication No 2010-22E, International Affairs, Trade and Finance Division, Parliamentary Information and Research Service, Library of Parliament http://www2.parl.gc.ca/Content/LOP/ResearchPublications/2010-22-e.htm (accessed 1 October 2013).

Fouquet, O. (2009) 'Fraude à la loi: l'explication du critère subjectif', *Droit fiscal*, 39: act 287.

House of Commons Debates, Canada (1987) 'Declaration of Minister of Finance on the 1987 Fiscal Reform', 33rd Legislature, 18 June.

Jérôme-Forget, M. (2009) 'A Word from the Minister', in Quebec Minister for Finance, *Aggressive Tax Planning*, Working Paper, January http://www.finances.gouv.qc.ca/documents/Autres/en/AUTEN_DocCons_PFA.pdf (accessed 1 October 2013).

Kjær, A.L. (2011) 'European Concepts in Scandinavian Law and Language', *Nordic Journal of International Law*, 80: 321–49.

Knight, K. (ed.) (1998) *The MacIntyre Reader*, Cambridge: Polity Press.

Lutz, C.S. (2012) *Reading Alasdair MacIntyre's After Virtue*, New York: Continuum.

MacIntyre A. (1988) *Whose Justice? Which Rationality?* London: Duckworth.

—— (2007) *After Virtue*, 3rd edn, London: Duckworth.

OECD (2011) *Tackling Aggressive Tax Planning through Improved Transparency and Disclosure*, OECD Publishing http://www.oecd.org/tax/exchange-of-tax-information/48322860.pdf (accessed 1 October 2013).

Russia G20 (2013) 'G20 Leaders' Declaration', Saint Petersburg Summit, September http://www.g20.org/news/20130906/782776427.html (accessed 1 October 2013).

Sherman, D.M. (1990) *Income Tax Act – Department of Finance – Technical Notes*, 2nd edn, Toronto: De Boo.

Smith, A. (1776) *The Wealth of Nations*, Oxford: Oxford University Press, 2008.

Tetley, W. (1994) 'Evasion/*Fraude à la loi* and Avoidance of the Law', *McGill Law Journal*, 39: 303–32.

Villey, M. (ed.) (1974) 'Préface', *Le Langage du droit*, Paris: Sirey (Archives de philosophie du droit, vol XIX).

Chapter 13

Withholding translation

Pierre Legrand

Askanted thinking matters. By way of counterpoint to the principal theme of this volume perspicuously urging upon comparative legal studies to engage translation such as to overcome the woeful under-theorisation that continues to plague the field, I want to argue that there must remain situations where translation ought not to govern, where the prevailing motion rather needs to be one of circumspection, restraint and, indeed, avoidance. In other words, I claim that there are instances of *overtranslation* that must be eschewed. 'Legal-origins' theory, which emerged in the late 1990s, offers a prominent example of the predicament I wish to address (La Porta, Lopez-de-Silanes and Shleifer 1998, 2008; Glaeser and Shleifer 2002; Beck, Demirgüç-Kunt and Levin 2003). Briefly, proponents of this model defend the existence of isomorphs between traditionary legal allegiance and economic development. More specifically, they suggest that law can be recast in terms of economic indicators showing common law jurisdictions to be better at 'doing business' than countries hailing from the civil law world – this expression having become the title of an annual report produced by the World Bank since 2003 and purporting to offer a comparative ranking of local regulatory environments according to an 'ease-of-doing-business' index (World Bank 2004). The chief assumption informing 'legal-origins' theory in general and the World Bank's *Doing Business* reports in particular is that law can unproblematically be converted into economics in order to generate 'objective' data, allowing for a comparative appreciation of the legal mercifully free of the ambiguity – the *play* – that otherwise characterises life-in-the-law.

   From the standpoint of analysts undertaking this repurposing of law into the language of economics, their initiative is unassailably productive. For these individuals, the reformulation of law they offer must be seen as a sophisticated striation of the legal into measurable units, allowing it to be harnessed towards the rightful attainment of modern opportunity (where to start a firm? where to buy real estate? where to invest in stocks?).[1] While the proponents of 'legal origins' assume an unalloyed gain, I want to argue that in the way law is made to undergo the kind of massive reductionism that deprives it of its experiential fabric, the process features, in fact, a huge detriment. Indeed, I claim that the mobilisation of 'legal origins', and the attendant articulation of the legal into a strictly computational language, assumes a disparagement of law through the imposition of purposive form so serious as to disqualify this approach as an epistemological operator for comparative purposes. Rather than be given free rein, the desire for unalloyed mathematisation of the law ought to be refrained. In other words, *translation must be withheld*.

But I want to refute more than the intoxicating hubris leading to the utter impoverishment of the law-world. I also object to the threshold assumption positing an easy relationality between two monolingualisms (law and economics) even as these languages are so discrepant as to reveal no rapport, originary or otherwise. While I hold that there cannot be a translation that could ever be called 'true' (Glanert and Legrand 2013: 513–32) – so that I do not fault 'legal origins' for not offering a true rendition of the laws it chooses to scrutinise – I defend the view that there can be mistranslations or, more accurately, *overtranslations*. I have in mind situations where the transformation to which the source-text is being subjected acts as an unacceptable betrayal of it. As it defects from the source-text, as it fails to abide by the cardinal translative goals of recognition and respect, as it does so much violence to the source-text as to move to a beyond of the inescapable translative disjointure, 'translation' emerges as the enemy of singularity. When, as with 'legal origins', two languages (law and economics) are conjugated in one declension only (economics), when 'translation' in fact purports to efface the source-language, when 'translation' becomes a celebration of univocity, it is not effectively performing as *trans-lation* but perpetrating linguicide – and, indeed, epistemicide.

Apart perhaps from some stray Luddites, few observers would be willing to doubt the importance of economic measurement in the ways of the world. For my part, I do not propose to challenge the opinion that numbers hold identifiable virtues.[2] Nor is it the case that I want to reify the matter of *adaequatio* or emphasise stylistic or semantic conformity. It is not, then, that I require commensurability or similarity or likeness across languages in order to warrant translation. And it is certainly not that I aim to fetishise law as language, that I pursue anything like legal fixity or essentialism. I do not seek a kind of 'semantic zoning' whereby languages – say, the legal and the economic – would be solipsistically quarantined in their own worlds (Apter 2006: 3).

While I note that the idealised rationalism on offer from the partisans of 'legal origins' very much reveals itself as an exercise in (transcendental or theological) governmentality, which benefits rather than contests anglobalisation – the worldwide spread of capital and accompanying authoritarian surveillance mechanisms – my immediate epistemological concerns lie elsewhere (although I cannot fail to emphasise without further ado how there is no part of 'legal origins' that is not thoroughly shaped by cultural processes or that escapes cultural politics). I argue that when it purports to say the legal by way of economics, 'legal origins''s articulation is so partial – so *deficient* and so *biased* – that it assimilates or appropriates this other language (law) such as to destroy its identity (a point I make bearing in mind many of the concerns latterly associated with the idea of 'identity').

To be sure, any statement having, say, a law as its object, is bound, even as it is uttered, ultimately to act as a self-reformulation and thus as a modification of what there is, there – Jacques Derrida aptly remarks that 'everything that is given to me in the light seems to be given to me by myself' (1967: 136).[3] However, 'legal origins's' alteration of alterity, its radical demotion of the source-text, the loss it countenances, is so excessive as to prove uncreditable. The inscription of 'legal origins's' model of 'translation' politics is tantamount to a writing of disaster.

While I want to confine myself to the matter of 'legal origins' as a notable example of overtranslation, as a situation where withholding ought to have obtained, the idea of 'translation' as metaphorical/organisational frame could easily prompt further reflection, for example, regarding legal migration. Is the 2004 French enactment of provisions whereby, under certain circumstances, an individual charged with a criminal offence can negotiate sentencing against a guilty plea a *translation* of the US law of 'plea bargain'? Is the 2008 French implementation of constitutional review, pursuant to specific modalities, a *translation* of the US model? Although fascinating in their own right, these permutations on the theme of 'translation' must fall beyond the remit of my intervention on this occasion.[4] Instead, I propose to reconsider a brief text I devoted to 'legal origins' when I was commissioned by a law journal a few years ago to write for a focus section it was organising on this topic (Legrand 2009: 215–22). As it appears here, this argument has undergone a certain degree of re-signification, of *translation*, so that it can legitimately claim to appear as a *contribution* to this book.

*   *   *

'The reduction of all qualities to quantities is nonsense'
Nietzsche (†1901: § 564 p 304)[5]

For most comparatists-at-law, comparison resolves itself as a generalising activity directed towards one form or other of normative integration. It thus succumbs to the Hegelian temptation of sublating contradiction, that is, of assimilating the singular. I am critical of this disciplinary stance, and I have long sought to forestall this appropriative tendency – which, to my mind, can only be based on fictional relationality across laws. Because it is unavoidably artificial, obstinately instrumental and, indeed, determinedly hegemonic, I want to suspend the connection between comparison and measure. In other words, I advocate processes of comparison that are no longer bound to commensuration. I argue in favour of incommensurability as the primordial absence of common ground between different orders of legal knowledge. 'Common ground', any 'common ground', must assume a metalanguage; but the empirical fact is that there is *no* language that can dispense with idiomaticity. What there is across laws, and all that there is, is an abyss – an impassable abyss. For me, comparison is thus the site of a problem rather than a solution.

Place, then, is not a mere static backdrop to legal meaning: it is a dynamic constituent of it. In other words, place is not simply a physicalist conception: it is also an existential notion. Law emerges only in and through place (an assertion that does not entail an essentialist, exclusionary, reactionary, conservative or immobile understanding of 'place' – one can, indeed, approach 'place' as source rather than terminus, as that from which something begins in its unfolding rather than that at which it comes to a stop). Law and place are inextricably enmeshed, which means, incidentally, that law can be constitutive of place in its turn. In the same way as there is no ungrounded language, there is no ungrounded law. For law, any law, to be 'as law', it must stand forth in terms of an experience of place. It must *dwell*. If I may be allowed to draw on the possibilities displayed by the German language, I make, in short, a claim for *Ortung* in contradistinction to the seemingly relentless drive for ever more *Ordnung* being promoted by the large majority of comparatists-at-law, who would have us believe that the world today is so mobile, so interconnected and so integrated that it is, in one prominent popular assessment, 'flat' (Friedman 2005).

Those who claim to have elicited a common denominator transcending laws and the places of laws, allowing for a mathematisation of law partaking in some sort of epistemological bilingualism and ultimately permitting a rigorous Archimedean assessment (and ranking) of laws in terms of 'efficiency' only, are, in effect, positing a range of audacious postulates. They argue that they can ascertain, understand and formulate 'the law' governing, say, the sale of real estate in France, both accurately and exhaustively (without their enunciation's being coloured by any pre-understanding of French law that they might carry as a result of their own prior socialisation into 'their' law); that there exists a 'referential' language called 'economics'; that 'the law' governing the sale of real estate in France is translatable into 'economics'; that 'the law' concerning the sale of real estate in France can be translated into 'economics' by economists in a manner that involves no distortion of it; that economists can reiterate precisely the same sequence (ascertainment, understanding, formulation, translation into a 'referential' language) with respect to, say, the law of real estate in England; that economists can then engage assiduously in *wertfreie* comparison and reach *wertfreie* conclusions with respect to the relative 'efficiency' of each law; and that economists can therefore ground their identification of the 'better' law on unassailable (economic) foundations.

The general idea underwriting these various heuristic motions is an apprehension of comparatism as dialectical resolution favouring the progression, through immersion in a utility-maximising framework of calculation, towards a position of knowledge of law-as-price that would enclose local epistemologies – their anachronism, their irrationality – within a fixed system withstanding 'contamination' by culture, offering technically guaranteed meaning and resting knowledge on secure rational ground not unlike the way in which gold once validated banknotes.

While law is, indeed, thoroughly cultural, as any serious archaeological research must reveal, economics is taken to operate on a more elevated plane, and on a higher ethical plane also, within a 'beyond' of culture, if you will, and specifically within a beyond of the law's naïveté or capriciousness as it manifests itself locally. Whereas law must contend with an economy – an *oikos* – such is deemed not to be the case for economics, which wishes to be taken as a strictly descriptive endeavour, as being able to tell it *like it is*. After property, contract, torts, procedure, corporate law, bankruptcy, secured transactions and criminal law, economists have come to consider that they can scientificise comparative legal studies by purporting to move it away from the legal pluralism and attendant relativism in which it has been (oh so distressingly!) mired, the pluralistic and relativistic agendas being antagonistic to the capitalist axiomatic, which, in sum, embraces the primacy of private profit, market-pricing mechanisms and the commodity form. Indeed, '*[h]omo œconomicus* is always a rational, maximizing individual, without a history, an unconscious or a class identity, enjoying perfect information about prices and responding only to them' (Rist 2011: 37).

But no matter how dogmatically it asserts itself in its desire to supplant *anarchia* (law's disorder) with an *archia* (a foundation), economics cannot exempt itself from contingency. It is saturated with culture, both in terms of its specific language and as regards any particular use of that language by any economist, which suggests something like a double bind, that is, embeddedness *squared*. In effect, the enculturation of economics has always already begun – the Heideggerian temporal metaphor indicating that ultimately economics is simply unenvisageable otherwise than as culturally-informed discourse: indeed, the fact that even economic 'truth' varies with ideological affiliation shows how it is unsurpassably woven into the cultural fabric (ibid: 5). Structurally, so to speak, economics is therefore but a language, a theoretical matrix, an epistemological construct. Thus, a politics is always implied, and economics cannot exist as an independent test of value. In fact, each of the postulates I have outlined is inevitably predicated on hidden predispositions and predilections, including a specific conception of 'the law', of 'understanding', of 'enunciation', of 'referentiality', of 'economics', of 'translation' and of 'comparison'.

These conceptualisations can aptly be termed 'metaphysical', at least in the sense that they entail surreptitious appeals to unsustained – and, in my view, unsustainable – assumptions: for instance, the possibility of the law's being fully present at the graphical or scriptural level of the law-texts incorporating it; the possibility of the interpreter's fully ascertaining the meaning of the law; the possibility of a referential language; the possibility of identifying a full correspondence between the languages of law and economics; the possibility of comparison between French 'real estate' (*bien immeuble* seems to come closest to the English designation) and English 'real estate', between a French 'sale' (or, rather, *vente*) and an English 'sale'; and the possibility of reaching conclusions about law's 'efficiency' that would be *sans* distortion.

In sum, there is no economic reading of the law that can materialise outside of the scholarly 'discoveries' that have punctuated technical advances in mathematics.[6] Nor can any economic reading of the law escape the specific institutional structures and social formations that have legitimated the articulation of an argument imbricating the rationalisation of society and the maximisation of wealth, whether in the Marquis de Condorcet's 18th century texts on social mathematics or in Baron Kelvin's later musings.[7] As much as economics would have us forget about the conditions under which it necessarily engages in a compromising relationship with rhetoric – albeit in disguised, displaced or policed form – when it claims to be speaking authoritatively on behalf of 'what there is', it cannot occlude the *mise en scène* characteristic of every discourse, of every fiction. In economics too, '[m]odel-making is a creative activity' (Morgan 2012: 158).

To be sure, numbers assume significant performative value. Thus, '[n]umbers provide the comforting illusion that incommensurables can be weighted against each other, because arithmetic always "works". Given some numbers to start with, arithmetic yields answers. Numbers force a common denominator where there is none'. Also, 'numbers are symbols of precision, accuracy, and objectivity. They suggest mechanical selection, dictated by the nature of the objects, even though all counting involves judgment and discretion. [...] Numerals hide all the difficult choices that go into a count. And certain kinds of numbers – big ones, ones with decimal points, ones that are not multiples of ten – not only conceal the underlying choices but seemingly advertize the prowess of the measurer. To offer one of these numbers is by itself a gesture of authority' (Stone 1988: 136–37).[8] However, epistemologically, economic thought remains caught in a network of irreducibly and structurally mediated intelligibility that is no more privileged or unconditioned (and no more stable) than any other network of mediated intelligibility (mathematical appearances notwithstanding).

Where economic thought perhaps differs from many other interpretive frames is in its active and strenuous attempt to repress the general state of mediation that necessarily underlies it in order violently to promote a certain set of capitalistic values.[9] Indeed, the way in which economics seeks to marginalise culture is neither innocent nor accidental. It is but the symptom of a much deeper prejudice in favour of (arithmetical) essentialism. In this respect, it is not unlike legal positivism, which apprehends law-texts as (quasi-)'natural' entities and contents itself with a focus on definition and description, demarcation and classification, conceptualisation and formalisation, clarification and exemplification, exposition and summarisation. Like positivism too, economics displays conservative affinities (Teles 2008: 90–134, 181–219). It entails a glorification of empiricism, a kind of ascetic endorsement of reification, a brand of religiosity sacralising its object of study (lawyers revere texts, economists numbers) and the assertion of a will to power. There is more. Behind a veneer of disinterest and while purporting to move the debate to an out-of-culture in the name of intellectual hygiene,[10] the quest for low transaction costs does, in fact, rotate the axis of our public conversation via the exaltation of numbers that it effectively propounds. As it instrumentalises values, economic analysis speaks to our conception of ourselves as moral beings. Along the way, it significantly impoverishes us (Golumbia 2009).

None of these observations, of course, is to suggest that when it comes to law one can somehow dispense with the question of cost (nor are my remarks meant to deny that markets can be credited with promoting economic growth, which, in turn, deserves to be ascribed various 'goods'). Rather, my point is to accept that economics is not a referent, that it has *its* referents in the name of which it imposes large-scale technical reductionism on what it has made into its object of study, a proceeding that involves a *partial* process of selection, abstraction and naming. The 'what there is' whereof economics alleges to speak is not in fact 'what there is' but, rather, its conceptualisation of 'what there is' such that ulti-mately, the delusion of total explicability notwithstanding, economics is talking about *economic constructions.*

I am certainly not suggesting that this brand of disciplinary solipsism is unique to economics. My main argument, again, is that economics enjoys no particular competence to minimise the inevitable gap between 'what there is' and 'what is being said about what there is'. Indeed, why should the frames embraced by eco-nomics be entitled to any epistemic privilege by virtue of embodying a message to the effect that (boundless?) consumption is the goal of life; that markets – as they collectively allocate resources, set prices and determine distribution of incomes – make society as prosperous as possible given the resources available; that markets are therefore good for people; that imperfections in a market can be overcome by the design of a new and improved market (the idea being that if the market for electricity fails to maximise wellbeing because a local utility enjoys a monopoly over price, monopoly can be replaced with competition); that individuals are to be understood as rational calculators of their self-interest – even while recognis-ing a role for 'behavioural' elements in the relevant equations so that people who act irrationally can be said to have good reasons for doing it (Rist 2011: 49); and that a politics of individual aspiration in a minimally regulated, self-equilibrating market system is worthy of support?

As it makes these contentions, economics advances not only an epistemological argument but also an ontological claim. Having initially posited capitalistic ration-ality, economics determines that what does not meet the standard of efficiency *it* has set – for example, the hapless French law of 'real estate' transactions – must be challenged in its very being. It must cease to exist as it is and be turned into, for example, the English law of real estate transactions.[11] Efficiency thus becomes a programme. An objective and a necessity, it is the only foundation for modern law, complete with the attendant immunity pertaining to fundamentalist, dog-matic discourse: 'Just as doctors are taught to value human life above other goals, economists are trained to value efficiency above other goods' (Woods 2006: 54). Human life aside, what is, indeed, more worthy than to reach and maintain efficiency? What is worse than to be inefficient? So why blame economists for con-structing a theory purporting to optimise efficiency? Is one not bound to prefer the efficient to the inefficient? Even the 'ordinariness' of the term, the way in which it is seen so readily to pertain to 'common sense', helps to make it acceptable. There is a process of 'naturalization' removing the concept from critical scrutiny: what is stated is propounded as being eminently normative, and everyone behaves as if what is stated is, in effect, the case: *one must always be efficient*.

The incompatibility of 'better-law' economics with comparative legal studies can be further shown through the matter of references to foreign law in the context of adjudication – an illustration that I deploy here in an exemplary capacity. In brief, comparatists cannot refrain from wanting foreign decisions in a judicial opinion. However, the cycle of self-reinforcing activity characteristic of path-dependent processes – such as adjudication – suggests that, in line with the idea of increasing returns (or decreasing cost conditions), incremental change is heavily weighted in favour of decisions that are consistent with the existing institutional framework. In as much as it constitutes a derogation from settled judicial practice, '[i]ncluding extraneous statements in an opinion invites later reliance on those statements and thus multiplies the costs of a nonergodic common law system'. Path-dependence therefore 'counsels judges to include in an opinion no more than what is necessary to decide the case at hand thoroughly and completely' – a claim that clearly militates against reference to foreign materials as being inefficient.

Indeed, the bounded rationality within which any institution operates becomes particularly problematic in the context of reference to foreign law, for in this instance the imperfect or incomplete character of the information available to legal actors (say, judges) proves even more debilitating than usual (Hathaway 2001: 663).[12] Yet, in the name of the recognition and respect owed to other laws (let us say, on account of a politics *for* alterity), references to foreign law need to be included not only as being 'crucial to the formation of a critical consciousness and the improvement of knowledge production by giving an area of knowledge greater range and depth' (Cheah 2009: 523), but also because they hold normative value as persuasive authority. I claim that the dilemma between economics and comparative legal studies must likewise resolve itself in favour of comparison. *Homo œconomicus*'s response would no doubt be at variance with mine.

*   *   *

I mentioned incommensurability. Note that incommensurability is not unintelligibility. The other law can be intelligible to me; but it can only ever be intelligible *to me* – that is, it can only ever be intelligible to me *on my terms* – no matter how mathematically that law is framed. In the end, all I have when it comes to an understanding of the other law is *my* reading, which can only be happening where *I* am and on the basis of who *I* am.[13] The fact is that I am always already 'there' – so much so that I cannot imagine myself bereft of 'thereness'. I am situated-in-the-world, I am 'in place'. And the further fact is that the other law, which as a comparatist I make into the object of my study, is also located somewhere in the world, although, by definition (so to speak), elsewhere than where I am (comparatism operates across places). Because all I have is 'emplaced' reading, that is, reading that is distant from the other law's 'emplacement', the only understanding I can ever have of the other law is but conjecture and hypothesis.[14] No attempt at commensuration, no matter how sophisticated, can overcome the estrangement of spatial dislocation – whether one has in mind so-called 'legal transplants', international conventions, international law or economics. Any argument that one law is 'better' than another because it entails lower transaction costs (or for any other reason) is but a claim for someone's understanding of what makes law 'better', based on that person's understanding of the meaning and relevance of transaction costs (or whatever).

In sum, I defend the hospitable harkening to otherness-in-the-law that fosters recognition and respect for different perspectives and that ultimately allows one to test one's assumptions, one's angle on the law-world. Whatever disruption or anxiety otherness generates along the way thus fulfils edifying ends. And I claim that such charitable comparison ought not to be translated into a divisive configuration having so little to do with the ethical negotiations between self and other and so very much to do with the generalisation of conflict into a hierarchical economy of domination where difference is subjected to a calculative technology purporting to achieve an increase of resources, including enhancement of capital, through various indicators reducing human beings to the same lowest common denominator of (allegedly) computable basic needs and interests. To those who like economics with their dinner, then, I respond that economics can contribute little to our quest for a deep or thick understanding of law as long as it continues to suck life out of the law and persists in approaching the law at a level of abstraction detached from its life-world (Woods 2006: 54), as long as it lacks 'sufficient granularity' (Morgan 2012: 392).

*   *   *

At this stage, I am aware that some readers, perhaps not so attuned to economic analysis of law, might find my critique of the economic mindset and its utilitarian concoctions unduly harsh. Thus, I want not-to-close with a good example of how implausible the matter can rapidly become when it is assumed that law and economics can be tallied on a single scale and when a quantitative assessment, a matter of more or less, is substituted for an examination of the qualitative differences between self and other.

The relevant case is *Lindh v Surman*,[15] in which the Supreme Court of Pennsylvania held that where an engagement ring has been offered by a man who subsequently breaks the engagement, the ring must be returned. As far as the Court was concerned, the particular circumstances surrounding the termination of the engagement ought not to matter as such. Reversing its earlier practice, the Court thus adopted a 'no-fault' approach. Consider the following case note subsequently published in the *Harvard Law Review*, which features a line of reasoning that, far from being unusual, typifies economic analyses of law:

Donors of engagement rings in no-fault states now have no financial disincentive to propose marriage casually. Moreover, the desire to enjoy the relational privileges of engagement may drive donors to devise schemes to reap those benefits – at no cost to themselves. Because it gives donors less incentive to take care, the [*Lindh*] rule will likely lead to an increase in broken engagements, with all their attendant emotional and economic harms. Such a result would counteract whatever policy goals a strict application of the no-fault rule advances'.

(Note 2000: 1880–81)

Indeed!

Notes

1 For an extensive discussion of 'striated space' see Gilles Deleuze and Félix Guattari (1980: 592–625).

2 The suggestion that I would discard any economic analysis of law whatsoever – as in Ralf Michaels (2009: 783 n 87) – does not capture my stance.

3 The original text reads as follows: '*Tout ce qui m'est donné dans la lumière paraît m'être donné à moi-même par moi-même*'.

4 I have addressed such issues in Pierre Legrand (1997).

5 The original text reads as follows: '*Die Reduktion aller Qualitäten auf Quantitäten ist Unsinn*'.

6 Cf: 'Economists' models offer mathematical accounts of the world, but there is nothing even that guarantees that mathematics in its various forms offers accurate ways to describe the economic world' (Morgan 2012: 408).

7 For a compilation of Condorcet's writings on point, see Condorcet (1765–93). See generally Jacqueline Feldman (2005). The reference to Baron Kelvin is to William Thomson (1883: 73): 'When you can measure what you are speaking about, and express it in numbers, you know something about it; but when you cannot measure it, when you cannot express it in numbers, your knowledge is of a meagre and unsatisfactory kind'.

8 For comprehensive arguments along these lines, see Janice Stein (2001); Stephen Marglin (2008).

9 For a compelling demonstration of economics's resilience, see Gilbert Rist (2011).

10 For an attempt at an economic 'displacement' of the idea of 'legal culture' see Anthony Ogus (2002). While this article relieves us from the tedious banality of so-called 'comparative-law-and-economics', its contentions remain obscure, although they make evident the economist's habitual obsession with rationalisation in general and with cost considerations in particular. But the fact remains, as has been helpfully underscored in an analysis of economic integration in North America in the wake of the 1993 North American Free Trade Agreement (NAFTA), that '[c]ultural practices do not always follow the structure of markets and incentives, which, however powerful, often fail to overcome countervailing pressures': Dan Schiller and Vincent Mosco (2001: 29).

11 Observe that the identification of the common law tradition as the teleological framework by which to assess all other laws (and to find them all to be wanting) and the correlative elevation of the United States into the developmental

benchmark towards which all other countries ought to aspire is spectacularly undermined in Dan Puchniak, Harald Baum and Michael Ewing-Chow (2012) – to refer to one illustration only. Aptly, some commentators thus hold that 'legal origins turn out to have little power to explain the effectiveness of legal institutions' (Milhaupt and Pistor 2008: 21). For another critique, see Daniel Klerman and others (2011).

12 This text offers persuasive remarks regarding the intricate relationship between path-dependence theory and common law adjudication.

13 For the purposes of this argument, I leave to one side any sustained investigation of the meaning of 'I'. But I want to observe that I am in significant ways the recipient of an ascribed identity, not least as the result of the structuring process of incorporation of professional attitudes that I was made to undergo in law school while being taught to think 'like a lawyer' (that is, while being encouraged to obliterate 'my' moral or social frames of apprehension). In fulfilling a regulatory function by setting the limits of what was and was not acceptable, the power of discursive authority acted on me and subordinated me to it and to its domination. This authoritative discourse thus constituted me – and continues to constitute me – into the individual, the lawyer and the comparatist-at-law that I am, which means that, through it, I am actively (and incessantly) engaged in the fashioning of my 'own' identity. The history 'I' call 'mine' thus very much stands as the unfolding of circumstances that were given to me.

14 I explore this issue at greater length in Pierre Legrand (2012).

15 742 A.2d 643 (Pa. 1999).

Bibliography

Apter, E. (2006) *The Translation Zone*, Princeton, NJ: Princeton University Press.

Beck, T., Demirgüç-Kunt, A. and Levin, R. (2003) 'Law and Finance: Why Does Legal Origin Matter?', *Journal of Comparative Economics*, 31: 653–75.

Cheah, P. (2009) 'The Material World of Comparison', *New Literary History*, 40: 523–45.

Condorcet, N. de (1765–93) *Mathématique et société*, R. Rashed (ed.), Paris: Hermann, 1974.

Deleuze, G. and Guattari, F. (1980) *Mille plateaux*, Paris: Éditions de Minuit.

Derrida, J. (1967) *L'Écriture et la différence*, Paris: Éditions de Minuit.

Feldman, J. (2005) 'Condorcet et la mathématique sociale: enthousiasmes et bémols', *Mathématiques et sciences humaines*, 4: 7–41.

Friedman, T.L. (2005) *The World Is Flat*, New York: Farrar, Straus and Giroux.

Glaeser, E.L. and Shleifer, A. (2002) 'Legal Origins', *Quarterly Journal of Economics*, 117: 1193–229.

Glanert, S. and Legrand, P. (2013) 'Foreign Law in Translation: If Truth Be Told ...', in M. Freeman and F. Smith (eds) *Law and Language*, Oxford: Oxford University Press.

Golumbia, D. (2009) *The Cultural Logic of Computation*, Cambridge, MA: Harvard University Press.

Hathaway, O.A. (2001) 'Path Dependence in the Law: The Course and Pattern of Legal Change in a Common Law System', *Iowa Law Review*, 86: 601–65.

Klerman, D.M. and others (2011) 'Legal Origin or Colonial History?', *Journal of Legal Analysis*, 3: 379–409.

La Porta, R., Lopez-de-Silanes, F. and Shleifer, A. (1998) 'Law and Finance', *Journal of Political Economy*, 106: 1113–55.

—— (2008) 'The Economic Consequences of Legal Origins', *Journal of Economic Literature*, 46: 285–332.

Legrand, P. (1997) 'The Impossibility of "Legal Transplants"', *Maastricht Journal of European and Comparative Law*, 4: 111–24.

—— (2009) 'Econocentrism', *University of Toronto Law Journal*, 59: 215–22.

—— (2012) 'Foreign Law in the Third Space', *Juridikum*, 4: 32–43.

Marglin, S.A. (2008) *The Dismal Science*, Cambridge, MA: Harvard University Press.

Michaels, R. (2009) 'Comparative Law by Numbers? Legal Origins Thesis, *Doing Business* Reports, and the Silence of Traditional Comparative Law', *American Journal of Comparative Law*, 57: 765–95.

Milhaupt, C.J. and Pistor, K. (2008) *Law and Capitalism*, Chicago: University of Chicago Press.

Morgan, M.S. (2012) *The World in the Model*, Cambridge: Cambridge University Press.

Nietzsche, F. (†1901) *The Will to Power*, W. Kaufmann (ed.), trans. W. Kaufmann and R.J. Hollingdale, New York: Vintage, 1968.

Note (2000) 'Property Law – Pennsylvania Supreme Court Holds that Engagement Rings Must Be Returned Regardless of Who Broke the Engagement – *Lindh v Surman*, 742 A.2d 643 (Pa. 1999)', *Harvard Law Review*, 113: 1876–81.

Ogus, A. (2002) 'The Economic Basis of Legal Culture: Networks and Monopolization', *Oxford Journal of Legal Studies*, 22: 419–34.

Puchniak, D.W., Baum, H. and Ewing-Chow, M. (eds) (2012) *The Derivative Action in Asia*, Cambridge: Cambridge University Press.

Rist, G. (2011) *The Delusions of Economics*, trans. P. Camiller, London: Zed Books.

Schiller, D. and Mosco, V. (2001) 'Integrating a Continent for a Transnational World', in V. Mosco and D. Schiller (eds) *Continental Order?*, Lanham, MD: Rowman and Littlefield.

Stein, J.G. (2001) *The Cult of Efficiency*, Toronto: Anansi.

Stone, D.A. (1988) *Policy Paradox and Political Reason*, New York: Harper Collins.

Teles, S.M. (2008) *The Rise of the Conservative Legal Movement*, Princeton, NJ: Princeton University Press.

Thomson, W. [Baron Kelvin] (1883) *Popular Lectures and Addresses*, vol I, London: Macmillan, 1891.

Woods, N. (2006) *The Globalizers*, Ithaca, NY: Cornell University Press.

World Bank (2004) *Doing Business* http://www.doingbusiness.org (accessed 1 October 2013).

Index

Intro   -   why translate?

- hermeneutics
- culture (perhaps first paragraph as it
           will be a constant theme.)
- Holy texts.
- difficulties
- methods
- current scholarship-
- translation and law.